Praise for *Living On A Thin Line*

'This powerful tell-all from the Kinks guitarist puts the spotlight on his own bad behaviour, dalliances with the occult and his recovery from a stroke.' – *Observer*

'Heartfelt, hilarious, revealing, insightful and astonishingly candid. Boy, you really got me Dave. I can't wait to read it again.' – Mark Hamill

'Bold and busy autobiography . . . testament to the tumult of life in the Kinks.' – *The Times*

DAVE DAVIES

LIVING ON A THIN LINE

HEADLINE

First published in 2022 by
HEADLINE PUBLISHING GROUP

First published in paperback in 2023 by
HEADLINE PUBLISHING GROUP

1

Cataloguing in Publication Data is available from the British Library

ISBN 978 1 4722 8979 7

PICTURE CREDITS

First plate section: p. 3 (middle) © Art Lubin; p. 5 (bottom) © Reprise Records/
Warner Bros./Courtesy of Getty Images; p. 7 (both) © Janne Bäckman.

Second plate section: p. 1 (bottom) © Lisa S. Johnson; p. 2 (top) © Rebecca G. Wilson; p. 3
(bottom) © Rebecca Wilson; p. 4 (top) © Al Pereira; p. 5 (top) © Rebecca G. Wilson;
p. 6 (top) © Steven Busby; p. 8 (top) and (middle left) © Rebecca G. Wilson

Typeset in 10.58/14.72pt Bell MT Std by Jouve (UK), Milton Keynes

Printed and bound in Great Britain by Clays Ltd, Elcograf S.p.A.

Headline's policy is to use papers that are natural, renewable and recyclable
products and made from wood grown in well-managed forests and other
controlled sources. The logging and manufacturing processes are expected
to conform to the environmental regulations of the country of origin.

HEADLINE PUBLISHING GROUP
An Hachette UK Company
Carmelite House
50 Victoria Embankment
London
EC4Y 0DZ

www.headline.co.uk
www.hachette.co.uk

To my dear Mum and Dad who started
me out, then nurtured me, on this journey.
Annie Florence Davies (Willmore)
Frederick George Davies.

PREFACE

A WAKING DREAM

I was standing near a hilltop monastery with four Tibetan priests who were all dressed in white robes. One of them handed me a plate of rice. I looked over and saw another man who looked like he needed to eat, so I gave him the dish. He gulped the rice down, handed back the empty plate, and from nowhere, it was filled with food again. At this point I realised I was having a vision and thought I should wake up. It was about four in the morning, and as I slowly edged back to full consciousness, I heard these words in my head: 'Lest ye become as little children ye shall not enter the kingdom of heaven.'

In my state of semi-wakefulness, after that very intense dream, I understood the power and magic of those words. I had given the rice to this starving man in a selfless, childlike manner, and my surrender and trust in the universe had created a second state of consciousness, what I call entry into a Zen-like state. I was overwhelmed by the knowledge of this feeling, which stayed with me as I went about my morning routine. We must recognise that the energies and forces surrounding us are very potent and affect our lives, and the lives of others, in profound ways. One time I saw an old woman and was overcome with sadness. I could see her life unravelling in front of my eyes; all her pain, anguish and sorrow. I wanted to speak to her, to do something to make her feel happier. And just as I was about to say hello, another woman greeted her. They both smiled happily and her face suddenly became radiant and filled with joy. It was heart-warming to witness.

We are living through difficult times, but no one should doubt the power of kindness and compassion — a single thought, a word or even a smile can help, and the words 'trust', 'compassion' and 'surrender' keep echoing through my mind. The opportunity to help each other, and the world around us, as never before is great. We need to surrender to the higher good that is all around us, and inside us. Letting go of all the hate and prejudices, and then transmuting that pain, is essential. Negative thoughts and emotions that contaminate our true being will be transformed into positive energies if given a chance. We can help the world with pure loving intent and we will receive help from the universe to do so; this is what the bowl of rice symbolised in my dream. There is a sort of loving code within the universe which stimulates the energies of the mind. If we have a deep desire to help and support other people we can effect change. As I look around me, everyone seems to be carrying a sadness, or a loneliness, and we really have to support and nurture each other to make our lives richer and more meaningful.

The power lies in that Zen state I mentioned earlier, that 'second state of consciousness' which affects mind and physical matter. This state is in operation all the time, and can be summoned into being by surrendering like a child. To enter into this state of awareness, we need to reach beyond our most painful emotions. When we wallow too much in pain it is difficult to reach this second stage, where the real healing and magick can take place. Endurance, acceptance, surrender; we must trust that all will be well, just like a child. It sounds so simple, and it can be if we believe and trust in the power. We are all alchemists and should meditate upon this.

PROLOGUE

30 June 2004

I called the album I was promoting at the time *Bug*. It was a record about a woman who thinks she has an implant in her brain, and I had actually met a Kinks fan, named Ellen, who sincerely believed that aliens had put implants inside her head. What a great subject for a record, I thought. I was living in Los Angeles and I'd flown back to London to do interviews and PR for the album. Which was when I realised, can you believe it, that there was something wrong with my own brain.

A few days after I landed I suffered a couple of episodes of what they call a TIA, like a very mild version of a stroke. I collapsed after the first one and wondered what was going on. Had my collapse been caused by fatigue? By too much flying and gallivanting all over the place? I hoped by slowing down I might recover my strength, but then the same thing happened again. Although I could walk and function fairly well, I was also partly paralysed. I went to the Royal Free Hospital in Hampstead and, when a doctor touched my hands to see how I felt, the effects of the TIA evaporated. How that happened remains a mystery. Ordinarily I'm not a great lover of medication, but I felt I could trust the doctor, and I followed her advice to take the blood-thinning pills she prescribed, and I felt normal again. Big relief.

On 30 June, I was booked for some interviews about *Bug* at the BBC. I made it through the first one but didn't feel great. The second interview was with Danny Baker, who didn't make me feel very comfortable, and during the interview I started to feel ill. My son Christian was managing all the interviews, and I keeled over as the lift was taking us back to the ground floor. I was fully aware of what was happening and didn't lose consciousness, but had lost all my mobility.

Christian helped me out into the street, at the back of Broadcasting House. The pub on the corner was shut, so I sat on the pavement instead and told Christian to call an ambulance immediately. It felt like I was having one of those TIA episodes, with a severity that made me fear it could be something much worse. While we waited, a strange phenomenon came over me where suddenly it felt like everyone I interacted with, whether an ambulance driver or passer-by, was someone I knew already – very strange indeed.

I was driven by ambulance to University College Hospital, and the doctor there who examined me said I should go straight away to Queen's Square Hospital, near Russell Square, where they specialise in neurosurgery. After scanning and examining me, a doctor explained what had happened. I'd had what they call an infarct, a burst blood vessel, on the left side of my brain, and that had caused a stroke.

By this time I was in a hospital bed and my right side was hopelessly weak. I couldn't stand and a male nurse had to lift me up to go to the toilet. My body was in a heightened state of sensitivity, reacting to what had just happened, and I felt like I was watching a movie – or three movies in one. One section, over on the left side, was what had already happened in the past. The central part was what was going on now, and the other overlapping part, on the right in my perception, was the future. I knew who was about to call, or who was going to turn up, before it happened. It was actually illuminating, like barriers between the past and the future had melted away.

In a way I felt good. I wasn't panicking or feeling isolated, or having any especially negative thoughts. Instead I became ultra-sensitive to everybody's feelings. I watched the staff, and one nurse in particular, who had just started her shift, freaked me out. As she walked past me, I could see the people who were making her unhappy. She wasn't just carrying emotional baggage, I could actually see the weight upon her. I had enough problems of my own and thought, Please don't come near me! This phenomenon of seeing inside people's pain became a song called 'God in my Brain', which I included on an album released soon after I left hospital called *Fractured Mindz*.

Some of the doctors and nurses proved skilled at putting me at ease. When I had to go to the bathroom or felt hungry, I needed the help of my favourite male nurse. When he wasn't around I felt very anxious and I'd keep a lookout for him. He would see me poke my head around the side of the cubicle, nod back, and it made me feel so reassured to see him. I thought carefully about how we experience and interact with other people, a subject which preyed on my mind when my elder sisters wanted to visit. They were anxious about what had happened, and I loved them dearly, but I didn't want them to see me in this condition. I couldn't have women around me. I preferred the company of men, and my sons were an enormous help. I found that women made me feel too centred and too vulnerable. My sisters had always been loving and supportive of what my brother Ray and I did with The Kinks, but I feared now they would be too gushing and overprotective, which would have become oppressive.

In those very early days I had some great physiotherapy, and I talked to brain experts and psychiatrists. I asked if they could find a space where I could meditate and a very kind doctor found me a side room where I put a chair and my own objects of meditation. I had my Ganesha with me and I did my meditations, which really helped. Although I couldn't do my proper breathing practice as normal, meditating helped me get back into shape, psychologically and mentally. I would mediate for twenty minutes, and those twenty minutes felt like hours!

It was tough being on my own, but I had already learned about the importance of being on your own when I had a nervous breakdown in the early seventies. I had realised then that the only person who can really help you is yourself. We find help from wherever we can in that situation, from other people and from medical experts, but I needed to spend time on my own, to find out what the fuck was going on inside my head. 'What's the next step forward?' 'How do I climb out of this place I'm in?' Knowledgeable people can offer ideas, but in the end we all have to do it ourselves. We're born alone and we die alone. It's sad, but that's life.

I told the therapists that I liked to paint, and painting became my saviour. Painting is all about intuition and creativity, and that, I decided, was going to pull me through. I couldn't use my right hand, so I used my left instead. Once I got used to it, my left hand became much stronger than my right; I realised then that all those years playing guitar had built up reflexes and muscles in unexpected places. For three weeks I had physiotherapy each morning, little tasks like picking pins and other small objects up from the floor and stretching exercises that were designed to reconnect the wires in the brain, what they call the synapses. And in the afternoons, I painted.

My consultant explained to me how we can re-programme the brain, and I started thinking this is what the media does and how commercials operate, programming our minds until we give in and think: I'll buy that! Recently, I came across the work of an American neurologist, Dr Richard Davidson, who has written extensively about what he calls neuroplasticity. The brain is like a sponge. To re-educate the brain after a stroke, you do exercises like putting a pin into a hole and then you have to keep up a repetitive motion, putting that pin back into the same hole again and again. It's like learning times tables at school; repeating the numbers until they stick. This is why I'm heavily into yoga and meditation, because those are areas of the mind and brain that we all need to work on.

I began to see noticeable improvement after I'd asked one of my sons to bring me a guitar. I didn't have the strength or the coordination to play it, but I realised how important the smell of the instrument was to me, and also touch; just putting my fingers on the strings triggered muscle memory. Eventually I would have to learn to play guitar all over again, although muscles, and the brain, do retain memory. So I talked to my body and asked for its help. I had met patients in hospital who had MS and brain cysts, and all sorts of traumatic illnesses, and usually the worse the illness the more positive I found people were. One woman with MS talked to me about Buddha and about how positive thoughts can build the inner self and I found that really helpful. I'd been hospitalised for about two months in total and learned a lot being with all those remarkable people.

After being discharged, I stayed with Ray for two weeks, which was nice for a couple of days, but soon became a nightmare. My brother is very talented and gifted, and I don't want to be mean so soon, but I sometimes feel he's like a vampire the way he draws so much energy from people. True enough, that's helped him become a great songwriter and he knows how to channel his ability to use people in a creative way. I'm glad he has always been part of my life, but you need to be strong around him. The way he was absorbing my energy during those two weeks, eventually I thought: For fuck's sake! Ray, I love you, but really I don't have much to give at the moment.

So I went to stay with my sister, Dolly, who lived near North-ampton. She had always been like a second mum to me, and Joe, her husband, was an older guy. The nurturing from my sister, and the strength I gained from Joe, proved to be just what I needed and I stayed at their place for another couple of months. My partner at the time, Kate, was living in Los Angeles, and she flew in to see me at the hospital. She also spent time at Dolly's house and offered me her unconditional love and support.

During my recovery, I listened to all kinds of music, from Tibetan mantras to Charlie Byrd and Jo Stafford, to Berlioz, and Dvořák, whose Serenade in D Minor comforted me like a blanket. Debussy also became important to me. I felt his music feeding that part of me beyond conscious thought. We like to think we are thinking creatures, but that, I believe, is only a very small part of us. Another example: I fell in love with Beethoven's 'Pastoral' Symphony. Listening to it, you can see the birds in the morning when you look out the window, and you hear the wind blowing through the music. It is music in touch with naturalness: with life, nature, animals and trees. I also devoured Beethoven's Seventh Symphony. I was thinking a lot about yoga and learning to walk again, and that Beethoven piece – with its rhythms and its energy – made me appreciate dancing again. Dancing can help rebuild the neuroplasticity of the brain, not necessarily fully back to normal, but to a point where you can work with things again. Dancing connects the physical with the mental.

All my life I've researched the psychic world. I remember being six years old and my mum couldn't stop me talking: 'Oh David, you do go on! I think you were born old!' But I knew there were other energies beyond mundane objects like the table, the teacup, the knife and fork. I discovered, as I got older, that we were quite a psychic family and my mum was very psychic, although she wouldn't have called it that.

Psychic energy, I believe, reaches out to people like the internet. One of the reasons we're here is because we're all a bit fucking mad. We're trying to join the pieces together and in life you meet people who help to fix bits of the jigsaw. An example . . . in the late 1980s, I had a meeting in Los Angeles with Simon Heath, who'd worked as part of the production team on *Die Hard*. He had been helping me knock a film script into shape and, during a drunken conversation at a bar in Burbank, he told me how important The Kinks had been to him growing up in Australia, in the outback of some little town. He'd turned on the radio when he was a kid and heard our song 'All Day and All of the Night'. It was like a coded message, he said, and made him think, I'm going to play in a band. No! I want to make films!

I was a rebel at school. The teachers couldn't teach me anything, because I felt like I knew more than them, although I couldn't explain why. That's where music came into its own because, through sound, I could express my feelings and impressions without needing to write anything down. Music is everywhere and we have to tap into it. How amazing that a kid in small-town Australia heard The Kinks – then all those years later we're sitting together in a bar in Los Angeles talking about a film script.

Music needs to be structured because we work with materials; making a song is like moulding clay. We must build machines too, but we need to be careful not to let the machines take over. Modern society is so focused around that consumerist way of perceiving things. But feelings matter too. When you've been in hospital alongside people who can't speak, but find other ways to use energy and express themselves, that much becomes clear.

The stroke, the illness, my recovery – it was a new opening for me. When you see people in wheelchairs, because of the task they have in life, these people are often giants spiritually, mentally and emotionally. You don't need a church to get inspiration about life and spirituality. Go to a hospital, where there are people in wheelchairs, and that should give you all the inspiration you need. We learn from each other all the time. As human beings, we try to help each other.

As kids growing up, Ray was withdrawn and reticent about getting involved in anything. I was more outgoing and I learned to read and write and play football at school, but when I wanted to know something important I'd buy a book, or borrow books from the library in Muswell Hill. There were cheap books they wanted to get rid of at the library, and I was intrigued by all the date stamps on the inside page. Looking at the stamps and the dates, I thought: There's a whole story before you even open the book itself. I bought *The Devil Rides Out* by Dennis Wheatley, and the story he told of different worlds that affect our world made me think, this is where I'm at! That's when I first really started to perceive spiritual, psychic stuff.

My mum used to read tea leaves. You leave them in the cup as you turn it upside down, then study the shapes in the tea leaves. From that you can deduce all kinds of things from the shapes and the symbols.

Lying in hospital for all those weeks handed me a precious opportunity to reflect on my life for the first time since The Kinks became popular in 1964 – some forty years earlier.

I thought about how important my family had been when I was growing up. I had been surrounded by my six sisters, by my mum and dad and my extended family – by the energy of all these women. They stimulated my emotions, my intuition, my senses and my psychic inner-life, and I felt privileged to have grown up around that. We didn't have money, but it was such a nurturing environment.

Looking back through the whole Kinks catalogue, most of our songs and albums were stimulated by family, by Ray writing about our family. Ray was born in 1944 and I was born in 1947, and we were surrounded by stories of the war and of people who had died and suffered. Working-class families had come through two world wars and the Blitz, and those experiences had made them very resilient and insightful.

I tried to connect everything that had happened in my life and thought about what an ancient Zen guru had once taught, that the world is like an ocean through which pieces of land pop up at random. But dive deep into the ocean and then you see that everything is connected – and the deeper you dive, the more connections you can see.

CHAPTER ONE

FORTIS GREEN

Mum would gaze into her tea leaves and tell us all sorts. Looking into the leaves myself, I might see shapes like a crown, or a man smoking a pipe, or a dog. But Mum knew how to interpret what she saw. She described people I'd meet in the future, and others best avoided, and would also warn me not to go to certain places because bad things happen there.

You can't just read a PG Tips tea bag, of course. Proper old-fashioned loose-leaf tea is what's needed, and after pouring the tea into the cup, and stirring in the milk and sugar, you keep the leaves. Working-class Londoners, like my family, latched on to this ritual that stretched back to tea ceremonies in ancient China, and to Gypsies, and also the Irish, who brought leaf-reading to England when they came here looking for work. My mum would often read the leaves with my aunt, and the images created a psychic impression: if she saw a shape like a bouquet of flowers, she might conclude that someone in the family was about to get married.

Once we kids were in bed, the women in the family would partake in seances with the letters of the alphabet written on pieces of paper, and a glass, trying to contact relatives who had died. They'd arrange the letters in a circle around the glass, and everybody put a finger on the glass and it moved of its own accord, sliding around the table, spelling out words formed by the spirits. When I was older, that got me into Tarot cards. The Tarot comes from very ancient traditions, and the cards look beautiful, and trigger ideas, thoughts and feelings in the psychic brain of the reader, finding a kind of order within apparently random thoughts.

My mother was Annie Florence Willmore and my dad was Frederick George Davies. Mum's mum, my grandmother, was called Catherine, but we'd call her Big Gran, and she married Albert who had actually come from money. Albert had been in the army, but he hated it, and his family had money enough to buy out his commission so that he could start over again. Later they turned on him. Big Gran had been abandoned as a baby. Her parents had wanted a boy, so they left her as a newborn with an elderly aunt – literally in a basket on the doorstep. When Albert's family heard that he was marrying not only a working-class girl, but an orphan, they cut him off completely. He ended up without two pennies to rub together. Big Gran looked like Queen Victoria and the cartoonesque caricature of Queen Victoria on the cover of The Kinks' album *Arthur (Or the Decline and Fall of the British Empire)* always reminded me of her. For a while they lived on Blundell Street in Islington, just opposite Pentonville Prison. Perhaps to compensate for growing up without siblings they ended up having twenty-one living kids, including some who died at birth. So I had lots of aunts and uncles.

When Mum was born they were living near the Caledonian Road – or the 'Calley' as they called it – around the back of King's Cross station. Albert, after he left the army, worked as a horse-and-cart driver on the railway, and that is why I always had such an affinity with the American blues and country music, and Hank Williams' 'Lonesome Whistle', because blues singers used to sing about working on trains and the railway. America was built on railroads and a lot of the great backbeats in music are like trains.

King's Cross was important in another way too, as it happened to be where my mum got fired from her first job. She worked in a bronzing factory and dropped off to sleep one day and her bosses didn't like it, and she was sacked. Back then, difficult to believe it now, there was a cattle market around the back of the rail station. Mum found a job in a little café there and that's where she met my dad, who'd come in to buy a cup of tea after his shift. He asked her out and a little while later they got married. Dad's side of the family had originated from Ireland. His mum was Amy, and we'd call her Little Gran. She ended up working as a servant in London where she met my grandfather, Harry Davies, who was from the Rhondda Valley in Wales.

One other thing that's hard to believe these days: when eventually my family moved to East Finchley, that was considered moving *outside* London. After they married, my parents lived in various places around King's Cross and Farringdon. My sisters – Rosie, Gwen, Dolly, Joyce, Peggy and Irene – were mostly born in a block on Cumming Street, between King's Cross and St Pancras stations, but living there very nearly ended in tragedy. When she was a toddler, Peggy was playing in the street with her friends. Suddenly a lorry, which had been stolen from St Pancras station, ripped around the corner and drove straight into the children. Peggy was slammed against the railings and very badly injured. She was in and out of hospital for months and suffered permanent hearing loss and a damaged arm. After that trauma, my family moved to nearby Rodney Place, until the war started. In 1939 the question arose as to whether my sisters should be evacuated to the countryside. At first Mum thought they should; then in the end she couldn't bring herself to do it. So that's when the idea came to move everyone to East Finchley. The first house they lived in, on Huntington Road, was big. Little Gran moved in too, with her daughter Rosie, my dad's sister. But the neighbours started complaining about all the noise and commotion. The other kids from the street had been evacuated already and the old folks who were left were enjoying the peace. And then my family turned up!

Mum eventually realised it was a hopeless situation and, at the start of 1940, she moved the family to 6 Denmark Terrace, on Fortis Green, the road that leads from East Finchley to Muswell Hill, the house where Ray and I were born. Muswell Hill was a lot shabbier and rougher than it is now, but the place had a good feeling about it. Down the road there was a greengrocer called Churches where my mum was always getting stuff 'on tick', on credit. We lived next door to a baker in the days when they made real bread: now it's an Indian restaurant. Every Friday night we would stay up late and hang around behind the baker's, watching them knead the dough. The smell was great! And everything we needed was in Muswell Hill. There was a funeral directors which was always busy, and is still open. Near to our house was a tuck shop, a sweet shop, where you could also buy newspapers. It was called Jones's, and the son of the family who ran the shop, Peter, became my friend. He sang with Ray and I in the very early days as Pete Jones and we called him Jonah; and in more recent years he became a pop singer who was very popular in Canada.

Denmark Terrace was a little working-class row of houses, and our house was a tiny semi-detached at the end of the row; another reason to move to a smaller house – no room for Little Granny, who drove my mum nuts.

After the war, my sister Rene married Bob, a Canadian serviceman, and moved to Ontario. She would send us letters and photos of fancy cars – and pictures of refrigerators! A refrigerator – what was that?

At 6 Denmark Terrace, Ray and I shared a bedroom at the top front. People would congregate downstairs where there was a fire. We called that room 'the kitchen', but really it was the dining room, lounge and kitchen rolled into one. There was a curtain leading in from the kitchen, and behind that was a sink and cooker. We didn't have a proper bathroom. Instead we had an annexe to the kitchen, which we called the scullery, where we'd take turns washing down. There was no hot water on tap, so water was boiled on the stove then poured into a tin bath. On occasion I peered through the curtain and would catch an eyeful when my sisters were washing and getting dressed up. They were all beautiful and this was the first time I learned anything about the female form. Thinking about this now, it sounds more like Victorian times.

The house was barely big enough for all of us, but it was always packed with aunts, uncles and cousins, and my mum's brother, Uncle Frank, who was closest to my mum, was always at our house. He was a real character, an archetypal Cockney geezer, the very essence of Max Miller. My mum and dad, and Frank, loved the music halls, Vaudeville and Gus Elen in particular, who was a working-class music hall entertainer. When my dad was pissed, which was often, he would play the banjo and sing Gus Elen's 'It's A Great Big Shame'. It went 'It's a great big shame, and if she belonged to me, I'd let her know who's who/Nagging at a fellow, who is six foot three, and her only four foot two/They hadn't been married but a month or more, when underneath the thumb goes Jim/Oh isn't it a pity that the likes of her, should put upon the likes of him?' He'd sing it as a joke about my mum, because he was definitely under her thumb.

Mum was very much the centre of things, making sure everyone was happy. My dad went out to work, and my mum ran the house: food, clothes, children, everything. If clothes needed a repair job, she'd do it. She was very industrious and resourceful, and it was a very matriarchal household. She was well versed in the world and smart, and always knew what was going on. She was also highly intuitive. She knew what people thought and what they really meant. She could look at someone and suss them out right away. This is what people were like then, that's how they grew up. They weren't necessarily well read, but they were well versed in real life.

Many years later, when I took acid, I communicated with a voice in my head that I used to call 'The Captain'. If my mind was going somewhere really weird, he would say: 'No, don't go there, go here.' It was this psychic, higher-self thing that I had, but was it also an impression of my mum saying, 'Don't do that,' or 'Avoid that!'?

Dad was not sent to war. He had learned to be a slaughterman from his dad, Harry, who had originally been a coalminer in Wales, but then took a job at an abattoir. During the war, slaughtermen were considered a reserved occupation; no matter how bad things got, people needed to eat. When I was eleven he took me to the abattoir where he worked, in Codicote, near Stevenage. These animals would be knocked unconscious by a knocking gun and then have their throats cut. The smell of animal blood stayed with me for years and that's why I became vegetarian.

Later in life, during his retirement, Dad became a gardener, always at the bottom of the garden in his greenhouse and he also had allotments. He told me, as dads did in those days, that I was born under the gooseberry bush. And I took it literally! It bothered me right up until I was thirteen – how am I going to tell people I was born under a gooseberry bush? He became an insightful old man. He'd grow beetroot, potatoes, sweet peas and he was also very keen on growing flowers, and developed a fantasy life – he would say he talked to the fairies under the gooseberry bush, and he was serious. I was a kid, so he felt safe telling me, but I'm sure he wouldn't have talked to his mates up the pub about fairies.

By the time I came along, in 1947, 6 Denmark Terrace was already bursting at the seams. I was the youngest. After having all those other children, Mum was rather large by the time I came along and kept this latest pregnancy to herself; my dad knew and that was about it. She felt self-conscious about becoming pregnant *again* in her forties, and when I turned up everyone was surprised, and I joined what was already a very full house. Dolly and Joe lived in the house; also Joyce and her family, who eventually moved into number 5 next door. One night Peggy went dancing in Soho and met Billy Baker, who was a merchant seaman from Senegal. They had an affair and she became pregnant. At that time having a baby out of wedlock was completely unimaginable, and having a mixed-race baby, sadly, added to the problems. By the time Peggy gave birth – to Jackie – Billy wasn't around. I'd thought for years that he'd been deported to France because he was in the country illegally, but talking to Jackie recently, I realise there was a lot going on behind the scenes that I wasn't aware of.

Billy had tried to come back and see Jackie, but no one would let him near Peggy. So all of a sudden there was this little black girl living in the house. She was Peggy's child, so my niece, but I thought of her as my sweet little sister and I looked after her. I would walk her to school, and the abuse we got! As much from grown-ups as from kids. Now Jackie lives in Los Angeles, and whenever I see her, she reminds me of my mum. Mum took Jackie's birth in her stride, and brought her up as one of her own because Peggy was always out working hard and trying to meet guys. The day Mum found out that Jackie's nursery teacher had been locking her in a cupboard, she raced around to her house and gave her a slap. She was furious that somebody had dared abuse a member of our family. Mum always made sure everyone was OK.

Ray also adored Jackie, and the different generations in our house all rubbed along together. My sisters had children who were the same age as Ray and me, and cousins, siblings . . . it was all the same thing.

Ray and I got on well at that stage, but in a weird way. We had our own language. At the cinema in Muswell Hill, we had seen a bizarre French film about a man calling himself Lion, who had alienated himself from society. He had huge hair, like a mane, and he'd made a world of his own in which to live because the real world was so cruel and judgemental. For most of the film, he'd be running around speaking his own language, ranting in shop doorways. Ray and I, at our age, missed the tragedy of the film of course. We thought Lion was hilarious and Ray started drawing funny, absurd-ist cartoons about him. And from that, a made-up language of our own emerged. We'd say things like 'Balam kusu baa!', just silly words that naturally came out, but we knew what we meant. Already we were playing with words and sounds, as a framework for survival. Despite the problems we'd have over the years – all the fighting and disagreeing – we do share a very similar sense of humour. At a young age, humour opens people up and it helped me and Ray communi-cate. Through humour you can find out what someone's really thinking. It would be like telepathy – I'd say to Ray, 'Ballo ballo, shiga shuga la ballo,' and he'd know exactly what I meant.

Ray and I both had our difficulties, and sharing this made-up language helped us. I didn't even know I had dyslexia until one of my sons, Simon, was diagnosed with it many years later. When I was a kid, I would see d's and b's as the same letter: not ideal if your name happens to be David Davies – or was it Bavid Bavies? I enjoyed school when I was younger, but when I got to eleven, twelve, thirteen, I didn't like the way teachers talked down to me. I thought, they're meant to be teachers and nurture children. But it felt like they were a race apart, and had no understanding of dys-lexia. If you were dyslexic, it was called stupid. And I was stupid *and* working class. I had an instinct for words but I couldn't articu-late them, and music saved my life and helped my growth. Music, football and meeting girls were my three obsessions as a maturing child from age twelve. Without music, perhaps I'd have been rob-bing shops.

I always felt Ray had a special bond with our sister Rosie who had an uncanny ability to empathise with his troubles, and break through the barriers he put up. Ray kept himself to himself, and he was able to withdraw completely. He was never into playing with other kids, his brother included. The biggest laughs we had were playing with our invented, gibberish words. Then Ray was comfortable because this language we made up put a degree of separation between him and the real world, but goodness knows what else was going through his mind. He had real problems sleeping. When we were still sharing a bedroom, one night he shot up in bed and began staring into the room, with eyes as big as plates. I asked if he was OK, and he started yelling. Next thing he's running down the stairs and out into the garden. By now, everyone in the house was awake. It was scary to see my big brother so distressed. He started shouting about how a tiger was chasing him. Then Mum held him firm and gave him a hard shake. Ray snapped out of it and looked as surprised as everybody else that he was standing in the garden in the dead of night. Sleepwalking became a major problem for him, and he never had any clue he was doing it.

He was the older brother, but I could see his vulnerabilities and I knew I'd have to look after him. I remember my dad, when I was seven or eight years old, holding my hand and saying, 'David, you've got strong hands. I worry about your brother because his hands feel really soft.' I thought: Shit, I'd better keep an eye on Ray, and felt very protective towards him. Mum became so concerned that she started taking him to see a psychologist, which was not usual for 1950s working-class Muswell Hill at all. Mental health just wasn't talked about and there was very little understanding of psychiatry. Mum would talk about taking Ray 'up the clinic' and was clued-up enough to recognise he seemed unusually depressed and withdrawn for someone so young. I always thought he was fearful of the world but, later, learned to articulate what he saw, like a journalist or a reporter. Music helps draw out who you are as a person.

Often I wonder how those personal differences we have never quite resolved had their origins in our earliest childhood. My sisters say that before I came along, Ray was more sociable as a toddler. He'd love to sing and dance at parties, and would run into the room singing 'Temptation', waving his arms in the air like Jerry Colonna. Later he became really good at mimicking people. He did a great impersonation of the comedian Jerry Lewis, and even looked like him a little bit, and his Buddy Holly was uncanny. Mimicry was how he started to sing.

Being the baby of the family, my sisters and aunts used to coo over me and, to be fair, I was spoilt rotten. Ray was loved just as much, but went from being the youngest and the only boy to, in his eyes, competing with me for affection, like I'd rained on his parade. Whenever there was an outbreak of jealousy or bitterness later on, connected to The Kinks, I believe it was because of underlying resentment from years earlier.

Music saved us, but the fact we were both drawn towards music and the guitar didn't help our rivalry; had one of us been a painter or writer things might have been different. I was into Eddie Cochran and blues singers like Leadbelly and Big Bill Broonzy, and I used the guitar to pick out chords and riffs I heard on records. I was self-taught and put things together myself, and my playing was no doubt considered rougher and cruder than my brother's. Ray had lessons from Peggy's husband Mike Picker, who was a very talented guy. He was really clever with electronic gadgets, and household stuff, but he also messed around with gramophones and recording tape. He also played great guitar, and his interests in music and gadgets interlinked. Mike showed Ray some classical guitar techniques and he took to it right away. He also started learning how to read music and was far ahead of me on that.

When me and Ray went to Mike's flat he'd show us picking, country and western style, and play us all these great records: Earl Scruggs, Lester Flatt and Bert Weedon, who I loved in particular because he played a version of a tune called 'Guitar Boogie', by another guitar player called Charlie Gracie. It was easy to play by ear and, as kids, we found learning the boogie easier than scales. When I tried to learn scales I used to cheat, but boogie patterns felt fundamental and sat well on the guitar, or left-hand piano. Mike also played jazz guitar, influenced by people like Barney Kessel, Tal Farlow and Charlie Christian, and had records by Django Reinhardt, which were dazzling, and had some Super 8 film of Big Bill Broonzy performing in a nightclub in Paris. He was playing 'Hey Hey' and I was utterly transfixed. Halfway through the performance you see a woman smoking a cigarette. There's an ashtray on the corner of the piano or table, and she knocks it on the floor. Bill stops playing and everyone gasps; a moment I've never forgotten. I wanted to be like Big Bill Broonzy. He had great style and a great voice, and was musically far ahead of the game.

Before I even knew who Big Bill or Lead Belly were, Lonnie Donegan was introducing Britain to the blues. He played banjo and guitar in Chris Barber's trad jazz band, when Barber had the great Ken Colyer on cornet, who modelled his playing strictly around the pure New Orleans style. During the intervals in concerts, Donegan began singing old American folk and blues songs by people like Lead Belly and Woody Guthrie, with backing from a washboard and a bass made from a tea-chest, played by plucking strings stretched along a broomstick nailed to its side. Skiffle was born and everybody loved it, Ray and me included. Lonnie's hit record 'Rock Island Line' was a jived-up version of a Lead Belly song. Through Donegan, jazz, blues and boogie met and crossed over. Skiffle was easy to play and very rhythmical, and opened up that world of blues and folk. Ray always used to say, during the very early days of The Kinks, that I did the research and I knew what he meant. I was always intrigued about where music came from as much as where it was going. Lonnie helped me join up all the connections.

Music also awakened the senses and opened up whole new

experiences; being a kid is hard, but now I had a way to express feelings I couldn't otherwise explain. I had a friend at school called Johnny Burnett. His family had spent time in America, and he had American records. I went to his house and he played me 'Sweet Little Sixteen' by Chuck Berry: I was gobsmacked. We didn't have a TV until the Coronation in 1953, and I used to hear other stuff by playing with my mum's wireless, pretending I was a disc jockey, messing around with the BBC Home Service. One day I heard César Franck's Symphony in D minor and it stopped me dead in my tracks; I was hypnotised by this music of such depth that could affect my whole being.

I used to play a game about running a record company of my own. As I listened to Jerry Lee Lewis, Little Richard and Buddy Holly, I'd make up names that sounded like them, such as 'Eddie Richard' or 'Jerry Lee Jones' and write into a little notebook the records of theirs I was going to release. I gave each of them their own little riff or signature tune.

Like so many experiences in my childhood, my sisters played an important part in my discovery of music. Rene would send from Canada records by Fats Domino, Pat Boone and Elvis Presley before they were released in Britain. And my sisters here loved ballroom dancing: Victor Sylvester and Joe Loss, long before trad jazz arrived. Joyce joined a dance club called The Arcadia that was in Finchley Central and went five nights a week sometimes, dancing foxtrots and waltzes. She also became a pretty good pianist and the piano was the centre of things in our front room; Gwen also played, but Rene was the best. There was also a wind-up gramophone and records started appearing in the house. Judy Garland, Gene Kelly and Bing Crosby, then Dolly discovered Fats Domino, Hank Williams and Slim Whitman, and I listened avidly too. All my sisters, but Dolly in particular, loved Jo Stafford, that velvety, warm voice drawing you in. I have quite a high voice and I tried to copy her song 'No Other Love', which she based on a piano piece by Chopin. Something about her voice was really quite mystical. Also in the house were records of *South Pacific* and *Oklahoma!* which my sisters played all the time. I thought for years that *South Pacific* was 'girls' music'. It wasn't until later that I realised what an incredible piece of music it is. I loved the theatre, the dancing and the movement. So stimulating for a young boy. I had my sisters around me all the time, and they were always dancing.

Every Saturday night, the whole family – aunts, cousins, Uncle Frank was always there – would descend on Denmark Terrace for a singsong around the piano, a good old-fashioned knees-up. Dad would arrive from The Clissold Arms with his mates and a crate or two of beer. Mum would lay on some sandwiches. Then the entertainment would begin! Dad would get his banjo out and sing his Gus Elen songs, and everyone would do their party-piece until three or four in the morning. My sisters would dance. People would sing songs from the thirties: 'If You Were The Only Girl In The World', 'Knees Up Mother Brown' and 'My Old Man Said Follow The Van'. Rene was always great on the piano. They knocked a wall through when my sister Gwen got married to make a larger room out of the front room and the adjacent back room, and the space ended up divided by a big curtain. It looked like a mini-theatre and we called it 'The Mini Palladium'. The tribe of kids would crowd around the curtain and we'd tell jokes and sing, and perform skits we'd worked out. We'd also sneak little sips of beer.

I was around five when I met Rene for the first time. Her married name was Whitbread but her marriage to Bob had run into trouble, and she returned to London from Canada, bringing her young son Bobby who was around my age and quickly became part of the family. Rene was a very impressive young woman and reminded me of a laughing, bubbly Hollywood actress, with classic fifties horn-rimmed glasses. She spoke with a part Cockney, part American-Canadian accent. She'd always had health troubles and had a delicate constitution to match. Born with a diseased heart, she then contracted rheumatic fever when she was young, which left her with a hole in her heart. Meeting Bob and moving to Canada in 1946, when Mum was pregnant with me, must have felt like a great opportunity to start a new life – especially given the state London was in after the war. But my mum and sisters quickly became aware that not all was well. Bob drank far too much, and Rene's fragility and her illness frustrated him. I believe he had affairs with other women, and used to beat Rene when already she was so weak. Eventually she had enough of his bullying and womanising, and came back to her family, and found a job in the optician's shop on the High Road. She moved into Denmark Terrace initially, then found her own place on Eastern Road in East Finchley.

The first time I met Bobby, we walked by each other in the street. Rene and he had just arrived at Denmark Terrace and Mum sent him to meet me halfway when I was walking home from school. I walked past this weird-looking kid, with his hair cropped, wearing a leather jacket and walking with a swagger, looking completely out of place in mid-1950s Muswell Hill; we knew Marty Wilde and Cliff Richard, but that American swagger was something else. We managed to recognise each other somehow and I swear, from the first time he opened his mouth, he never stopped talking and we became really good buddies. We made our own magazine called *The Epic* that was packed with silly drawings, crossword puzzles and cartoon characters. There was a footballer called Dave Donaldson, and a detective called Hank Lynstone who smoked a pipe. We became good at drawing these characters, and spent lots of time together doing that. Bobby had obviously witnessed his dad hitting Rene and, one day, completely out of the blue, said, 'When I grow up I'm going to kill my dad.' At the time, I thought, what a strange thing to say. I was stunned.

After a year or so, Rene heard about a cardiac specialist in Canada who was working on pioneering surgery to repair heart valves. She had high hopes that this operation could change her life, and went back to Canada to meet with the surgeon then have the operation. After she returned, she told us a remarkable story around the dinner table in Denmark Terrace, and we all listened, open-mouthed. She had been lying on the operating table under general anaesthetic, and all of a sudden felt she was floating out of her body and up to the ceiling. She spoke about looking down at her own body below, and seeing lights shining in the distance. One was red, the other was green. To survive the operation, she told us, she knew she had to stop these two coloured lights from touching: 'If they collided, I knew I would die,' she said. 'I needed to use all my powers of concentration to move them apart.'

I was mesmerised by her story. There was a book by Dennis Wheatley that I got hold of a couple of years later, called *The Ka of Gifford Hillary*, taken from an Egyptian word for 'spirit'. It's about a guy who they think is dead, and they bury him but he's not dead really. His Ka is still linked to his body. That fascinated me and drew me into ideas about reincarnation. Rene insisted that when she died she wanted to be reincarnated. The idea cropped up again a few years later when I saw an episode of *The Twilight Zone*, about a guy who died, and they were going to put him in the mortuary, and he was in the spirit world saying: 'I'm not dead.' A nurse, who was tidying-up the body, noticed a tear in his eye. If he's dead, why is he crying? That got me thinking about otherworldliness and about Rene – her body being lifeless when she was having her operation, but she wasn't dead and she had to keep those lights apart.

Despite the operation, and the expectations that came with it, Rene's health situation did not improve; she felt herself becoming weaker and sicker. On 21 June 1957, when she was thirty, Rene travelled into town and we never saw her again. She went dancing at the Lyceum Ballroom on Wellington Street, just off The Strand in central London. She loved dancing there, and that is how she left the world. She suffered a fatal heart attack on the dance floor and collapsed into the arms of a complete stranger. Rene and Bobby had taken the front bedroom that Ray and I had shared, and I was sleeping in the back, upstairs room. At around seven o'clock the next morning, suddenly I heard terrible wailing. I was wondering what was going on, when I heard this clippety-clop coming up the stairs; my dad always wore big, brown, working man's boots. He came into the room and I looked at him. 'Rene,' he said, and I knew what had happened even before he spoke. He was trying to be a tough guy, and sat at the end of the bed, held my hand and told me that Rene had died. He broke down completely and I felt like the father: my dad was at the end of my bed, crying, and all the father–son barriers came crashing down.

I quickly got dressed and went downstairs with my dad, and my mum was distraught, rolling around in an armchair, waving her arms around, screaming, 'She fucking died on the fucking dance floor in a stranger's arms.' Those words always stuck with me. There was nothing I could have said. I was a scared little kid. It was awful.

Years later I realised the effect that Rene's death had on me, and my family. All these personas we think we're supposed to have when, in the end, we're stuck with ourselves and the frailty and dis-appointment of life. But we came from a working-class family and the attitude was very much that we're tough enough to deal with this. Soon enough my dad conformed to type, back to his role as the tough working-class dad. All I can remember is wanting to care for my mother and poor little Bobby. He and I bonded a lot more after Rene died. I felt a distinct need to help people, my family especially, much more than I had previously. It had all been about me before, but now I had been pulled out of one emotional state and thrown into another.

The funeral was harrowing. They wouldn't let the kids go, so we all had to stay in the house, and Mum blamed Bob for putting Rene, as she said, in an early grave. Later, Bobby traced his dad to a hospital in Canada, where he was in the last stages of alcoholism, his body crumbling and his faculties dimmed by dementia. Somehow he managed to write a letter back to Bobby, one of the hospital staff perhaps helped him, and Bobby told me it was one of the saddest things he'd read – filled with remorse and self-loathing.

21 June that year also happened to be Ray's thirteenth birthday. In Canada, Rene had worked as a teacher. She knew how to cope with troubled children and had taken Ray under her wing. Rene recognised that spark of musical talent within him and patiently nurtured him; they sat together at the piano for hours, she showing him chords and teaching him little tunes. For months Ray had been eyeing up a guitar in the window of Les Aldrich, the music shop on Muswell Hill Broadway that is still there today. He never stopped talking about that damn instrument, and Rene helped Mum pay for the guitar as a thirteenth-birthday present. Whereas my instinct had been to look after my family when Rene died, Ray turned in on himself even more. He had not only lost a sister, he had lost someone who really understood his problems, and who was a source of comfort and inspiration. The thrill of becoming a teenager, and being handed his first guitar on his thirteenth birthday – that pleasure was taken away from him too.

There's a song on *Bug*, the album I was promoting when I was taken ill, called 'Fortis Green', which is all about reconnecting with my past and my family and the place where it all started. It was written as the world was entering into a new millennium and took me back to my roots, in an album that was otherwise about alien implants in the brain. In our minds we can go anywhere, but touching base is always important.

The opening song on the album, 'Who's Foolin' Who', was all about manipulation. I sang about 'Brain dead, paranoid, the mutant factor's activated/Acting out just automated/Forked tongues everywhere, can't believe a word they're saying/In the news, on the net, channel hopping, mind popping'. The title song of *Bug* opens with lines about 'There's a bug in my brain and driving me sane/ There's a bug in my mind of an alien kind/All the right is all wrong and the wrong is all right/Gotta act, get it back, I'm losing my track.' It's hard rock, like The Kinks' *Low Budget* album, except harder. Then 'Fortis Green' appears in the running order, like a 'missing' song from *The Kinks Are The Village Green Preservation Society*, or the B-side to 'Autumn Almanac', bringing a whole other sort of music to the album. My vocal is backed by a brass brand, and I had put myself back into an imaginary space that allowed the memories to flood back. 'Fortis Green' reminded me that I wasn't going fucking crazy; I could still relate to this world and my background. Other songs on the album like 'True Phenomenon' and 'De-Bug', where I looped jagged, abstract techno beats, were about exploring new worlds. My son Russell helped me with those tracks. But keeping one hand fixed on the past, thinking about where you've come from, can form a safety net.

The song 'Fortis Green' began with a line lifted from real life: 'Mum would shout and scream when dad would come home drunk/ When she asked him where he'd been, he'd say Up the Clissold Arms/Chatting up some hussy, but he didn't mean no harm.' This is what life was like. The Clissold Arms was the local boozer and is still there today, directly opposite 6 Denmark Terrace. My dad was always in the pub with his mates, chatting up the bar staff and some floozy or other. I would sometimes stand outside waiting for him, catching his eye through the window, and he'd bring me a bag of crisps. One day, when my sisters were still babies, my mum was so cross with Dad being in the pub, when they lived near the Caledonian Road, that she put the kids in the pram and went to the boozer where he was knocking back a pint of Guinness and chatting up a barmaid. She pushed the pram at him and said: 'Now *you* look after the bloody kids. I'm going out!' Then poured his pint over his head.

My dad always reckoned the owner at The Clissold Arms watered down the beer, so he started going to another local pub called The Alexandra, which is gone now. But The Clissold Arms has gone down in history as the place where Ray and I played our first gigs. These days it's a posh bistro, but the new owners have been very sweet and tried to keep the mood of The Kinks. There's a 'Kinks Room' with old posters, record covers and photographs displayed on the wall. Back in the fifties, though, the place was much rougher, with sawdust on the floor – a proper working-class local. My dad drank in what they called the public bar, and next to that was a saloon bar, which was much posher, where you could take your 'missus'. It was the culture of the time that men congregated in the public bar, and it wasn't considered sexist. It happened all over England: take your wife to the pub and you would use the saloon bar or sit at tables at the back of the bar. There was also a big room, that is now the restaurant, which was called 'the lounge' and it was *so* posh that you had to pay a couple of pence extra for your pint. It had a little stage and this was the room where Ray and I played, invited by the owner of the pub – helped along by my dad's persuasion.

We were just kids. I would have been eleven or twelve, Ray fourteen or fifteen. I was probably wearing short trousers, but I knew five chords and thought I could play anything. It was just the two of us – there was no drummer and we didn't meet Pete Quaife, who played bass in The Kinks, until a few years later at school. Starting to play in public didn't feel like such a big leap from playing in the front room at home, and I liked the sensation of performing in front of an audience, feeling that connection with them. We'd mimic songs we heard on the radio and that we played on our radiogram: the Everly Brothers, The Ventures, Johnny and the Hurricanes, that kind of thing. Ray would sing and play the lead parts; I would keep the rhythm going as best I could. Ray also started to write an instrumental that circled around F and G, with a Chet Atkins country vibe, that he called 'South', which later became the basis of the Kinks song 'Tired of Waiting'.

It could be that Ray and I played at The Clissold Arms only two or three times. Confidence was never a problem for us and soon we wanted bigger places to play, especially once Pete had come on board. Then we were three guitars, and often played at our school hall. Ray's fantastic Buddy Holly style came in very useful; and we also played Jerry Lee Lewis hits, even though we didn't have a piano. We weren't 'The Kinks' yet, of course. If someone booked us to play and they knew Pete, we'd turn up as the Pete Quaife Trio; the Ray Davies Quartet became another popular name. In those earliest days, though, we were just kids having fun, messing around with music we'd picked up on records and from the radio. Ray's instrumental evolved into 'Tired of Waiting' and all the information we needed for what would become The Kinks was already in the Muswell Hill air – all we had to do was sniff it out.

By my early teens I *loved* guitars and experimenting with amplifiers, working out the different sounds I could coax out of them. The radio shop on Fortis Green near our house, Ted Davis, was a treasure trove from where I bought an Elpico: a tiny ten-watt amplifier, with a seven-inch speaker and two different controls, one for volume and another for tone. Messing around one afternoon, I thought what a great idea it would be to collect all my amplifiers together and experiment with them. I also had a sixty-watt Linear amp, a much-beloved Vox AC 30 and an old radiogram. So I carried them all down into the front room at Denmark Terrace and started messing with them.

What would happen, I asked myself, if I plugged my guitar into the Elpico, then fed that through my Linear amp? What sound would I hear? I took the wires hanging out of the back of the Elpico, put jack-plugs on the ends, and plugged them into the Linear. Then I wired the radiogram and the AC 30 through the Elpico, and stood back and admired my handiwork before walking over to the wall and flicking on the switch. For a split second I heard fantastic crackling, static distortion – and then all hell broke loose. I had managed to overload the mains and there was an almighty bang. Next thing I know, I'm lying on the other side of the room, thrown there by the force of the explosion, and my mum is bursting through the door wondering what the hell is going on. The electricity fused and I had plunged the house into darkness – and I was bloody lucky not to have electrocuted myself.

Then, after a while, a brainwave. How about if I slashed the speaker inside the Elpico with a razor blade? What difference would that make? I tried – and wow! Where I had cut the speaker cone, the edges vibrated against the outside shell of the speaker, unleashing a visceral, jagged roar when I played my guitar. Then I plugged it through the input sockets of the AC 30, causing the green amp to act as a pre-amp, which made it even louder. I had created this whole new sound, but I couldn't have guessed how much that moment would change my life – and Ray's too.

Whenever we played a live show, I used the set-up and it rarely went without mention: 'What *the fuck* was that?' was a common reaction, although other people loved it right away. Ray and I went to see the film *Jazz On A Summer's Day*, a jazz documentary that was shot during the 1958 Newport Jazz Festival on Rhode Island and featured a load of great jazz stars, including Thelonious Monk, Gerry Mulligan, Anita O'Day, Louis Armstrong and Eric Dolphy. But two performances stuck in our minds. Chuck Berry sang 'Sweet Little Sixteen' backed by some jazz musicians who couldn't really hear his brilliance. They were almost chuckling at him behind his back, because he wasn't playing their idea of sophisticated jazz. But Ray and I got what he was doing right away, and felt the music deeply. The other standout performance was by Jimmy Giuffre, who was primarily a clarinettist, but was featured in the film playing tenor saxophone on a song called 'The Train and the River'. Ray and I were awestruck by the riff he played and we sang it all the way home.

A while later, in the front room in Denmark Terrace, Ray was playing some jazz riffs on the piano, no doubt with 'The Train and the River' in mind, while I was playing my guitar. I was obsessed with my new guitar sound, and was trying all sorts of different permutations of heavy, three-fingered barre chords. Suddenly Ray said, 'Hey, come listen to this!' He was playing a riff, looping back to the beginning once he reached the end. It sounded great – the 'You Really Got Me' riff had suddenly appeared in the world. Ray was picking it out with two fingers, and I picked up my guitar and gave it the full barre-chord treatment, with my new amp sound. It roared, and Ray and I stared at each other – it was like a magic spell had filled the room. Ray then shifted the riff up one tone of the scale, and I moved with him; we didn't need to talk it through, it just felt instinctively right. A few days later, Ray came back with a lyric – 'Girl, you really got me going, you got me so I don't know what I'm doing' – and there was 'You Really Got Me'. Little did we know we'd still be playing it all these years later.

CHAPTER TWO

SCHOOLBOYS IN DISGRACE

I was learning about life from music and from the books I was reading – and school was a very poor second best, a complete waste of time, in fact. My first day at school set the pattern. At age five, I was sent to St James's Primary School, at the top of Fortis Green, and on the first day the teachers made me stack up toyboxes. What's the point of this? I thought. I'm not coming back here. So after a couple of hours I left and went home to Denmark Terrace. I walked into the house and said to my mum: 'Look, I've been to school and I don't like it.' She went completely barmy, called me a little bleeder and dragged me screaming back to school. Then my memory fades for a couple of years. Once I'd learned to read and could add up, found my love of football and started going out with girls, I thought: That's it, that's all I'm interested in.

Also, the more fascinated I became with music, the less interesting school became. At the age of eleven, I took the eleven-plus exam, which determined whether I'd follow the academic route by going to a grammar school for kids considered 'clever' or spend the next few years of my life in the comprehensive system. It goes without saying that I failed the eleven-plus spectacularly, as had Ray a few years earlier, and we both ended up at the local comp, called William Grimshaw School, which we nicknamed Willy Grim. The horrible thing about the eleven-plus is that it succeeded only in breeding failure. The teachers had spent years making me feel like

I was stupid, destined to go nowhere in life, which set me up to fail. The morning I walked into the hall to sit the exam, I was so wound-up and terrified, my mind went completely blank. And my undiagnosed dyslexia didn't help. Of course I was going to fail.

School was an uncomfortable, knockabout environment. It felt safer to be in a little gang and, eventually, I formed a gang with my best mate, George Harris, which we called The Black Hand Gang. To be in our gang you needed to wear a black glove on your right hand; then you were in. During my first day at William Grimshaw, I nearly had a taste of how thuggish some of the kids could be. The initiation ceremony one gang had dreamed up involved stretching a new kid along the wire-mesh fences that surrounded the playground, pushing so hard that the edges cut through the skin. But this was a bullet I managed to dodge. Ray was already a few years ahead of me at the school and, along with his friends, made sure that I was kept out of harm's way.

I was happy to find other lads who wanted to play football, that was one good thing about school, and for a while I took up boxing, although this sudden interest was not strictly to do with sport. My English and French teacher was Miss Joshua, who was a very beautiful young woman. I was smitten. And I was certain: she was the girl for me, and I did my very best to impress her, even concentrating unusually hard in my English and French lessons. My interest in boxing was all about impressing Miss Joshua. At the end of my first year at William Grimshaw, Ray and I were chosen to represent the school in the annual Middlesex School Boxing Championships. The teachers liked to go along to offer support and Miss Joshua was certain to be there, and here was my chance to impress. But I was petrified. My opponent and his mates were hanging around in the dressing room before the match and gave me a bit of a slap around and were telling me that, after his last match, the guy he knocked out ended up in hospital. Whether that was true or not, if their aim was to dent my confidence, it worked. Not that I had much confidence to dent.

Dolly's husband Joe owned boxing gloves – his nephew had been an amateur boxer – and Ray and I decided to have a boxing match in the front room in an attempt to sharpen our skills. Midway through I got lucky. Ray's defences were down momentarily and I slipped a punch past him. He fell across the room and whacked the side of his head against the piano and pretended to lie absolutely motionless. I thought, bloody hell, I've killed my own brother. How to explain this to my mum? I was panicking and starting to tear up as I leaned over him, just willing him to wake up. I put my ear to his chest to listen to his breathing . . . then suddenly he opened his eyes, roared with fury and punched me straight in the mouth. Old gullible me!

In the boxing ring the day of the championships, my knees were knocking together with terror. Through one eye I could see my opponent, who looked like someone not to be messed with. Out of the other I could see the lovely Miss Joshua, who returned my gaze with warmth and encouragement. The bell rang for the first round and I dragged myself reluctantly towards the centre of the ring. My opponent looked like a monster but, fortified by Miss Joshua's presence, I mustered up all the aggression I could find and lashed out. Then I became like a man possessed. All sense of time drifted away. I was completely in the zone, fists flying. I don't know how long we fought, but eventually the referee blew his whistle to stop the fight and my opponent was a crumpled heap on the floor. I'd beaten the crap out of him. I'd won! Victory was sweet. But Miss Joshua's radiant smile as she clapped and looked at me was even sweeter. That moment unlocked something inside me; for the first time I understood about men and women.

But my infatuation with Miss Joshua was to be short-lived. When I returned to school after the summer holidays, she'd left.

Apparently she had got married and moved away from the area, and all that enthusiasm I'd had for English and French evaporated instantly; school became a fucking grind again, and I regarded the other teachers with contempt. Art lessons could be enjoyable because I liked to draw, but I remember drawing a picture I was really proud of, and the teacher taking the piss out of it. I thought: What's the matter with you? Why would you want to make me feel so bad? When my friend George Harris got kicked out of school a little while later, my rage intensified. His father had died unexpectedly and George was playing hooky all the time. He was eventually expelled for truancy, but nobody thought to ask *why* he didn't want to go to school.

With Miss Joshua gone school felt unimaginably boring, like there was no point in it. Boxing stopped too. After my own triumph, I'd watched Ray lose to a champion boxer from another school, and I winced each time he was hit. I also realised I had better hold on to my good looks if I wanted a girlfriend – I didn't want a squashed misshapen nose or cauliflower ears. So I threw all my energies into football and music. And then I met Susan Sheehan and everything changed.

Sue was the first girl I loved properly. She was friends with a classmate of mine called Christine Hussey, but went to a posh girls' grammar school up the road in Temple Fortune called Henrietta Barnett. I met Sue in a little park across the road from what was then called the John Baird pub, now the Village Green pub, on Fortis Green Road, just along from the Les Aldrich music shop where Ray had eyed up his first guitar. The instant I saw her, I was dumbstruck. Her intelligence, her beauty, her figure – she was perfection and no other girl I'd met could match her style. After our first kiss, she was all I could think about. Her family situation could hardly have been more different from mine. She lived in a well-heeled part of Muswell Hill, in a big house on Duke's Avenue. Sue was an only child and her parents were stiff and formal; it didn't take much to irritate them, and they both glared at me with utter disdain. But Sue and I were together, and there was nothing they could do about it.

We'd love to hang out in Muswell Hill. The El Toro coffee bar had opened on Fortis Green Road, which was one of the first coffee bars outside central London: a slice of Soho brought to Muswell Hill. Sue finished school before I did and would run to William Grimshaw in time to meet me at the gates, and she loved coming back with me to Denmark Terrace. Unlike her sleepy, quiet house, mine was bursting with activity: relatives coming and going, animated conversations and lots of fun. Sue and my mum adored each other. She and I were never apart. Whenever we played at the school hall, or some other local venue, Sue would come along. One time, at a school dance, she jumped up onstage and belted out 'There's A Hole In My Bucket'. She was in great voice.

One evening after drinking frothy coffee with friends at El Toro, Sue and I went back to her parents' house. Her dad was in bed already and, just as we sat down in the kitchen with a cup of tea, her mum walked in to say goodnight. The house was still. Sue and I looked at each other, like we knew what was about to happen. We moved our chairs closer and started kissing, our tongues going forever deeper. Then Sue faced me on my lap, lifted up her skirt, and we made love for the first time. It was an exquisite moment, bringing us closer than ever. After that evening we'd go for walks in Highgate Woods and find quiet places to have sex – there was an incline at the back of the woods, dug out for the railway – although the sofa in the front room at Denmark Terrace also did the trick, as did various park benches around Muswell Hill and East Finchley.

Given even half an excuse, Sue and I would very happily bunk off school together. And the arrival of summer, the hot weather and longer days, gave us all the excuse we needed. One morning in June

1962, with the day promising to be a hot one, and no desire to be in school, we decided to spend the whole day together. We ran along Fortis Green, towards East Finchley, laughing and holding hands. Then we talked and walked. And walked and talked some more, and before we knew it, we'd reached Kenwood House and Hampstead Heath – a massive park, where we thought we'd lose ourselves easily and nobody would ever spot us. The Heath is one of the highest vantage points in London. You can see right over into the city, and we gorged on the amazing view, but something else was on our mind – we wanted to find a quiet place to make love. As Sue used to say, 'We never have anywhere to go.'

The last time we'd ended up on the Heath, the grass had grown high, and now we ran to that same place. But the grass had just been cut, spoiling our plans but doing precisely nothing to dampen our ardour. Eventually we found a bushy area surrounded by trees, nice and quiet. We sat down and started kissing and stroking each other, and Sue put her hand inside my pants and the intensity began to build . . . then, completely out of nowhere, two men in officious-looking raincoats ran out from behind the shrubbery and started shouting at us. We were stunned, completely shocked. As we scrambled to zip ourselves up, putting our bits and pieces away, they were demanding to know why we weren't at school. We found out later that they were truant officers who had followed us all the way to Hampstead Heath, and waited to find the best moment to pounce. Sue couldn't cope with the humiliation and burst into tears. I was a cocky fifteen-year-old, but the shame of being caught hit me immediately.

That was the end of my school career – Sue's too. The truant officers reported back to our schools, and the end came quickly. School contacted my mum and we both waited outside the headmaster's office feeling doom-laden – what was he going to say? When we were called in, the cruel fucker, called Mr Loads, caned me hard across the palm of my hand and I noticed my mum's bottom lip start to tremble as he said those dreaded words: 'Davies, you're expelled.' As we walked out through the gates of Willy Grim for the last time I felt mixed emotions. Mum was in floods of tears and I hated upsetting her and it had been a very embarrassing episode – but at the same time, I was free at last! The deadening routine of school, and those drab, uninspiring teachers, had never suited me. Now I was free to lead the life I wanted. As we walked home, I kept reassuring her, 'Don't worry, Mum, everything will work out, it's all going to be fine.'

Sue had been expelled too, and her parents proved less forgiving. As far as they were concerned, she had thrown away a superior education and academic prospects over some fifteen-year-old lad with probably no future. They decreed that we must stop seeing each other immediately, but we carried on anyway – in fact it was a great opportunity to see each other more. I would tell my mum I was going to the Labour Exchange and, instead, Sue and I would get the 134 bus to the West End. That's how I discovered Dobell's Jazz Record Shop on Charing Cross Road, which was an education in itself. Walking through the door, you might hear records by Ella Fitzgerald, Duke Ellington or Django Reinhardt – and also the bebop guys like Charlie Parker and Dizzy Gillespie. They also had racks of fantastic blues records, people like Big Bill Broonzy and Lead Belly. It was paradise for a musically curious young man, and everything about Soho at that time, the Italian cafés and the shops, felt like an adventure. I was too young to get into jazz clubs like Ronnie Scott's, Studio 51 or the 100 Club, but Ray had joined a band led by the trombonist Dave Hunt. Ray played guitar, and his friend Hamilton King sang and played harmonica. They called themselves The Blues Messengers and played in a club on Gerrard Street, near Ronnie Scott's, called The Kaleidoscope, and also at The Scene in Ham Yard, near Piccadilly Circus. Ray would discreetly let me in through the back door and I'd soak up the music and the atmosphere. This was the tail end of the trad jazz crossover with the blues, and their playing was enthusiastic but a little stiff.

Sue and I both ended up with jobs in the West End, Sue working at Selfridges on Oxford Street, while I took a job at the warehouse of Selmer's music shop off Cambridge Circus; then we'd meet after work, at Leicester Square or Tottenham Court Road tube station, and take the Northern Line back to East Finchley. I worked in the Selmer warehouse cleaning musical instruments: trumpets, saxophones, trombones and the rest. One day Acker Bilk's clarinet came in for cleaning and it was filthy. Dried-up spit was blocking the mechanism and the instrument reeked of stale booze. But I enjoyed learning about the buttons, and gluing the covering over the holes on woodwind instruments – it was fascinating learning how instruments actually work. The routine did become tedious, but the boredom was alleviated by the guy I was working with, Derek Griffiths, who would later become an actor and presenter on children's television programmes. He was funny and off the wall, we were good company for each other. Derek also played really good clarinet, and during breaks we'd jam around, me on guitar, playing little blues or boogie pieces, or other things we'd play by ear like 'Stompin' at the Savoy' or 'Begin the Beguine'. He loved swing-era clarinettists like Artie Shaw, Benny Goodman and Woody Herman. And we totally thought we *were* Benny Goodman and Charlie Christian.

One day in August 1962, Sue suddenly became overwhelmed with emotion and sobbed, 'I'm pregnant, and I have no idea what to do.' I was stunned, left reeling. But I plucked up the courage and did what I thought was the right thing. I wanted to take responsibility for my girlfriend and our child. 'Let's get married,' I said, and the next day we went to Oxford Street to buy an engagement ring, which cost me £6. We both knew that telling Sue's parents our news was going to be an ordeal, but I trusted that my mum would be delighted for us – she had supported Peggy when Jackie was born, so why would it be any different for us? We marched through the front door, full of smiles and bursting with happiness, and took Mum into the front room to share the news of our engagement, fully expecting her to cry with the joy of the occasion. But it was not to be. I told her that we wanted to marry, and her face dropped and, where I'd expected to see happiness, I saw frustration. 'David, that's not possible,' she said, 'you're both far too young.' And then – mother's intuition, I guess – she pieced the rest together. She looked over towards Sue and suddenly shouted out, 'Oh my God, David, is Sue pregnant?' I nodded and Mum's frustration turned to real anger. She made me feel like a naughty child again, like I deserved a telling-off over some trivial transgression. Couldn't Mum see that we were in love? And wanted to marry, and bring up our baby together?

This is where the story gets dark. I thought it would all work out. That Mum would get over the shock, and Sue and I, with our baby, would all live happily ever after. But then she disappeared from my life for decades. Mum told me that Sue no longer wanted to see me, that it was all over: she no longer loved me, and I'd better get used to it, because that was the reality of the situation. The emptiness, the grief – the utter devastation felt like the day Rene died all over again. Sue and I had been seeing each other for two years, and had hardly spent a day apart in all that time. And now she had cut me out of her life, and with a baby on the way? How could this be true? What about all those plans we had made? Making sense of it all was a struggle and I desperately wanted to see Sue and talk the situation through. As darkness fell that night I walked to her house on Duke's Avenue, but couldn't bring myself to ring the doorbell. There was a passageway at the back of the house and, instead, I sat there and the tears flowed. Lights from the house were illuminating the garden and I couldn't help but wonder what Sue was doing inside. Exhausted by the day, eventually I fell into a deep sleep under the stars. In the morning I crept back home and told my mum that I had spent the night at my sister's place in Highgate.

Much later I found out the truth: the two sets of parents had concocted a plan to keep us apart. That night I sat outside her house, no doubt inside Sue was crying her heart out because she'd been told that I wanted nothing more to do with her. The pretence was kept up throughout her pregnancy. Somehow I managed to find out that she was staying at an institution called the Unmarried Mothers' Home in East Finchley, but the owners had been given strict instructions not to let me in. All I wanted to do was make sure that my girlfriend was OK. A few months later Mum sat me down and told me she had some news. Sue had given birth to a little girl – and her name was Tracey. I ran down to the home with flowers, but they wouldn't let me see Sue or Tracey. And it would be nearly thirty years before I saw Sue again and met Tracey. I loved my mum, of course I did, but I never forgave her for the brutal way Sue was taken out of my life. I was traumatised by the experience and my feelings for Sue, and the mystery of what had happened, would consume me for decades to come.

In a strange way, all these years later, I can see Mum's modus operandi. Ray and I were learning guitar, and she realised, I think, that music was a way for us to get out of the rut, and do something different. That's why my sisters, and Mum and Dad, were so encouraging. Experimenting with music was alien to most of my school friends, who wanted to be accountants and lawyers. Mum's famous intuition told her, if Sue and I married and the responsibilities of fatherhood came my way, I would be trapped. She knew that my natural instinct when trapped, as my experiences at school had demonstrated, was to break free.

And musically things were really starting to hot up. Pete Quaife had originally been Ray's classmate in Sixth Form at Willy Grim, and would come back to the house after school and at weekends. He was a funny guy, and very outgoing. The Quaifes lived on Steed's Road, on the Coldfall council estate, behind Coppetts Road in Muswell Hill. There were fields at the back where we would play football. Pete had a really annoying younger half-brother, and clearly felt a certain stigma because he avoided talking about his dad. His guitar was a Futurama, which was a cheap Japanese fake copy of a Stratocaster, but it was his first guitar and he was very proud of it. It had a little whammy bar attached to the bridge that stretched the pitch of a note up or down, except when he pressed it all the notes fell out of tune – he needed to be more careful about the pressure he applied. He'd say, and with a completely straight face, 'Yeah, but it's just the same as a Strat,' and that's one thing I loved about Pete – he was very good at convincing everyone about things that weren't necessarily true. I ended up with endless affection for him because he sat perfectly between Ray and me, and brought us together through music. They were older than me, of course, and when you're fifteen someone eighteen or nineteen feels a *lot* older. But Pete was always exceptionally kind and treated me more like a younger brother than Ray did. Ray was quiet and moody, often preferring to observe than participate, whereas I'd be wondering what was going on – and always I wanted to be at the centre of things. Immediately I liked that feeling of playing music with people.

Neither Ray nor I wanted to play bass, and Pete became a really good bass player because he was a guitarist first, and lots of people have said that he was really ahead of the game with the bass. Many years later, when I was talking to Noel Redding, who played bass in the Jimi Hendrix Experience while being primarily a guitar player, he told me that was why he played a lot in the higher octave. It was 'the guitarist in my head' he said, and the same thing was true for Pete. He liked much of the same music as us, although he also had a penchant for Hank Marvin, Cliff Richard and the Shadows, and I wasn't very keen on those guys, although Cliff and the Shadows had an exceptional record, 'Move It', which had some fantastic guitar. He also introduced me to Marty Wilde and his band The Wildcats. Pete had a copy of Marty's 'Bad Boy', and it had a great melody, and that record became my personal theme for a while. The lyrics were relevant to what I was going through at the time: 'All the people down the street, whoever you meet/Say I'm a bad boy/Even dear old dad, when he gets mad/Says I'm a bad boy/ Well, you see now, I got a girl/And we stay out late, almost every night.'

In the beginning there were the three of us. We tried out various drummers, because our first drummer, who we knew from school, wasn't cutting it. His name was John Start and his family lived in a posh house near William Grimshaw, and we'd hang out at John's after school and thrash around. John had a really bad stutter and his parents thought it was good for him to play drums, and they encouraged us to rehearse at their house. Music certainly helped him, but at gigs he became shy and wasn't very good at interacting with people and being sociable. Another pupil in his class – a Scottish kid called Rod Stewart – also rehearsed with us on occasion, and perhaps played a gig or two. But his voice never really fitted with what we were trying to do. Then after a few months John's parents ended it. They were never comfortable with John disappearing into the night to play gigs, and they thought he should settle down and find a proper job. So we auditioned for drummers and eventually hired Mickey Willett, who was an older guy, and played big band drumming in the style of Gene Krupa or Buddy

Rich. We also found our first agent, Danny Haggerty, and made ourselves available to play weddings, bar mitzvahs and birthday parties.

Ray was already leading the life of a proper musician, playing gigs independently of me. He'd met Hamilton King through another regular gig, playing guitar with the Dave Hunt Rhythm & Blues Band, the one-time house band of The Crawdaddy Club in Richmond, Surrey. The band played R&B-flavoured jazz and Charlie Watts played drums with them at one point. The Crawdaddy was owned by Giorgio Gomelsky, who would later manage The Yardbirds, and brought in a young upcoming band called The Rolling Stones, who no one had heard of, to replace Hunt at his club. Gomelsky had also been involved with The Piccadilly Club in Ham Yard in Soho, where once The Scene club had been. He'd taken the room over from the trad jazz clarinettist Cy Laurie on Saturday nights and ran blues evenings, featuring bands like Alexis Korner's Blues Incorporated and The Rolling Stones. He'd pay his friends to stand outside the entrance to create an impression of a capacity crowd in the hope of drawing people in. But it was an illusion; the audiences usually were very small. Gomelsky had taken a shine to Ray's playing, and booked Hunt's band, with Ray, to play at The Piccadilly, and one evening The Stones opened for them. They were as raw as fuck and played with a restless, unpredictable energy. I was transfixed, glued to my chair. What a band!

Hamilton King was Hunt's vocalist and he also played pungent, earthy blues harmonica. The Blues Messengers felt like the real deal compared to Dave Hunt's band, properly authentic as opposed to a bunch of Londoners trying to be bluesmen. It's easy to forget how many musicians who would later be considered the cornerstones of British rock and blues were working clubs in Soho at around this time. Mick Fleetwood was one of them – I used to watch him play at a place called The Kaleidoscope at the end of

Gerrard Street in what is now Chinatown. Even then Mick knew how to hold a backbeat, and this is four years before Fleetwood Mac started. If you listen to 'It's So Easy' by Buddy Holly and the Crickets, the backbeat is so infectious. But holding down a solid backbeat is never as easy as it sounds, and not many British drummers at the time had the right feel. Mick was ahead of the pack.

Alexis Korner had a regular gig at The Marquee Club on Wardour Street and all sorts of great people passed through his band: Cyril Davies, Long John Baldry, Ginger Baker, Graham Bond and Jack Bruce. Brian Jones worked with Alexis for a while, before meeting Keith Richards and Mick Jagger and The Rolling Stones happened. When The Stones were getting their shit together, and before Charlie Watts appeared, they rehearsed with a young drummer from Surrey called Mick Avory. People were in and out of each other's bands, and we were all swapping ideas about blues and jazz. It was a fantastic scene.

Meanwhile, Ray, Pete and me – now with Mickey Willett – were gaining confidence, and had acquired a new name, The Ramrods. We were crazy about the American guitarist Duane Eddy, who had a string of hits, songs like 'Peter Gunn' and 'Shazam!', but the one that really captured our imagination was 'Ramrod' so we borrowed it for our band name. We loved those jangling riffs Duane used, and I adored that sound of his guitar! Some white rockers had a stiffer way with rhythm, not as naturally syncopated as the jazz stuff, but I loved that syncopated style you got from jazzers like Eddie Condon and Django Reinhardt. Duane's tone on his instrument derived from using the bottom strings and bass notes of the guitar, and something new grew out of that. Now that we had a proper and memorable name, our new agent, Danny Haggerty, found it much easier to secure us gigs, although rock and roll stardom had to wait a while yet. One of our brothers-in-law, Brian, acquired an old Daimler ambulance, and we'd all pile in together with the drums, guitars and amps. People's faces when we'd turn up at gigs in an ambulance!

Even getting on for twenty years after the war, there were still US air bases all over the place and Danny got The Ramrods into that circuit. A few times we backed Rick Wayne, who was a singer and bodybuilder. He had come to London from his native St Lucia and ended up auditioning for Joe Meek, who produced his single 'Hot Chick-A-Roo', with 'Don't Pick On Me' on the B-side. It wasn't the success he'd hoped for, but he was friendly towards us and always hilarious. We would open with a few instrumentals, then he'd come up onstage and flex his biceps in time to us playing a Johnny and the Hurricanes number. I was too busy chatting up girls and listening to blues records to get interested in bodybuilding myself, but back then it was a big deal: Charles Atlas was world renowned.

I learned years later that there's a craft involved with theatre and doing a show: create the right atmosphere and connection with the crowd and you can basically do whatever you like once you get onstage. When it went wrong, though, it went very wrong. One night we were booked alongside Rick and a pair of old strippers who, to be honest, should probably have given up ten years earlier. Rick did his stuff and the audience gasped in astonishment at his rippling muscles, then the strippers came on and that's the moment we noticed that this was a very different crowd. Wives and children had been invited too. The officers, sitting in their uniforms, started to sweat nervously as these old dears peeled their clothes off – then suddenly there was a mad dash for the exit, the wives shielding their kids' eyes from the naked dangly bits onstage. The strippers, livid that they couldn't finish their act, began swearing at the audience and, to top the farce, Rick got into a row with an officer.

The name 'The Ramrods' had been lucky for us. It coincided with a moment when the ambition of the band became grander than me, Ray and Pete copying stuff we'd heard on the radio and on records. We were focusing seriously on what we wanted the band to be, and the gig with the strippers, as it happened, was the last time we performed as The Ramrods. We needed a new name and proper management, someone who could find us better gigs and maybe even a record deal. We changed to 'The Boll Weevils' which I'd heard on an Eddie Cochran record, the 'Boll Weevil Song' – 'Ah well, the Boll Weevil and the little black bug/Come from a-Mexico, they say/Came all the way to Texas/Just a-lookin' for a place to stay.' Then we became The Ravens after I saw the horror film, *The Raven*, shortly after it came out in 1963. It was based on the poem by Edgar Allan Poe, and starred Vincent Price, Peter Lorre and the great Boris Karloff, and I loved that film, and also the name had echoes of 'rave on', so it was perfect. If I'm honest I always preferred the name 'The Ravens' to 'The Kinks', although history disagreed with me.

We let Danny Haggerty go, and thought carefully about the question of management. Then through Mickey Willett we met an extraordinary pair of characters, Grenville Collins and Robert Wace. Grenville and Robert were everything we were not: middle-class to upper-class and seemingly wealthy. They'd had a background in business, stocks and shares, but had precisely no experience of managing pop groups. But Robert fancied himself as a pop singer and Grenville agreed to be his manager. Robert was looking for a backing group and a mutual friend put him in touch with Mickey, and we met one Sunday afternoon for a rehearsal at the Athenaeum Ballroom in Muswell Hill. Robert and Grenville immediately had Ray eating out of their hands. Their upper-class airs and graces charmed him and they promised they could find us gigs playing society balls, well paid compared to the US air-base gigs, on one condition – that Robert could have a slot in every show singing with the band, which was fine, except as soon as he opened his mouth we realised it wasn't going to work, although we persevered for a bit.

Robert was a gangly upper-class toff, in a Savile Row-tailored suit, trying to sound like Buddy Holly. And it was even worse than that sounds, like Prince Charles trying to sing Little Richard. Dreadful. But signing with Robert and Grenville pulled us out of the rut of the air-base gigs, and playing those posh society dos came with its own fascination and rewards. Champagne was on tap and the debutantes were sexy and liked nothing better than talking to exotic pop musicians; one of Robert's friends even told me he could hook me up on a date with Princess Margaret for a small consideration.

My dad used to help out with the gear as part of the entourage in the van. Before one debutante party, he was carrying the drums when he was suddenly caught short. So he farted like a trooper in front of all these posh girls, then carried on with his work. He was completely unimpressed by these elevated surroundings and I admired him for remaining true to himself. Meanwhile, I came to like Grenville enormously. He'd suddenly drop into the conversation, in his cut-glass English accent, something like 'My wife's brother works for MI6!' and I feared we'd be on a government watchlist for a while. He adored my mum: 'She was the salt of the earth, David,' he told me. Mickey, however, could never bring himself to like either Robert or Grenville. He was of a mind to think that they were both oddball pretenders who were out for what they could get.

Robert's career as a pop singer came to an abrupt and ignominious end. One night, at the Grocer's Hall in London, during a debutante ball, he bounded onstage with puppy-dog enthusiasm to sing Buddy Holly's 'Rave On', and after only a few bars bashed the microphone into his mouth, knocking his top teeth out. He ran offstage much faster than he'd run on only moments before, and Ray scooped the microphone up from the floor and started singing. Afterwards, Robert was slumped in a chair looking very sorry for himself and Grenville gave it to him straight: his singing was just not up to it; in fact, with Ray singing he felt the band could go places. So Robert should go find himself a dentist, then stick to management.

Deciding to work with Robert and Grenville had represented a leap of faith; they were feeling their way as much as we were. But they proved as good as their word and possibilities started opening up for us. The Beatles put out their debut album, *Please Please Me*, at the start of 1963, and their follow-up, *With The Beatles*, was about to be released that autumn when Robert and Grenville brought Brian Epstein along to see us rehearse. He was, of course, the manager of The Beatles and at the time there was no bigger name in pop. For him to sign us would have been a dream. He walked into the Camden Head pub in Islington and this giant of pop was actually very unassuming, quietly spoken and shy. We played a set and all the signs were good. He told us how much he had enjoyed the music, some of the material we would soon be making into demos, and that he'd report back – but we never heard from him again.

Getting ourselves a record deal had become an urgent priority. This was the way we could up our game and move on from playing the society circuit and whichever other gigs came our way. We turned up at the Regent Sound Studio on Denmark Street in Soho one day in November 1963 and recorded a bunch of demos. There was a pub across the road from Denmark Street, on Charing Cross Road, called The George where all the musicians would hang about. We met there and walked over to Denmark Street, and the studio itself was very small, in the basement of the building. There was hardboard on the walls for soundproofing, and a small mixing board with sliders and faders, and you'd walk down narrow stairs to get there. I'd written a song called 'I Believed You' which I really liked, but it ended up sounding too much like a Beatles track. We liked messing around with riffs and experimenting with instrumental colour and tone. Ray and I went to see Sonny Boy at the Fairfield Hall in Croydon, and we absorbed that tone and vibe in a way that's impossible from the records. 'I Believed You' was one of the first songs I'd written.

That same day we recorded a Leiber and Stoller song called 'I'm a Hog for You, Baby', which had a strong rhythm-and-blues feel, and Pete did a great job on backing vocals. Back into the studio before Christmas, we recorded more demos, including Ray's 'I Took My Baby Home' – a song reminiscent of 'Twist and Shout' – that we would record again as The Kinks, and which ended up as the B-side of 'Long Tall Sally', our first single. We also had fun with a song called 'Ooba Diooba', not the deepest thing we ever recorded. But the sound of The Kinks – as opposed to kids messing around with stuff they'd heard on the radio – was definitely hovering in the air on those records. I didn't like playing harmonica myself, and Ray did it very well on some of the demos; I thought about learning tenor sax for a while, but it's hard on the mouth, and I liked to sing and you can't really do both.

By the time we set foot in the studio again, in January 1964, we had become The Kinks. Although we didn't know it at the time, The Ravens evolved into The Kinks on New Year's Eve, 1963. Grenville and Robert had got us a gig at a New Year party at a popular Chinese restaurant on Edgware Road, near Marble Arch, called the Lotus House. That was our second gig of the evening: earlier we'd played in Hornsey to celebrate Pete's twentieth birthday, then we dashed over to Marble Arch to set ourselves up in time to see out the old year. The Lotus House had become a haunt for music-industry people, and we were happy to see our new booking agent, Arthur Howes, had come down for the party. And watching us play that night, Arthur, apparently, had a light-bulb moment. The name 'The Kinks' popped into his head. In our leathers and capes, we were a world apart from the clean-cut image of, say, Cliff Richard. We were 'kinky' in the way we looked and dressed; everyone had sex on the brain, even more than usual. What had gone on between government minister John Profumo and call girl Christine Keeler? The Profumo scandal was all over the newspapers, and the press weren't holding back on the sexual intrigues, reporting about 'kinky sex' like they might not have done a few years earlier. Arthur reckoned our risqué new name would gain us attention, notoriety even.

When we heard a few days later that Arthur thought we should be called 'The Kinks', we all thought he had lost the plot. It was explained to us that, as a practical consideration, 'The Kinks' would stand out on playbills and record sleeves more than 'The Ravens'. Following the demo sessions recorded on Denmark Street, Robert and Grenville had made headway on the question of a recording contract, although progress had at first been frustratingly slow. Things started changing when Kassner Music took an interest. Edward Kassner was an Austrian music publisher, and a shrewd businessman. He had ended up in Britain after his Jewish family left Austria during the war; already on the British scene a long while, he had published Bill Haley's 'Rock Around The Clock' in the UK. By 1963, Kassner was eyeing up the success of The Beatles with envy and was actively on the lookout for other promising young bands. His business partner was Larry Page who, like Robert, had flopped in his attempts to become a pop singer – even though he had dyed his hair all sorts of colours and at one point called himself 'Larry Page, the Teenage Rage'. Kassner signed us and it became Larry's job to look after the publishing side of things day to day.

Even with Larry on the case working alongside Robert and Grenville, securing a record deal was proving stubbornly difficult.

It was a no from Philips, no from Decca, no from Parlophone: these labels had been swamped with new acts – promising bands like The Beatles, The Rolling Stones, The Yardbirds, Manfred Mann – and somehow our demos landed on desks always just that little too late. But then we heard that Pye Records was interested, and next thing we knew our management had clinched a deal. We were ecstatic. Enter another person who would become central to the early story of The Kinks. Shel Talmy was a record producer from Chicago who had recently arrived in London and initially worked for Decca, and then moved to Pye. Talmy really had faith in our music and it was through his intervention that we got the deal. He then became our producer, and worked on our first single – 'Long Tall Sally' with 'I Took My Baby Home' on the B-side – and then our first album, called simply *Kinks*.

My day job at Selmers had already ended. Following the example set by my mum at the bronzing factory all those years earlier, I'd fallen asleep at work and they sacked me; I'd been playing an all-nighter and had gone straight to work the next morning. Ray had been studying at Croydon College of Art but felt increasingly detached from his studies – his imagination was filled with music. Pete had taken a job at a fashion magazine called *The Outfitter*, based near Charing Cross station, and now we all had to commit fully to The Kinks.

Ray, Pete and I had strong ideas about what we wanted the band to be, but the one problem we'd never properly resolved was the drummer. Mickey Willett, nice guy that he was, suddenly didn't fit. Musically, although he could hold down a solid rock backbeat, he was just that little bit older and clashed with the image our management were trying to project. He had never hit it off with Robert, and didn't much like Larry either, and his position in the band had become untenable. Mickey was suspicious of Robert and Grenville's motives; in his paranoid way, Mickey's view was that he had been round the block long enough to suspect he was being exploited – I personally was never convinced of that. Another row blew up after he refused to stay late to play an extra set for which we would have been paid handsomely. He had to get up for work the next morning, he said, and enough was enough. Then one day he was gone. His parting shot to us was a warning: 'You should watch these guys.'

Finding a replacement was no easy matter. We needed a drummer who could sustain a solid, hard-hitting backbeat. Auditions were held, but the drummers who turned up were either in the big-band mould like Willett or leaned more towards jazz, and likely viewed what we were trying to do as inferior. Bob Henrit, who eventually joined us in 1984, was due to audition but he was working for Adam Faith at the time, who refused to give him time off. Faith clearly didn't want to lose his drummer. Another drummer, Viv Prince, who ended up playing with the Pretty Things, told me years later that he was so stoned he forgot to turn up. Had he done so, he might well have got the job.

The day Mick Avory showed up at the Camden Head to audition, he looked like another in a long list of no-hopers. We were dressed in our denims and leathers, and Mick, as Ray once said, looked like a Boy Scout with his neatly cut hair and pressed suit. He was so nervous and uptight about being confronted by all these new people. Had one of us said 'boo' he would have jumped out of his skin. But once he started playing he won Ray over immediately. Certainly he was the most promising drummer we'd heard, but whether he was an exact fit – the perfect drummer for The Kinks – I felt less sure, but we went ahead anyway, and the tension that has always existed between Mick and me can perhaps be traced back to that first day. However, the pressure was on, and Grenville convinced me he would look the part. We'd been booked to play a prized slot on the pop TV show *Ready Steady Go!* and Pye wanted us to record. We needed a permanent, reliable drummer. So we hired Mick, and played some low-key gigs to break him in. The first gig with the classic Kinks line-up was at Oxford Town Hall on 1 February 1964. Mick needed to feel his way into the music, the influences we were working with and the rhythmic feels we wanted – but beyond that he needed to look and act the part. We were The Kinks – The *Kinks* – and the clue was very much in our name. Mick needed to loosen up. Robert and Grenville told him to let his hair grow long to look less groomed, which he did.

But it took him longer to get used to our jokes. Pete had started impersonating the gay men he'd met while working at *The Outfitter*: effeminate wiggles, hands on the hips, pouting lips, and I joined in enthusiastically with the high camp. And Mick simply didn't know how to take it. He looked uncomfortable and squirmed, so we'd tease him even more. Within a few months, though, he was camper than any of us.

Before Mick joined, we had already started rehearsing in the studio, with Shel Talmy in the sound booth loving what we were doing. Pye Studios was a step up from the cramped basement on Denmark Street where we'd recorded our demos only a couple of months earlier. During our first session we cut 'You Do Something To Me', 'You Still Want Me', 'Long Tall Sally' and 'I Took My Baby Home'. It was 20 January 1964, and the session had been arranged in a hurry. Arthur Howes had been in Paris and heard The Beatles perform Little Richard's 'Long Tall Sally' and the audience went crazy. They were likely to record the song, he said, therefore we should record a version of our own and do so quickly. We wanted our version to sound heavier and slower than The Beatles' version. Two or three days later we were in the studio, and then Pye didn't hang around. Our first single – 'Long Tall Sally' and 'I Took My Baby Home' – was released on 7 February 1964, four days after my seventeenth birthday.

That same day, we went to the Rediffusion Studios near Holborn for *Ready Steady Go!*, where we appeared alongside Manfred Mann, Kiki Dee and Ben E. King. Even though we mimed to our own record – the studio was too small to juggle the logistics of multiple different bands playing live – I was absolutely terrified. Appearing on television was completely alien to us, and I was a bag of nerves. But as soon as we started performing, and I thought about all those people watching us – even though we weren't actually singing – a light bulb switched on in my head. This felt great, exactly what I wanted to be doing, and even now I think of it as one of the most exciting moments of my life. The next time we appeared on the programme, we performed 'You Really Got Me' and made a bit of history. But for now, even though our appearance grabbed us lots of attention, 'Long Tall Sally' didn't sell well. It managed to chart at number 42 in *Melody Maker* magazine, then sank pretty much without trace.

To capitalise on our television appearance, we were booked to play dates all over the country and Arthur Howes got us lots of gigs all around London and in Manchester, Leeds, Newcastle, Leicester and in Liverpool, where we were even billed once as 'The Kinks from Liverpool'. At the Liverpool Empire one night we opened for The Beatles, and the audience wouldn't let us leave the stage. John Lennon sulked and sneered at us from the wings: 'Get these fucking people off!' Although later I came to love John dearly, he could be really nasty when he wanted to be.

The first tour we did was in a package with The Dave Clark Five and The Hollies. We had opened for The Beatles and knew their music and The Dave Clark Five sounded to us like a poor imitation. Their lead singer, Mike Smith, was a pleasant guy, but was trying to sound more like John Lennon than John Lennon, and so many bands wanted to cash in on The Beatles. This was the first time we'd experience the adulation of groupies, and especially girls who would do anything to be with their pop idols. But right from the beginning, The Kinks always wanted to be approachable and welcoming to people who liked our music, and we've always had a close affinity with our fans. That attitude started, I think, because when Ray and I began playing in The Clissold Arms, it was like an extension of playing for our family in the front room of Denmark Terrace. It stayed with us, embedded deeply inside the group, and these days I'm on Twitter – @DaveDaviesKinks – and fans often fire questions at me about The Kinks and all sorts of other music. The internet has been a good and bad place. Sometimes I find the attention stressful, but it's allowed me to reconnect with old friends like Mike Quinn, the singers Jayne County – wonderful! – 'Weird Al' Yankovic and the DJ David Symonds from the BBC, one of the original line-up on Radio 1.

The Hollies had started a couple of years before us, and were older and more experienced. In 1964 they released two albums – *Stay With The Hollies* and *In The Hollies Style* – and their music, although drawing on some of the same influences, like Chuck Berry and Ray Charles, wasn't as raw as ours, but I really liked their harmonies; they had an approach totally of their own. Their bass player Eric Haydock and singer Graham Nash realised we were new to touring and tried to look after us, and make sure we didn't get into trouble – not too much trouble anyway. Arthur Howes, concerned perhaps that 'Long Tall Sally' hadn't raced to the top of the charts as we'd all hoped, hired what these days would be referred to as an 'image consultant' to sharpen us up, a guy called Hal Carter. He had worked with Billy Fury as his road manager and was well-meaning enough, but his attempts to choreograph childish dance routines for us – leaping from one side of the stage to the other, leaping on top of our amps – was embarrassing nonsense and showed that he had zero understanding of our music. And nor would he shut up about Billy Fury; Billy, apparently, was 'an artist' and we were nothing. One day Graham Nash was watching from the side of the stage as we were rehearsing and saw through the crap immediately. 'Hey, Hal,' he shouted, 'why don't you fuck off and leave them alone? They're great as they are and are going to be fine.' Graham gave us the confidence to stick with what we were doing.

As we toured, one thing became clear: the crowds loved 'You Really Got Me' and always screamed and clapped for more, could never get enough of the song. Our second single, 'You Still Want Me' and 'You Do Something To Me', which used up the remainder of the material we'd recorded in January alongside 'Long Tall Sally' and 'I Took My Baby Home', was released in April and did OK, but not as well as we'd hoped. Our initial contract with Pye was for three singles, and had number three also tanked, the future of the band would have been uncertain. With the sounds of audiences ringing in our ears, 'You Really Got Me' was the obvious thing to put on the A-side of the next single. We recorded a demo – which has since vanished from the face of the earth – and then ran into big trouble. All these years later, the idea of 'You Really Got Me' *not* being considered suitable for a single is unthinkable, but the message from Pye was that it would be a commercial flop; it was too raw and in-yer-face. Even Pete had his doubts.

Our first attempt at recording 'You Really Got Me', like the earlier demo, has gone missing. I get asked about it all the time, and while I understand the curiosity over this lost piece of Kinks history, believe me, it was horrible. Had Shel Talmy misunderstood the song, or was he trying to soften it to appease the record company? Either way he got it wrong. He failed to understand that the power and energy of the song spun out of the guitar riff, which he decided to nudge into the background. He'd become obsessed with Phil Spector and his 'wall of sound' and, having backgrounded the riff, he then swamped the song with reverb and stuff, which snuffed out that gritty, earthy sound we wanted. It was also much slower than the version everyone would come to know. After the session, Ray and I knew that the record, as it stood, was awful and could never be released. This landed us right in the shit. Pye had paid for studio time to record a song they were uncertain about – and our admission that it didn't work confirmed their worst suspicions. They wanted to drop it; Ray dug his heels in. The necessity to re-record 'You Really Got Me' was obvious, but Pye refused to put up the extra money, and a lot of people got very upset. Eventually Robert and Grenville agreed to pay for another session, and their £200 saved The Kinks. We'd have walked away rather than have Pye issue that dreadful record.

We assembled in the IBC Studios on Portland Place – one day in the middle of July 1964, a month or so after our first attempt – to make 'You Really Got Me' again. The atmosphere was tense. Shel produced again. He was professional and friendly as always, but an unspoken criticism hung in the air – he'd messed up a month earlier, and that's why we were in the studio for a second time. We all knew what was at stake. Get this wrong, and it was over. If we couldn't get it right this time – what then? Ray was wound up like a coiled spring, but I was more relaxed. This was our opportunity to get the song right, and to exorcise memories of the earlier version. We had our vision of what the song should be – and once we were allowed to follow our instincts, without any reverb or echo bullshit, slowly we heard it become a reality. That gave us a thrill. As every-one was fussing around, I began to get impatient. 'Let's just record it!' I remember screaming.

Our management was nervous about whether we could cut it. Mick was new into the band and had been doing well, but he wasn't experienced in playing the rock backbeat we needed for 'You Really Got Me'. Bobby Graham, a great session drummer, was brought in; he and a jazz guy called Phil Seaman were the top session drummers of the period. This was before the really great rock drummers came into being in this country, and Bobby was so kick-ass. The first time he came in with what drummers call a flam – a crushed shorter note, before the main hit – fucking hell, it roared! And just listen to the way he made our version of Chuck Berry's 'Beautiful Delilah', which we recorded the same day, swing. He was very generous and helpful too, and became the rhythmic glue that helped the record gel. There were other musicians hanging around in the background, and we didn't know why they were there. Now I realise it was insurance: studio time is very expensive and they were on hand to play if we needed. Over the years the myth has arisen that Jimmy Page – later of Led Zeppelin, and one of the musicians hanging around that day – played my solo on 'You Really Got Me'. It's completely untrue; Jimmy has acknowledged that too. I was an aggressive young kid who wanted to play. Nobody could have stopped me soloing that day! It was my guitar sound and my guitar solo.

The studio was plusher than Regent Sound Studio, and the sound was drier, which suited 'You Really Got Me' well – you could actually hear how the instruments sounded. Bobby Graham played behind a screen, much bigger than the screens at Regent Sound: this was to stop the sound of his drums swamping everything else. Ray, Pete and I had a microphone each, and I think they were Dynamic mics, which gave a more natural filter to the room's ambience and made the sound tighter. The engineer placed what we called a 'bum mic' behind where Bobby sat. It was a dynamic microphone which picked up the resonant bottom of the bass drum. We needed that thwack. The snare drum is very crisp and punchy on the record – this was a minimal miking technique that made an important difference. We also had Arthur Greenslade on piano, who never played live with us, but we wanted the flavour of eight-to-the-bar New Orleans-style piano on the record, like Fats

Domino, Little Richard or Chuck Berry's pianist, Johnnie Johnson.

Arthur's piano also helped outline the harmony. The song starts in G, but instead of a regular four-bar pattern in G, C and then D, 'You Really Got Me' modulates to A. A couple of years later, Leonard Bernstein, no less, appeared on American television, during one of his *Young People's Concerts*, and talked about this 'really terrific, barbaric song by The Kinks'. He even sang it, accompanying himself on the piano. He was lecturing the kids about modes and talked about 'You Really Got Me' as exemplifying the Mixolydian mode, which, I have to say, came as news to us. The energy of that chord shift – from G to A – was really based around a sexual feeling. The foreplay, the penetration, then the guitar solo was the ecstatic climax. Some people have said that Mick Avory ended up playing tambourine. I can't remember, but he had to learn on the job about rock backbeats, and quickly, because we had gigs to play.

Just before I started soloing, Ray shouted, 'Oh, no!' It was a purely spontaneous gesture, not something we'd worked out before, and this was a moment that said a lot about our relationship. On one level he was praying I wouldn't fuck up. He was uptight and projected that onto me – I was the one who somehow needed to be controlled and made to behave in a certain way. He was worried about studio time, and reaching the end of the session without finishing the record. Fair enough. But most of the time, especially with creative stuff, things work better when you leave them alone. Why couldn't he just fucking leave me alone? It irritated me that he said anything. I think Ray's always had a fear of the unknown or the unexpected, whereas music freed me – although Ray's skills for organising and refining meant he excelled at crafting his songs and arrangements.

Life was never the same again after Pye released 'You Really Got Me' on 4 August 1964. Within a few weeks it had reached number one in the UK singles chart, then we heard it was due to be released that September in the US. It stayed at number one for two weeks, toppling The Rolling Stones, The Beatles and Jim Reeves from the top spot. Only a year earlier we'd been playing posh society balls and weren't even called The Kinks, and now this. It felt like a dream, but achieving success like that, and so quickly, at the age of seventeen, was addictive. I wanted more and more success, and to play all the time. The moment it really hit me, I was driving back to Muswell Hill in my friend Jeff Francis' car after seeing Arthur Howes at his office on Greek Street, and suddenly there was our record on Radio Caroline. Caught unawares by our own record, I was able to hear it, momentarily admittedly, from an outsider's perspective. It was true to what we wanted to express, and so earthy you could have planted a tree in the sound. I was blown away by its trance-like hypnotic power.

Suddenly The Kinks were everywhere. In magazines like *Melody Maker*, the *NME* and *Fab* – also magazines devoted to fashion, newspapers too. We were on *Thank Your Lucky Stars* and *Top of the Pops*, which was filmed in Manchester, and we had a lot of fun doing live sessions. *Top of the Pops* has become synonymous with pop success, but back then *Ready Steady Go!* was the heart of the business and had the best atmosphere. The producer, Vicky Wickham, was totally on the side of The Kinks and we performed 'You Really Got Me', as Manfred Mann, The Four Pennies and Kenny Lynch looked on. Important to the atmosphere was the large studio where they filmed the show. All the bands listened to each other play. That's how I met Otis Redding, who I adored. I had imagined because of his voice he'd be rough and ready, but he was a gentleman, very accommodating and friendly, and he loved The Kinks. He also loved The Rolling Stones – he covered 'Satisfaction' on his 1965 album *Otis Blue/Otis Redding Sings Soul* – and was very in tune with that dirty, working-class energy. I also became good friends with Dionne Warwick. By this point Mick and I were sharing a house in Muswell Hill, on Connaught Gardens. Dionne would come back with me after shows and we had some great conversations. She was into spirituality, psychic stuff, ouija boards and the like. It was never a sexual thing, but we had a real affinity based around music and psychic energy.

I also met Gerry Marsden when Gerry and the Pacemakers played on *Ready Steady Go!*, and Cilla Black. There was a Liverpudlian vibe and a Manchester vibe. They joked around and drank just as much as the London groups, but they considered us to be very serious. Cilla was light-entertainment pop compared to someone like Dionne, but she was very funny, a bit of a tomboy and everyone's mate. Gerry always had more of an eye for Marianne Faithfull, who was very beautiful. Everyone tried to chat her up, but Gerry was always the most determined. Also around was Jimmy Savile, who we didn't take at all seriously because he was one of those DJs with a gift of the gab, and everything seemed a joke to him. I was shocked and appalled when, a few years ago, it was revealed what he was getting up to. I could never take him seriously, and to know how he was behaving in the background saddened me deeply.

The other force from Liverpool to be reckoned with was, of course, The Beatles. I'd had a girlfriend called Joan Glass, and I would play her Chuck Berry and blues, and she would say, 'Yeah, they're all right, but you need to listen to this.' And she played me The Beatles' first album, *Please Please Me*. Eventually she said she liked The Beatles better than The Kinks, which put me right off her. When I heard 'Love Me Do' for the first time, I thought quite honestly it was a novelty record. It was catchy, fair enough, but John Lennon's harmonica was jaunty and straight ahead. It didn't have any obvious blues inflection, that sliding tone, like how Ray or Hamilton King played. I thought it was Larry Adler, the light-music harmonica player who was always on the radio and had played on the soundtrack to the film *Genevieve*, a popular musician of a different ilk. But The Beatles couldn't be ignored. Pete Quaife was a big fan, and when I heard 'She Loves You' I understood how skilfully they were bringing a different tone and vibe to the regular pop song.

When we played The Cavern Club in Liverpool, all of a sudden Pete developed a Liverpudlian accent. 'Pete! Why are you talking like that?' I asked him. 'Oh, I don't know what you mean *like*,' he said, as though he was purebred Scouse. So many bands north of Watford were trying to be The Beatles, like The Mojos and Wayne Fontana and the Mindbenders. Billy J. Kramer was another, but he had a great voice and we became good friends, recognising that spirit of the lone rebel within each other. By the time we had a couple of hits, 'You Really Got Me' and 'All Day and All of the Night', under our belts, I honestly didn't feel any rivalry with The Beatles. It was the same with The Stones – they were different enough for rivalry not to be a problem. Talking to Paul McCartney one night at The Scotch of St James club, around the time 'See My Friends' came out, he said '*We* should have done that song.' And I said: 'But you didn't, did you?'

'See My Friends' was really the first rock record to evoke the flavour of Indian music, and was a real change of direction for us following 'You Really Got Me'. A lot of people adored that record, especially other musicians, and McCartney was very shrewd and was always taking everything in, listening carefully. I admired George Harrison's guitar playing and Ringo Starr's drumming very much but, especially George, they seemed like private people who preferred to be left alone.

John had a prickly exterior, and I wonder if that earlier experience in Liverpool, when The Kinks impressed what he considered to be *his* audience, had coloured his view of us as Cockney upstarts. But he was always happy to talk, and we discussed music and wider things. He and I shared a working-class background, and we could relate. It seemed to me he was lonely and shy, in pain even. Certainly I was shy, and increasingly I was using drugs and drink to mask my shyness, and I could come across as insufferably overbearing. One night at The Scotch of St James club, John slammed the table during one of our conversations and called me a 'cynical, obnoxious bastard'. And, to be fair, he had a point – the booze and the drugs could make me boorish and pushy, and now I regret somewhat how I behaved in those days.

Because I grew up around all those sisters, I was never shy around girls. When 'You Really Got Me' came out, I was still living with my parents on Denmark Terrace, but my habit of bringing girls home at all hours became a problem. Mum turned a blind eye to some of what happened at first, and she would discreetly check how old they were in case I landed myself in trouble. She tolerated lots of disruption and noise, but I realised the situation couldn't continue after she burst into my bedroom and found me in bed with a whole gang of female groupies. After that incident I got the house with Mick Avory on Connaught Gardens. The drugs and parties became so outrageous that even Mick couldn't deal with it and moved back with his mum for a while. There were always groupies in the house, and the bedrooms were never quiet.

After spending my life with very little money, suddenly the attention – recognised and praised wherever I went – was intoxicating, and I would swagger around the place, and often jump at the chance of showing off. People are attracted to success and the more you're told you are brilliant, the more you believe it. It's an unhealthy way to live, but behind my brazen confidence I knew shit and was frightened and I muddled along as best I could. I was an innocent in many ways. The first thing I bought with my newfound riches? Not a fancy apartment in a fashionable part of town, or an expensive car. I marched into a big department store in Holborn called Gamages, famous then for its large toy department, and bought a Scalextric car track. But I didn't just buy a few things – I bought everything the shop had. The attendant couldn't believe his luck, and a few days later it was delivered and I set it up in my bedroom, like I'd always dreamed I would when I was a kid. I also found I could acquire clothes by just walking into shops on Carnaby Street. They'd literally give me clothes in the hope I'd wear them on television.

Imagine me, man about town, swaggering into The Scotch of St James, often with a whole entourage of folks that somehow I'd managed to pick up on the way. The Scotch of St James was behind Piccadilly and was *the* place to be seen and hang out. This was where top musicians, people from the fashion industry, and showbiz types all came to party. Eric Burdon of The Animals had a flat above it; Jimi Hendrix played his first show in the UK there. This was where John Lennon had called me obnoxious, and where I became friends with Brian Jones from The Rolling Stones. I'd open a tab and buy drinks for everybody, and it was the best place in town to meet girls. Wannabe actresses and singers hung out there, hoping that the stardust might rub off. A night might start on Carnaby Street, trying to score drugs at one of the pubs, the Shakespeare's Head or Blue Post. A 'drink' was a cocktail of an amphetamine called Purple Hearts, washed down with either white wine or Coca-Cola, perhaps with a joint on the side. Then, once the pubs had closed, we might move on to a club like the Flamingo, Whisky A Go Go or Kaleidoscope; then finish the night at The Scotch of St James, often with an after-party back at my place in Muswell Hill, or crashing at the Ashburn Hotel in Kensington.

Going on, hanging out, getting high and finally to bed – that was the rhythm. Often after breakfast I'd feel surprisingly OK in the morning, and able to get on with the day. Drugs came into my life not in Soho, but at the El Toro coffee bar in Muswell Hill, where at one time I'd hung out with Sue. Sometimes Ray and I had played there as a duo, and that's when I discovered pot, then called 'reefers': marijuana rolled into cigarettes. It had become much easier for people of my generation to acquire drugs. The big difference with the earlier generation of musicians, especially the modern jazz set, was that we took drugs to make life seem more fun and exciting.

After a gig in Sheffield that summer, I noticed two girls hanging around at the stage door. I asked them if they'd like to come into the van and meet the boys. They were Rasa and Eileen, and Ray immediately paired off with Rasa, and Eileen came back to my hotel room. I liked Eileen a lot but never regarded her as 'my girlfriend', but Ray and Rasa became inseparable and a few months later they married. This was a period when Ray and I were getting along well, and me and Rasa also got on. She loved The Mamas & the Papas and sang their songs all the time, and had a very cool voice, and we used her as backing vocals on later Kinks records. She was brought up in Bradford and her best friend from that time was Kiki Dee, and Kiki used to come round all the time. Rasa – full name Rasa Emilija Halina Didzpetris – was the daughter of Lithuanian refugees, very serious and earnest people, with strong moral values and manners that were beyond reproach.

Our management wanted Ray to marry on the quiet. Had word got out that he was no longer available, the mystique would disappear and many of our female fans with it. So the wedding was held in Bradford, with a reception afterwards at the family home. Eileen was maid of honour and I was best man. We got to the house early for the reception and, as the guests were arriving, ran upstairs and started making out. After a while, we heard my sister Peggy calling my name, and the bedroom door opened. She froze with embarrassment and shock, and eventually spluttered out, 'David, everyone's waiting for the wedding toast and your best man's speech!' We managed to run down the stairs as we adjusted our clothes, and we smiled awkwardly as we ran into the room, with Eileen holding up her bouffant hair. By the time it came to give the speech I'd had far too much to drink, and winked naughtily at the vicar and called him Vic. He didn't see the funny side. Then I launched into some incoherent nonsense about how pissed I was – and how everyone else could do the same and have a fucking good time. Everyone laughed, apart from Rasa's family, who looked somewhat crestfallen. But they just got on with it.

Ray and I had always loved music growing up, but it wasn't the guitar that always interested us – it was the songs and how they affected people. Listening to The Mamas & the Papas, and also to The Byrds and Bob Dylan, it hit me that a whole new genre of American music had emerged: this wasn't the rock of Buddy Holly or Eddie Cochran, something new was happening. I loved The Byrds' 'Eight Miles High', their nod towards John Coltrane's influence, such a deliberately wild guitar solo that works beautifully. I was writing songs, but I was too busy having a good time and didn't take songwriting as seriously as I should have done. But Ray was honing his craft, and was drinking in all sorts of music: Charlie Parker, Motown, electric blues – he listened to it all. Larry Page would rub his hands together and say, 'We need more songs, Ray.' After they married, Ray and Rasa moved into an elegant Georgian house on Fortis Green, a short walk from Denmark Terrace. This was a very rich and creative period for us. Ray had a white upright piano in his back room, and we'd have intense sessions during which we'd work out arrangements, develop ideas into finished songs and work out vocal harmonies. Ray would call me whenever he wanted to get together.

So much had happened in 1964. Our lives had changed beyond anything we could have imagined, and the year ended on no less of a high. At the end of September 1964 we went into the studio to record 'All Day and All of the Night', which I feel, sonically, was much more powerful than 'You Really Got Me', simply because we were allowed to record the song as we wanted. The guitars bite, the attitude is wild and raw, and we recorded it without any fuss or disagreements. The same engineers who had sneered at my guitar set-up earlier in the year were now full of praise. Nobody could argue with the success of 'You Really Got Me'. 'All Day and All of the Night', and our debut album, *Kinks*, were released that October, and we went on a package promotional tour with The Yardbirds, whose guitarist Eric Clapton, before Jeff Beck turned up, was also playing rough and aggressive blues. 'You Really Got Me' and 'All Day and All of the Night' seemed to grab audiences instantly, more so than a more 'poppy' song like 'So Mystifying' that was on our album. It reached number two in the charts, and after all the uncertainty surrounding 'You Really Got Me', The Kinks were here to stay – although at that time, none of us could have guessed for how long, or the musical journey upon which we had embarked.

A few months earlier I'd been in a shop in Muswell Hill, and saw a man I recognised. Then I realised it was Mr Loads, the headmaster of Willy Grim, who I'd last seen in his office when he expelled me, and gave me the cane. He trotted over to me and told me how excited he was to see me on television, in words filled with insincerity. I glared back at him, then brushed past his shoulder and walked out the shop. I glanced back and his mouth was open with astonishment. But what had he expected? I also realised that he wasn't the big man I'd remembered. I thought, Fuck you. He'd told me I'd amount to nothing, but I had made a life for myself based on my skills and creativity. A schoolboy in disgrace, no longer.

CHAPTER THREE

EV'RYBODY'S GONNA BE HAPPY

When I was recovering from my stroke, taking time in hospital to think back over everything that had happened in my life over the previous thirty years or so, I learned that the brain constantly adapts itself to new situations. The doctor who looked after me was writing a book about neuroplasticity, the processes through which the brain is able to heal itself after a trauma. She used to tell me: at school, you don't learn the alphabet first time; it is repeated over and over until, finally, you remember it. The arrangement of the letters travels through nerves in the brain but, for that pattern to stick, permanent neuropathways have to be created – which is why the alphabet needs to be repeated like a mantra or ritual.

I related immediately to that because working with The Kinks had taught me about the power of rituals. Grooves have ritualistic energies, like they've been carved from sacred, mystical places, and that's the reason the 'You Really Got Me' and 'All Day and All of the Night' riffs connected with people. The blues speaks directly to us now, while also evoking something ancient and musically fundamental, harkening back to another time while also being time*less*. The Kinks had been about discovering new experiences in music and, it soon became clear, in life too. We were never interested in reheating old formulas or ideas; we wanted to open up new pathways, musically and expressively.

As a kid I was always interested in sci-fi movies from the 1950s and early 1960s like *It Came From Outer Space*, *The Day of the Triffids* and *1984* with Peter Cushing – what an actor! I was also a big fan of *Quatermass*, which terrified the crap out of people when it was on television. When *Star Trek* turned up on TV here around 1966, this was still the very early days of The Kinks and it all somehow felt connected. Watching those old shows now, it's amazing how they've stood the test of time. Long before *The Simpsons*, here was a drama that took on American society and was unafraid to take the piss a little. Gene Roddenberry, who created the show, was very much in tune with the way society was going and took lots of care in developing his characters. One week you might see a good philosophical story, and even if the next week was a little flimsy, and not especially deep, the episodes were always funny because his characters were so fully formed.

It's amazing, thinking back, that people were exploring psychological subjects using sci-fi as a way to tackle the esoteric on mainstream TV. Later, when I became interested in metaphysics – people who are into sci-fi are often interested in metaphysics – I began to appreciate *Star Trek* even more. Every great story starts with a great journey. Pythagoras and Plato had ideas about new universes, Jules Verne and H. G. Wells too. Ideas of journeying into the future also resonated with my interest in the blues: looking for a way out, journeying beyond the everyday. When I was a kid I had aspirations for another worldliness, and that's why I was interested in Tarot cards and my mum's tea-leaf reading. Discovering *Star Trek* seemed to encapsulate so many of these ideas, especially of going – boldly – on an adventure where 'no man has gone before'. One of my favourite *Star Trek* movies – with the original cast – is *Voyage Home*, and I love that film because it's about the clumsiness of being out of time. They've transported themselves from the future into the Bay area of the 1980s. Spock has to wear a headband to cover up his huge ears and Kirk explains, getting the language muddled: 'Don't mind him, he took too much LDS in the 1960s,' a line that always makes me laugh.

An undercurrent of sci-fi was young people exploring what was really going on, rather than accepting what they'd been told, like how we'd given ourselves permission to experiment with rock music. English pop music from the late 1950s often felt smarmy and phoney, pretending to be something it wasn't, and that same icky sentimentality bled over into the 1960s pop scene. Pat Boone was a tremendous singer, and lots of people liked him. But a Little Richard record in the early 1960s took you into unknown territory. You can't compare Pat Boone to the earthiness, dirt and reality of Little Richard, whose music was truly something else. In 1965, as part of a poll-winners' concert, we shared the bill with Tom Jones and, nice guy that he was, he was like a relic from the 1950s. His voice had an operatic boom, and the way he moved was stiff and overly choreographed. He wasn't very rock and roll, and I couldn't begin to understand how he had captured the popular imagination. But listen to Little Richard and you can't help but dance and move your ass, and dancing has always been tribal. It's an important centre of cultural expression, of who we are as human beings. Over recent years they've discovered that dancing, as well as yoga and other forms of exercise, can help build neuroplasticity, which creates new pathways within the brain.

So much pop music around that time was easy to understand, telling people they were safe and acting as a comfort blanket. But The Kinks were never motivated by comfort. We were working-class kids who had been soaking up the sounds of Little Richard, Leadbelly, Sonny Boy Williamson and Chuck Berry – music of a whole other magnitude. Towards the end of his life, Albert Einstein intimated that imaginations think up scientific ideas and therefore imagination is more important than science. Carl Jung intimated that Western teaching avoided delving deep into the subconscious, and he talked about the collective unconscious. Over the years I've investigated astrology and music and the mind – the conscious, super-conscious and subconscious mind – and these are areas that need to be talked about in everyday life. Music is a great way of connecting our emotions and our mind to the spirit world, because what we can learn from looking beyond the conscious mind is very valuable. The physical reflex response listening to Little Richard or Chuck Berry – or 'You Really Got Me' – try *not* tapping your foot – tells us of the power beyond our conscious mind. We get an idea and think, Right, that's it. I've done it!, but that's only the beginning. It's our conscious mind interfering that often screws things up. The conscious mind wants everything filed neatly in boxes, but the creative mind knows how to select what it needs from what other people might consider chaos. Maybe we need a measure of order and chaos to function.

Ray and I have a kind of telepathic understanding and he can be a bit of a perfectionist, but emotionally I always knew when a piece of music was ready. His instinct was usually to keep on cooking, and in the end sometimes cook the shit out of it. When a flower is growing, it flowers, it blossoms and eventually dies, but you need to catch it when it's ripe. Before it ripens an apple is sour, but if it's too ripe it goes all mushy. Knowing when something is ripe is a useful thing we can learn from nature and the earth – otherwise you end up making tiny, fiddly adjustments that take you further away from the thing you're trying to achieve. Talk about the spirit world and to some people you're weird but, the truth is, the universe knows more about what's going on than we do. When I was recovering from my illness and listening obsessively to classical music, to composers such as Berlioz and Haydn, and especially to Beethoven's Seventh Symphony, those chords that open his slow movement felt like the end and the beginning of something all at the same time, a perfect unity. It was spiritual nourishment to me during a troubled period.

As The Kinks became successful, I started to think carefully about how music affects moods. One reason I got into astrology, Tarot and mystical things was because of my brother and trying to make sense of his behaviour and how we interacted. I couldn't always fathom his meaning. And I started to question *why* people say one thing while thinking another. I was coming to terms with my own sense of intuition, inherited from my mum. In Western society, lies flourish just as much as truth and beauty. When people sound like they're speaking eloquently, often they might be lying; and I can usually tell. Music and feelings, and intuition, are all connected. Why did I gravitate to The Ventures more than to The Shadows? In my mind I thought that The Ventures was a musically authentic group, not that I knew why at the time.

Youth culture wasn't only concerned with music, of course. Similar movements were afoot in film, the visual arts, literature, theatre and comedy. I saw *The Loneliness of the Long-Distance Runner* at the cinema. Its star, Tom Courtenay, was a truly remarkable actor, I thought, and, it turned out, a very good footballer too. We both played a few times on the Showbiz Eleven football team, and there was an immediate kinship between us. When I met Albert Finney, most likely at a party, we also shared an immediate understanding. He was from working-class Manchester, but it was like meeting someone from my own family. As we chatted about football and what we could get away with at school, there was an immediate emotional connection. I'd greatly admired his performance in *Saturday Night and Sunday Morning* and, although the film was shot in Nottingham, it could easily have been set in Muswell Hill. Shirley Anne Field's character reminded me of my sister Gwen; that same look, and they talked in a similar way, albeit with their different accents.

The music The Kinks made – and all the music I most admired, Little Richard and all the rest – was in touch with the earth. In essence 'You Really Got Me' is a song about a guy wanting to lay his girlfriend, and there are so many questions asked in that record about how to put those primal feelings and that emotion into sound. That's why I got into music: because feelings are so essential and immediate. Practising yoga is a deep learning process, and one of the things I learned is the deep connection between sex and the nervous system. We make the connection physically through sex and love and emotion, and the union of marriage is mystically an enlightening experience. The mystical practices of yoga work constantly to build that connection between body, mind and spirit.

I discovered that the basis of astrology is the elements: earth, fire, water and air. Astrology is a pinpoint point-of-view into the cosmos. Every element in the cosmos, and in your life, you see through the prism of your own perspective. The *Kabalah* offers keys to a micro as well as a macro universe. Even if two people were born at precisely the same moment and place, everybody has a different point of reference, and a point of perception – a point of where you are in the cosmos and the universe. I believe that the human body knows us better than the mind, because the mind is more changeable than the body. There's an exercise based on a concept called Psychokinesis. Stand up and put your arms out, and move them up and down. Then put one arm out and hold something you suspect is unhealthy – like a cigarette – in the other. Ask someone to pull your arm down and try to resist. If it's easy for them to push your arm down, then that's your body saying 'this is not healthy'. But if you were holding a flower, you would feel your arm becoming strong, and that's our body talking to us, not through language but through action. Music is a big part of that. Little Richard was born by a railway track and knew how to make a backbeat sound like a train coming down the track. Him screaming 'Tutti Frutti' was pumping fresh energy into the world.

Real investigation into music extends our understanding of sound, and there is no right or wrong way to find out what's going on. They talk about Aleister Crowley as though he was a 'black magician', but he was merely creating devices to wake people up into new ways of thinking. Too often people will call what they can't understand 'evil', but art sometimes needs to explore unpalatable truths. Crowley had an exceptional mind. The spirit of that era was adventure and experiment, and people opening their minds to new experiences, whether musically, sexually or through drugs.

The Kinks started performing a lot in Paris, and I had a French girlfriend called Su-Su. After a drunken night on the town, Su-Su and I ended up back at my hotel near the Moulin Rouge. We kissed and undressed each other and made love. Afterwards, as the dawn broke, Su-Su talked to me about other sexual experiences, and it turned out one of her other lovers was Brian Jones. They would get together whenever The Rolling Stones played in Paris. My lover was telling me she enjoyed going to bed with someone else, a friend of mine, but there was no jealousy; I was, in fact, excited and turned on. I told her that I had always fancied Brian – I used to say, he was the only other man in London who knew how to dress! – and thought what fun it would be, if ever we were all in Paris at the same time, to have a threesome. Brian, she said, had mentioned that he fancied me, although the next time I saw him in London we avoided the subject.

But my mind had been opened to sexual encounters with men and I happily explored the possibilities without ever attaching labels like 'gay' or 'bisexual' to what I was doing. The relationships I had taught me lots about men and my attitudes to sex. The love I'd had for Sue, and for other women later in my life, was special and unique but, if you genuinely respect and love another human being, does it matter if they happen to be male or female? Most people would simply prefer to know that someone loves and is caring for them. The most important thing I learned is sensitivity. Men have feelings too and no one should ever make fun of people's emotions. I was flamboyant and cocky, and fucking around with a sweet guy was fun. Maybe he kissed nice and I enjoyed the way he touched me. But I came to understand that having relationships with men who considered themselves gay, and wanted commitment beyond sex, was dishonest and too often led to distressing situations. That's why messing with people's emotions is a bad idea. When I came to the conclusion that I was hurting people, and abusing their feelings, I stopped because it was fake and dishonest. Emotions can be powerful but also extremely fragile. My dad had grown up at the tail end of that era when a man had to be 'a man', but I had learned *not necessarily*. My dad ended up nurturing flowers, and I nurtured sounds and feelings. Men can be nurturing without having to sleep with each other. It is nurturing that encourages the intuitive and spiritual part of us, but creativity is more important than anything, because through the creative process we can find solutions, maybe to everything.

Back in the 1960s, pop music was, of course, entertainment and whatever lofty ideas I might have been incubating were best kept to myself. They had no place on *Ready Steady Go!* or *Top of the Pops*. When Robert told us his latest bright idea – that we had to wear white frilly shirts and pink hunting outfits – I didn't feel comfortable about the prospect, but went along with the idea so we could reach the next stop on the journey. Robert acted like he was better off than he was and used to buy all his clothes on Savile Row, and no doubt mixed socially with the hunting set. He would take us to check out the riding stables behind St George's Hospital where posher people used to go horse riding. Robert liked the fact, I think, that we looked part of that world with which he was familiar.

He and Grenville liked to show us the aspects of their lives that they thought would impress us.

For a band inspired by Sonny Boy Williamson, Lead Belly and Chuck Berry, wearing hunting outfits associated with the English upper classes was unquestionably an odd thing to do. But that was the theatre of pop and it gave us a distinctive look. Pete and I always thought about fashion – the elegance of hipster trousers, jackets, boots and belts. I loved Oscar Wilde's style. Wilde's hair was parted down the middle, which was nice to see because every new band seemed to copy The Beatles' signature haircut: 'Oh no, not again!' The first time we were in Germany we met a band called The Lords, a German band that had existed before The Beatles. Then they saw *A Hard Day's Night* and wanted to be a German equivalent of The Beatles – and that included copying that fucking stupid haircut and it looked like they were all wearing German helmets. Yet they thought they were cool.

Ray and Mick weren't into fashion at first and their ideas about clothes came from me and Pete. Left to his own devices, Mick was happy wearing baggy jumpers and Ray wasn't a very good dresser either. I remember Robert saying you cannot always develop a taste for good fashion and a style; some people just have a knack for fashion. He said I could wear the curtains and look good, but Ray always looked awkward and needed to grab something extra, like a hat, for the same costume to work. I guess costumes had a long history in British popular music, dating back to Acker Bilk and his waistcoats, and wearing the hunting jackets was fun the first few times. But by the time we got to Perth and Sydney in Australia, playing Bondi Beach in 120 degrees, we came to realise that the joke was over and in danger of becoming a parody. Shit, it was hot in those jackets.

My musicality has been driven always by something that I can't attain, and by feelings that I can't fully explain. Because the human body knows us better than the mind, my body tells me when the music feels right. Over many years there have been occasions when Ray and I have been in the studio or onstage, and something extraordinary and unexpected happens. Moments like that are gone before you realise they've happened, and can never be repeated. Those particular moments – maybe just a millisecond – of inspiration feel set in a time frame of their own, like a gateway has opened up, and new inspiration and fresh energy have crept in. There might be an album title – like *The Kinks Are The Village Green Preservation Society* or *Bug* – and also an idea of the themes or characters I want to touch on, but I never see a new album all at once; I only find out what an album is through making it.

Who's to say some of the places in these albums aren't actually real? They can't all be in your imagination, and it is a creative person's job to access this information in as honest a way as possible. We all add little creative touches to real life, and creative people do it more. An image in a Picasso painting could have been actual while, at the same time, suggesting other dimensions of his consciousness. His paintings were often about what was really happening and what he thought *might* happen. This is why paintings contain more real life than photographs. Painting connects us to other levels of consciousness, and that is the great expression of artistic experiment. You keep looking at a painting because it hands you different information each time. This is in part what meditation is about, unravelling aspects of yourself that you might be ready for. You don't start life like a book, on page one and moving forwards from there. You start off with a feeling. When you're young you know stuff without necessarily being able to express it, but as we grow older we can learn to be more in touch with our feelings. It's normal to ask questions like 'Where are we in the cosmos?' In the early days people thought I was a bit crazy, but nowadays I'm as crazy as everybody else.

*

By the middle of 1964 our first album, *Kinks*, had reached number four in the charts and stayed there for twenty-three weeks, which was considered a real achievement. And then the pressure was on not only for new songs, but for a whole new album: if 1964 had been busy, everything cranked up a gear in 1965. At the end of 1964 we had toured in a package with Gerry and the Pacemakers, Gene Pitney, Marianne Faithfull, The Mike Cotton Sound and The Manish Boys, a group that included a young tenor saxophone player and singer called Davie Jones, who later did pretty well when he renamed himself David Bowie. Then we toured the UK in May for the first time as a headline act, in a package with The Yardbirds, Goldie and the Gingerbreads and The Riot Squad. And we toured internationally, all over Scandinavia and Australia and New Zealand, France, Hong Kong, Singapore, Switzerland, Holland, Germany and the US. It felt like we were never at home, yet Ray and I worked together with tremendous focus and discipline during this period.

The crazy touring schedule and my partying never got in the way of the music. Material prepared in Ray's music room in Fortis Green bounced into life once we were in the studio, and much of our second album – *Kinda Kinks* – was recorded over just a few days, between 16 and 18 February 1965.

There was also the question of our next single, and what could possibly follow 'All Day and All of the Night'. Should we attempt another song in that vein, or strike out with something new? 'Tired of Waiting' had been left over from the August session the previous year, when finally we cracked 'You Really Got Me', but the word from our management had been, it's a very nice song, but too different from 'You Really Got Me' to release as a follow-up; if the point was to create a clear identity for The Kinks, maybe this was the wrong way to go. A year later, though, we had established ourselves and the time felt right for 'Tired of Waiting', to which I had added a modified guitar part using the 'You Really Got Me' and 'All Day and All of the Night' distorted tone. We were so busy touring we couldn't relish its success, but our new single went to number one after only a few weeks and was a game-changing record for The Kinks. The worry in the studio had been that my heavy guitar sound might drag down this song that was already slow-moving, but once we worked out how to balance the sounds it was recorded quickly, the throb of my guitar actually adding a hard-boiled emotional intensity.

Lots of people didn't like The Kinks, considering us too in-yer-face and brash. When pop embraced rhythm and blues, licence was given to be less buttoned-up, which I liked even if I was in the minority. I loved the raunchy feel of R&B, and I have always thought 'All Day and All of the Night' was a better record than 'You Really Got Me', which sounded constrictive in comparison. 'All Day and All of the Night' was freer, because we knew what we were doing and were in charge of the sound. Making the music we recorded for *Kinda Kinks*, and the singles we recorded around the same time, it felt like our music was taking off in a multitude of fresh directions. 'Tired of Waiting for You' represented what I considered to be the perfect pop song, and even while we were recording it, a long time before it came out, somehow I knew that the record was going to become number one. It had been brewing in our imaginations for a long, long time. The song had grown out of 'South', the instrumental piece of Ray's that dated back to the period when we were playing as a duo in The Clissold Arms. 'South' had been a country and western-style piece, and 'Tired of Waiting' became a blend of everything that inspired us: country, blues, rock, R&B – the track was total Kinks.

Ideas for singles flowed, although our next one demonstrated that we were not invincible. 'Ev'rybody's Gonna Be Happy', with 'Who'll Be Next In Line' on the B-side, fared very poorly compared to 'Tired of Waiting'. The song developed out of a jazzy riff that Pete had been obsessed with since we toured in a package with a singer from Detroit called Kim Weston, backed by The Earl Van Dyke Band. Earl's organ doubled the bass line, like funk before funk existed, and we would sit at the side of the stage and watch every night, soaking up their feel. Pete felt inspired enough by Earl's left-hand vibe to come up with the riff which became the basis of Ray's song 'Ev'rybody's Gonna Be Happy', and its nervy chromaticism was quite a change from the earth and the grit of 'You Really Got Me' and 'All Day and All of the Night'. We pieced the song together in the studio through improvising and jamming. I put some funky syncopated chords to Pete's riff, and Mick worked out a drum part that nailed down all the accents, all of which suggested a lyric to Ray. We came back from New York to promote the single and Ray was convinced we'd have another hit, but it was way ahead of its time. People weren't ready for those funky, jazz-flavoured syncopations.

Our next single, 'Set Me Free' with 'I Need You' on the B-side, released in May 1965, put us on more secure ground. It was rushed out only three months after the indifferent response to 'Ev'rybody's Gonna Be Happy' in an attempt to swing back favour in our direction. We performed the song on *Thank Your Lucky Stars* in Birmingham just before the release date and the reaction was positive enough to convince me we'd hit gold again. But its structure sounded awkward to me; it didn't flow seamlessly like a lot of our songs. 'You Really Got Me', 'All Day and All of the Night' and 'Tired of Waiting' had all been in the key of G, which suited the range of Ray's voice well, and G always cast a spell for The Kinks. The key of G is magical on the guitar, as is E, which is the most basic key on the rock guitar. When I first heard Chuck Berry play, I thought: How come he's playing in B flat? Then I found out his piano player, Johnnie Johnson, favoured that key and obviously

Chuck was influenced by his playing. 'Set Me Free' was actually in A minor, but I wasn't about to argue with its success. It boosted our confidence after 'Ev'rybody's Gonna Be Happy' didn't do too well.

No doubts at all about our next single! 'See My Friends', with 'Never Met A Girl Like You Before' on the B-side, followed that July and remains one of my favourite Kinks tracks. In contrast to the stiff structure of 'Set Me Free', 'See My Friends' flowed with unfussy and direct simplicity, and the purity of its expression touched hearts and minds. Ray had really excelled himself with this song which, to me, spoke of deeply felt loss, of a friendship or who knows what else, and its power transcended the words. The song invoked the sound of Indian classical music at a time when Ravi Shankar had become popular, and we seriously considered using a sitar – but realised none of us knew how to play it.

We worked very hard to get the unique sound of 'See My Friends' right. Once we'd dismissed the idea of using a sitar, we experimented with altering the natural tunings on our guitars to create sustained drones, which was something brand new in British pop. But after a few takes, and while we were listening to the playback, the song wasn't quite living up to our vision somehow. We were expecting to be taken towards some unknown, all-encompassing cosmos – instead it sounded detached and frosty. Nothing wrong with the playing, but the flatness of the recording was sucking all the emotion out of the song. We scratched our heads, trying to figure out what exactly had gone wrong. Shel was as puzzled as anybody else, and it took a while before the penny dropped. The sound we were aiming for was so specific and unique that none of the conventional recording methods worked. It needed something *beyond* that, and one of the engineers, Alan MacKenzie, suggested overloading the levels of the two master compressors, which added a push-pull effect. We tried – and eureka. That technique gave the song that otherworldly quality we had been searching for.

On the *Kinda Kinks* album, 'Tired of Waiting' ended the A-side, and covers of 'Naggin' Woman' and 'Dancing in the Street' dropped back into our roots in American music. But also in the mix were 'So Long' and 'Nothin' In The World Can Stop Me Worryin' 'Bout That Girl', which emerged out of our folk and country influences. Although Ray never had formal classical training, he had learned some classical guitar pieces from Mike Picker, things like *Romance d'Amour*, and you can definitely hear that influence on his delicate, poised introduction to 'Nothin' In The World Can Stop Me Worryin' 'Bout That Girl'. When the rest of us come in our beats sound like they have been spring-loaded – couldn't be more different from the thunder of 'All Day and All of the Night'. 'So Long' was also light on its feet, like a madrigal, and perhaps this song was saying 'so long' to the past, to an idea of a fading England, which sowed the seeds for *The Kinks Are The Village Green Preservation Society*, recorded three years later. This song gave our music a noticeably reflective tone.

We had been listening to a fantastic album called *Folk, Blues and Beyond* by the British blues singer and guitarist Davey Graham, which was also released in 1965. Davey performed songs reminiscent of blues influences, and also contemporary material by Charles Mingus and Bob Dylan, and developed his own distinctive voice. Davey also liked using unconventional tunings, which evoked a blend of the East and the blues. He was a good friend of Ray's and, although it took me a while, I came to admire his music enormously. He travelled to Morocco and India, learned different modes of playing, and brought all those influences to London. Also he had what I'd call a 'non-singer' style of singing, somewhere between singing and talking, which I loved – so much colour and edge. The composer Ralph Vaughan Williams was also important to my appreciation of folk music, and I marvelled at how he borrowed ideas from folk music and integrated them into a classical landscape. His music sounds like a yearning for a country that is beyond what we know. Is it real? Or existing in a fantasy? You want to go there but you don't know where it is in space or time. I always had the feeling that, similarly, The Kinks may be time travellers.

So much pop music at the time used what I call the 'Walk Don't Run' chords, after the song by The Ventures – A minor, G, F, E. We used that chord sequence ourselves many times right up to 'Come Dancing' in 1983, but it did drive me insane. In the 1950s and early 1960s, it seemed like every record you heard used that same chord sequence. Amazing music did come out of those chords, but songs like 'Tired of Waiting' and 'See My Friends', and a folk-influenced song like 'So Long', told everyone that there were other chord sequences. 'Set Me Free' hovered around A minor and G. But Ray was honing his craft as a songwriter and I felt like I should be allowed to explore whatever he came up with.

In our personal lives, Ray and I were entering different phases. His first daughter, Louisa, my niece, was born in May 1965, and time at home with Rasa and their new baby was becoming increasingly important to him. Meanwhile I had begun an intense affair with Michael Aldred, one of the presenters on *Ready Steady Go!* who I'd met during our second appearance on the show. Eventually Michael moved into the house on Connaught Gardens alongside Mick and me, which proved an unwise decision. Michael was fully fledged gay and although he reconciled himself to my wandering eye when it came to the opposite sex, if I so much as looked at another man he went nuts. I found Michael attractive. He reminded me of a young Dirk Bogarde, with his dark good looks and deep brown eyes which were filled always, I thought, with mystery. But we wanted different things from the relationship, and sex became difficult. I could never suppress my rapacious desire for women, whereas Michael really loved me. Because I was so young and full of myself, I thought we could play around at sex without ever appreciating the extent to which I was hurting Michael's feelings. For me it was a frivolous bit of fun, for him it was much more serious. Then I started avoiding intimacy with him, hoping we could enjoy the closeness of sharing time together in other ways. But I was deluding myself.

Late one night, when I arrived home with my old pal Mike Quinn, the tensions came to a head. Mike and I had had quite a guys' night out, and he had already told me that he didn't feel comfortable with Michael's lifestyle; there was friction because Michael once made a pass at him. Mike was a DJ and owned a boutique on Carnaby Street where lots of folks involved in pop and show business bought their clothes. The evening had begun with a scrap in a parking lot in Soho after we got into a disagreement with a pair of hooligans who were trying to score drugs off us. We shook them off and ended up in a bar on Greek Street until about 1 a.m., then we rolled blind drunk into a cab and headed back to Muswell Hill.

Only when we approached the house did I remember, shit, Michael had promised to make me dinner. I had become so involved in the craziness of that night, I'd forgotten completely. He was furious – that I'd forgotten and that I had turned up with another man. He was standing at the front door wearing an apron, and quivered with anger.

He screamed and swore at us both and glared at Mike with utter contempt. Mike, sensing trouble, disappeared as quickly as he could. Michael ripped his apron off dramatically and threw it into my face. 'This was meant to be *our* night, you bastard,' he howled. 'Your food's in the bin. I'm out of here.' I explained Mike and I had only been for a drink, and that we had lost track of time. But nothing I could say gave him any solace. The resentment continued to boil over. Mike and I were friends, nothing more, but Michael made it clear he didn't want me to see him again. 'You're a complete fucking slut, Dave, you'd fuck anything that moves,' he screamed, like he was in genuine pain. He tore his shoes off and hurled them at my head, then ran into the garden sobbing hysterically.

When I walked into the house, Michael ran back inside and grabbed me from behind, and started swinging his fists around. I tried to deflect his punches, but he caught me on the side of the head and, by now, I was the one getting angry. I pushed him off and said 'Fuck you, I'm off to bed.' But he grabbed me again on the stairs and suddenly his fury switched to deep sorrow. He gripped me in a bear hug and wailed. He was very strong and not in control of his emotions, and I started to worry that he might do me serious harm. So I held his hand gently and we walked into my bedroom, where we sat on the bed and the emotion poured out of him. This was the moment I realised how out of control this relationship had become; I had to end it. After a while I pretended everything was OK and asked Michael if he wouldn't mind fixing me a drink downstairs while I got ready for bed. Then I locked my bedroom door and a few minutes later heard him come back with the drinks, and then crumple on the floor outside my room when he realised what I'd done. He mewled and whimpered like an animal in pain all night. It was agonising, and the next day he packed his bags and moved out. We kept our distance after that, but Michael always had a special place in my heart and his tragic early death, aged fifty, from an HIV-related illness was a very sad moment indeed. He had been living in San Francisco, and I hadn't realised how sick he had been.

Sexual boundaries were being questioned. I had male friends, like Mike Quinn, who were friends and no more, and I also had male friends with whom I was intimate and shared things, without it necessarily becoming serious. But if you happened to be a member of a successful rock band, sex was everywhere. I met a guy called Allen at a sex party in Chelsea, hosted by the television personality Ned Sherrin who was my friend and Ray's. He made sure there were equal numbers of men and women and, late into the evening, he'd put weird stuff into the drinks and people started to lose their inhibitions. The first time I went along I couldn't believe how dizzy and out of it I felt – and I was used to taking drugs – and, next thing I knew, there was a naked man sitting on the sofa next to me, massaging my arms. Eventually he went off with someone else, but that's where I met Allen and we were together for a while.

Clubs – The Scotch of St James and all the rest – were also places I met partners. The great thing about The Cromwellian in Kensington, apart from its plush décor, was the hours it kept. It didn't close until four in the morning, and often I was the last to leave. Sometimes I'd head there after a night out in Soho for a final round of drinks before it closed. One night I turned up with a girl I was dating called Jane, who managed a leading fashion store of the time on the King's Road. She was very sweet and stylish, and had been brought up around Kensington and spoke with a slight lisp which I found very sexy. We walked into The Cromwellian and found Eddie Thornton, who played trumpet with Georgie Fame, nursing a drink at the bar. Eddie always seemed contented and I was very fond of him. He also knew where to score the best pot in all of London; and when he was properly stoned his West Indian accent became so strong he became impossible to understand – unless you were as stoned as him and then, miraculously, everything he said became clear.

Eddie's flat was a short cab ride away from The Cromwellian, and the three of us headed to his place at 4 a.m. once the club had closed. The flat was tiny, more of a bedsit, but very cosy. Eddie fixed some drinks and unwrapped a packet of especially potent smokes – best not to ask how he came across it – and he rolled huge joints for the three of us. He put on a mellow Chet Baker record,

Denmark Terrace, early 1950s. At the back: Joyce, Little Grannie – my dad's mum – and Gwen. At the front: Irene, me, Jackie and Mum.

Ray, Terry and me, late 1940s/ early '50s.

Me in the backyard of Denmark Terrace, aged 5 or so.

Our first family car, which we called Bessie, taken outside Denmark Terrace, with the Clissold Arms sign to the right. Rosie, Mum, Dad, me and Jackie.

Me and Mum, early 1950s, at the seaside.

Sisters Gwen and Rene on the beach on holiday – early to mid-1950s.

Me and my nephew Bobby on a fishing trip, with Dad and Arthur – off camera – early 1960s.

My sister Peggy and me at our sister Rose's house, Yeatman Road, Highgate. Early 1960s.

Me with Ray, phone booth picture — early-1960s.

Ray Davies — Muswell Hill Broadway, 1966.

Me in Muswell Hill, 1966.

This is my all-time favourite photograph of Pete Quaife from my own personal collection, taken April, 1965 on the flight to New York, before our first American tour.

Classic Kinks photo – Tower Bridge, London 1964.

Me, Rasa and my sister Rose at Ray and Rasa's house, Fortis Green. Late 1960s.

Simon, Dad, Christian, and Lisbet, at Ashurst Road, Cockfosters, 1973. This was the first house I bought, where I wrote the song 'Strangers'. My dad used to enjoy doing gardening for us.

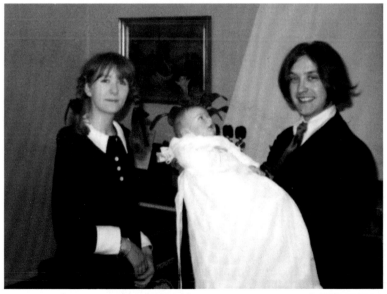

Lisbet and me at Martin's christening. December 1967, Copenhagen.

Me with The Kinks, Stockholm
Concert Hall, March 26, 1976.

The Kinks – Gordon
Edwards, Ray, Mick
Avory, Jim Rodford
and me – at Stanley
Theatre, Pittsburgh,
June 1, 1978.

Kinks, Universal Amphitheatre, 1979 – Mick Avory, Ray, Jim Rodford and me.

Me, Daniel, Lana and Nancy in Watchet, North Devon, 1980s.

Me and my son Martin on his 14th birthday, September 1981. In Southgate, London.

With Lana at a Kinks video shoot, 1989.

The four stroke paintings – I painted these in Queen's Square Hospital while recovering from my stroke in 2004.

'Acceptance'

'Stroke'

'Hope'

'Healing'

followed by some Miles Davis, and the three of us blissed out on the music and the smoke. Jane and I started kissing and stroking each other, and then we undressed. Eddie enjoyed the sight of these two naked people in his living room, as his head nodded appreciatively to Miles and Chet. I caught Eddie's eye as Jane licked my chest and moved down to my stomach, and then started giving me the most delicate blowjob I could imagine. But even by my standards I'd overdone the alcohol and the drugs. My head started spinning, and I was overwhelmed with sickness. As Jane continued the task at hand, I threw up all over her. Instantly, we all snapped out of our dream-state. Eddie rushed to the bathroom and came back with a towel to mop up, and Jane looked at me with utter bewilderment. And rightly so: who could blame her? I couldn't wait to get out of there and ordered a cab while she showered. We left quickly and Eddie handed me a bag of dope on the way out. 'No worries, man,' he kept saying, to reassure me. Jane said she thought I looked sexy when I was stoned, but she didn't plan for this. I couldn't apologise to her enough.

Jeff Beck, Long John Baldry, Keith Relf and Eric Burdon were all regulars at The Cromwellian, and also The Searchers' drummer Chris Curtis who had a fetish for what he called 'ugly waiters', and at times would hang around hoping to pull. It was a schlep to Muswell Hill from Kensington, and I found a quiet little hotel around the corner called The Ashburn to crash. I got to know the doorman well and he welcomed me, always discreetly, when I'd show up with a different girl – and occasionally a boy. The most he ever said was 'Good to see you again' if he recognised my partner from an earlier visit.

One night I took Long John Baldry back with me. Long John loved The Cromwellian and we would often talk late into the night about great blues singers – John Lee Hooker, Muddy Waters, Lead Belly. That night he'd more to drink than was wise and I worried about him making it home safely. I suggested he come back with me to The Ashburn to sleep it off. I had no idea he was gay, and to avoid any misunderstanding I asked for a room with two single beds. But once we were in the room the chemistry changed. We kissed each other tenderly and held hands, but there was no sexual intent behind that kiss. It was a kiss that said how deeply we understood each other and we spent the night in each other's arms. It was a life-enhancing experience, one that taught me about how compassionate and caring two men can be – something that needs to be acknowledged in society more often.

Hotels were about to become an inescapable part of my life. Being away from home, in a different city and hotel every night, might sound like fun, and it was for a while, but soon enough it messes with your mind. The package tour we did in 1965 – with Gerry and the Pacemakers, Gene Pitney, Marianne Faithfull, The Mike Cotton Sound and The Manish Boys with Davie Jones – taught me exactly what it meant to be a raver. What a mix of personalities! Marianne Faithfull was part of the circle surrounding The Rolling Stones. The record she was promoting was 'As Tears Go By' (with 'Greensleeves' on the B-side), a song by Mick Jagger and Keith Richards which The Stones had yet to record – their version would follow a year later. At the time Marianne was having relationships, on/off, with Jagger and with Brian Jones, and she certainly made her presence felt on the tour coach. She made it clear that she knew she was sexy and the sound of her posh, Sloane Square accent bounced off the walls – she was a bit of a tease. It can't have been easy for her spending all day, every day with a bunch of rowdy, randy young lads, away from home and looking for fun.

Davie Jones I found was quiet and thoughtful, and he was very much learning the ropes; by the end of the year he had adopted the name 'Bowie' to avoid muddling his name with Davy Jones of The Monkees. He was intrigued by The Kinks' music and latched on to me I think because I was more of a star than he was. We talked about girls and drugs, and about songs we liked; and he was very good at picking out the girls from the crowd, who were hanging around in the hotel, who I had my eye on, and bringing them up to the room to meet me. After that tour I never saw him again. Many years later, when I lived in Los Angeles, I used to frequent the same bar as Reeves Gabrels, the guitarist from Bowie's Tin Machine band, where I would also play pool with my dear friend and film director John Carpenter. Naturally Reeves and I would talk about Bowie and I said I'd like to pop by and see him, but Reeves would say how miserable and unsure of himself David was. He also told me that, whenever Tin Machine rehearsed, Bowie would invariably start off with a few Kinks songs to warm up.

Gerry Marsden and I had already met when The Kinks performed on *Ready Steady Go!*, and we hit it off really well: I guess we saw something of ourselves in each other. Gerry was a genuinely funny guy and could rave with the best of them. One night, when the tour reached Taunton, we arrived back at the Grand Hotel after the gig, desperate for a drink, and with two girls. The hotel could have saved themselves a lot of bother had they served us a drink and let us take the girls up to our rooms. When they refused we went upstairs and our fury stewed, then we thought, fuck this, let's go downstairs and smash into the bar. The lobby area was quiet, apart from the night porter who was looking at us anxiously. On our way into the hotel earlier I'd noticed an antique armoury display pinned to the wall, and I snatched an axe and Gerry took down a pair of swords – and the night porter ran off as we ran amok. I was taken aback by the weight of the axe and smashed it down in the middle of the reception desk, and ended up hanging from the chandelier. Revenge is sweet and the sight of splinters of wood spiralling through the air was very satisfying.

Gerry grabbed the axe off me. He'd been trying to slash the

curtains and sofas with the swords, but they were blunt. My axe inflicted far more damage and Gerry kept up the furious pace I'd set, crashing the axe down and sending more of the reception desk hurtling towards the ceiling. When the night porter ran back, I smashed the light above my head with the sword, plunging the room into darkness, and Gerry and I ran out the main entrance and hid for half an hour or so until things quietened down. Then we skulked round the back of the building, found a back entrance and ran up to our rooms. The next morning we came down for breakfast and saw the scene of destruction, but acted like we knew nothing about it – strangely nobody mentioned a thing.

Looking back now I am, of course, ashamed at my destructive behaviour. Why did rock stars at that time acquire a reputation for trashing hotel rooms? We were kids, that's the first thing to remember. And kids who had been told we were something special, and had been given a load of money. So there was a misplaced sense of entitlement. We were free-spirited souls and we were living life through music, drugs and sex, and hotels could seem like stuffy relics of a faraway age, all cucumber sandwiches and stiff-upper-lip politeness. But for all my surface cockiness, I usually felt very homesick and afraid. Nobody knew how long The Kinks was going to last. The pop scene was filled with bands who had burned out after only a couple of records, and the pressure was on to give our best, always, every single night.

Even with our youthful energy this was exhausting and unsustainable – and hotel rooms often found themselves at the eye of any emotional storm. Bringing a girl back after the gig was about finding a beautiful human connection in between all the craziness. In Wigan I'd met a very attractive girl called Vivien. We got stoned on whiskey and amphetamines, then slept together. In the morning we were woken by someone shouting her name outside the window – 'Vivien, Vivien, Vivien!' – getting louder all the time. I rolled over and checked the time: 6 a.m. Vivien said, 'Shit, it's my dad.' She went to the window and told him she'd felt ill and was staying with a friend. But that didn't cut any mustard. He told her to come down now – *immediately* – and started screaming about her behaviour. She quickly got dressed and sped out the room. Having her taken away like that so infuriated me that I upturned the bed and threw chairs around the room. Then I pissed in the wardrobe, and to demonstrate my absolute fury, I crouched over the sink and left a huge turd behind. As with the incident involving Gerry Marsden in Taunton, I checked out like nothing had happened. But this one caught up with me – a few days later the hotel sent a bill to our management, including a charge for 'removal fees of excrement from the sink'. God, the embarrassment. I cringe at the thought.

Trouble did seem to follow us around. When we played for the first time in Denmark, at the Tivoli Theatre in Copenhagen on 9 April 1965, we found ourselves at the centre of a full-on riot and not one of our making. We were big in Scandinavia, our records had sold well, and it felt like every teenager and twenty-something in Denmark was crowded into that theatre: the roar when we walked onstage was unbelievable. The first few songs passed without incident, and we were pumping that hall with joy. Looking out into the crowd, I was happy to see the kids screaming and dancing in the aisles. There was a great buzz and we encouraged the audience to party, like we had at hundreds of other concerts.

Many in the crowd started to run to the front of the stage, where they continued to dance and have a great time. Again we had seen this many times and weren't fazed in the slightest, but apparently nobody had told the Danish authorities what to expect. Suddenly, out of nowhere, a whole troop of riot police burst in through the doors, armed with guns and batons, and began throwing their weight around. The police were pushing the kids to the ground, and beating them with their batons. We stopped playing and looked at the scene unfolding in front of our eyes with disbelief and alarm. What had been an utterly joyful room only a few minutes earlier had collapsed into bedlam. People were screaming for help and were running from the building as the police pursued them, thrashing out randomly with their batons, while others, who decided to stay and fight back, were getting crushed by their vicious brute force. The promoter sprinted onstage and guided us to the wings, where we were kept out of harm's way as we watched the scene descend into anarchy. Some kids were obviously very badly injured, while others turned their fury on the building itself, smashing windows and ripping seats out from the auditorium then throwing them above their heads.

We'd held a press conference the afternoon before the concert at a nightclub in Copenhagen called The Carousel, which was owned by a rich businessman, Kai Postien. Kai turned up with his daughter Beden and his niece Lisbet Thorkil-Peterson. The second Lisbet walked into the room, we were instantly attracted to each other. She exuded sophistication and intelligence, with a shyness that I found very appealing and sexy. Pete Quaife got together with Beden, and I invited Lisbet to attend our concert that night, and left her a ticket, not knowing, of course, how the evening was going to turn out. As we left the Tivoli Theatre following the riot I was really worried about Lisbet. Had she been hurt or set upon by the police? I had no idea and I was very thankful to find her waiting for me at the hotel. At the first hint of trouble, she explained, she'd made a run for it.

When it was judged to be safe, we were ushered through the building and into a car that was waiting to run us back to the hotel. The foyer of the theatre had been devastated, with shattered shards of glass and twisted bits of smashed furniture strewn over the floor, looking like a bomb had ripped through the place. I looked up and only one thing remained undamaged: a photograph of Jim Reeves was hanging lopsided on the wall, his smile radiating through the chaos like that famous photo of St Paul's Cathedral standing proud during the Blitz. We were shaken up, and very relieved once we arrived back safely at the hotel. It was an horrific experience, one that I would never forget, although I did have another reason to remember that night – 9 April 1965 was also the day I met the woman who would become my first wife.

We sat in the bar and talked through what had happened. I was upset and Lisbet comforted me. I just couldn't understand *why* the police had overreacted to such a degree, provoking a violent response from a crowd of young people who had simply gathered to enjoy the music. I could see the headlines now – 'Riot at Kinks concert' – and, of course, the blame would be aimed squarely at us, and not towards the police who had blundered into a situation they knew nothing about. I had plenty sorrows to drown, and drank more and more. And then sorrow turned to anger. I asked the barman for another drink, but he ignored me and started cleaning the tables. Behind the bar I noticed a full bottle of Rémy-Martin, my spirit of choice. When the barman was looking the other way, I leaned over the bar and pinched the bottle and poured the whole thing into a pint glass, which I glugged down like it was a long, cool glass of beer. I grabbed Lisbet's hand and we went back to my room. As a final two-fingered salute towards all the bad stuff that had happened that night, I picked up the empty bottle and threw it with maximum strength into an expensive-looking mirror that was hanging on the back wall of the bar.

By now the effects of the brandy were kicking in. My head was turning cartwheels and I was staggering around, and I hardly noticed the deafening clatter of glass as the mirror hit the ground. Lisbet and I made it upstairs without anyone stopping us. Once we were safely in the room, I made a drunken, ham-fisted pass at her.

But before anything could progress further, we heard a stern knock. When I opened the door, three sullen security guards were staring daggers back at me. As one of them questioned me about what I'd been doing that evening – whether I'd been in the bar and was aware of what he described as an 'incident' – another squeezed past me into the room and saw Lisbet sitting on the bed. Now they had two reasons to rip me apart. 'You realise our male guests are not allowed female visitors in their rooms?' one of the guards said in a tone that dripped with contempt. 'You must leave immediately, madam,' he continued. Meanwhile I was questioned about the 'incident' in the bar and I denied everything, frantically trying to overcompensate for my slurred words by being as polite and clear as possible. I must have sounded ridiculous.

Then the sheer injustice of the evening hit me. Our concert had been ruined by officious arseholes like these guys, and now I was being told I couldn't have a girl in my hotel room, like we were kids – this in a country that prided itself on taking a liberal attitude to sex. I started screaming at the guards to 'get out the fucking way'. I was not going to be parted from Lisbet, and I forced our way past the security guards, and into a lift. Once we reached the lobby, the place was crawling with armed policemen and I desperately pushed the buttons, hoping the lift would whiz back upstairs, winching us away from trouble.

It almost worked. But just as the lift doors were about to close, we were spotted. A policeman tried to throw himself against the door to stop it closing, but he was too late and we shot back upstairs again. Goodness knows on which floor we ended up, but I started banging on doors at random, thinking if I hit enough I'd find our tour manager, Jay Vicars, and he'd sort out this mess. Bleary-eyed guests were peering anxiously through their doors wondering, quite justifiably, who was this boorish drunken idiot who was disturbing their sleep. Perhaps some of them started ringing down to reception, worried about their safety. Next thing I knew, there were police everywhere. We gave them the slip briefly by hiding in a linen cupboard and turning off the light. But the door slammed open, and I was manhandled out and given a roughing-up.

Then I was taken back to the lobby where, much to my relief, I saw Grenville and Jay were trying to smooth things over. The police, however, were very riled up and banged me up in the back of their van, and pulled Jay in with me. I was yelling and swearing at them, but Jay remained cool and composed as he tried to calm the waters: he happened to speak a little Danish. As the van pulled away from the hotel I saw Grenville gently chaperoning Lisbet away, but what happened next cut me to the quick. I'd provoked all this shit by behaving like an idiot – but the police, for reasons I couldn't work out, decided to take it out on Jay, and started beating him up. When we arrived at the station, I tried to throw a punch at one of the officers, but my arms waved in the air with all the force of a *Thunderbirds* puppet. They grabbed me, put me into a choker hold, pushed me into a cell and slammed the door behind me. The next morning I woke up with a thumping headache but I was very lucky – Grenville had not only bailed me, he had persuaded the hotel not to press charges, and I was free to go.

When I went back the next morning to pack up my belongings, the hotel staff were hanging around in the foyer pretending to work, but really, I suspect, they wanted to see how I looked after a night in the cells. As I was about to leave, I saw the hotel manager walking the other way, and shouted after him, 'Fucking awful hotel, never wanted to stay here anyway.' The hotel staff laughed and applauded. I couldn't wait to board the plane and get out of there. But I did wonder what had happened to that gorgeous girl I'd met, and whether I'd ever see her again.

Not that there was time to think about Lisbet for too long. The very next day we played two shows in Exeter, and the next night we performed at the *New Musical Express* poll-winners' evening at the Empire Pool in Wembley. And what a cast it was! We performed alongside The Bachelors, Wayne Fontana, The Rolling Stones, The Rockin' Berries, Cilla Black, Donovan, Them, Georgie Fame, Twinkle, The Seekers, Herman's Hermits, The Ivy League, Sounds Incorporated, The Moody Blues, Freddie and the Dreamers, Tom Jones, The Searchers, Dusty Springfield, The Animals . . . oh, and The Beatles. Brian Epstein decided to mix things up a bit, and we appeared after The Beatles to finish the show. Epstein was a clever guy and was turning the tables on us after we stole some of The Beatles' limelight during our previous encounter. Following The Beatles was not an easy task. They went onstage, the audience screamed. By the time we came on, the atmosphere was flat – The Beatles had exhausted the crowd, taken away all their energy, and we had to work extra hard. But after a couple of songs we reignited their passion and I imagined John Lennon backstage packing away his guitar, thinking, That'll fucking teach 'em.

Whenever The Kinks and The Beatles appeared on the same bill, the tension between us was undeniable. John was still smarting from the night we'd opened for The Beatles in Liverpool, and he wasn't any happier now that we were following them in Wembley. No pleasing some folks, I guess. Before the show he had been tetchy and aloof. I tried to be friendly and engage him in conversation about guitars – but I got a shrug of the shoulders and he told me he didn't want any fucker messing with his guitar. Without John, The Beatles, I felt, would have been just another cute boy band, singing pretty songs. John brought a spiritual depth that would otherwise have been missing; he gave them attitude and grit. He was a difficult man, and he was clearly uncomfortable around The Kinks in case we stole their fab-four halo – but I deeply respected him as a musician and for what he brought to that band.

Tensions had also been stirring within The Kinks and were about to break into the open. The truth is, we were pissed off with each other and fed up of each other's company. We hadn't had a day off since 'You Really Got Me' was released in the summer of 1964, and the endless merry-go-round of touring, gigs and recording was taking its toll. In 1965 the idea that The Kinks might still have existed in 1966, let alone have a history that would stretch as far as 1996, seemed unlikely. Pop taste was notoriously fickle and the prospect it might all come crashing down added to our nerves. Pete and I were still close and never had a cross word, but things were far less rosy between me and Mick – and, of course, there was always friction between Ray and me.

In Taunton, on 18 May, we had argued about the set list. I wanted to change things around a bit but Ray disagreed, and Mick sat on his arse refusing to commit either way. That was so typical of Mick at the time, like all he wanted to do was sit behind his drums and not communicate anything he felt about the band. Thinking about it now, I guess we put him into an impossible position and he was trying to avoid being caught in the middle between two warring brothers. I told him to stop being so lazy and tell us what he thought, and our argument escalated into full-on fisticuffs. The road managers had to prise us apart, but not before we had started laying into each other.

That set the tone for the following evening in Cardiff which, after a glorious eighteen months in the spotlight, could have been the night The Kinks fell apart under the weight of battling egos. Mick and I had tried to stay out of each other's way that day, but by the time we arrived at the Capitol Theatre in Cardiff and went onstage, emotions were once again running very high. We opened with 'You Really Got Me' but something inside me snapped in the middle of the next number, 'Beautiful Delilah'. I glared at Mick. 'You're a useless cunt,' I yelled, before telling him that his playing was shit and that his drums would sound better if he played them with his cock. I made a gesture, like he was wanking on his drums, then kicked over his bass drum and the rest of his kit fell like dominoes. I turned back to the microphone and started singing again, like nothing had happened.

Suddenly I'm lying on my back in the dressing room backstage, blood pouring from my head. I learned later that Mick had picked up his hi-hat and thwacked me on the back of my head. He considered his drums to be like sacred objects, and he took what I'd done very badly, like I had assaulted him personally. Apparently the audience had howled with laughter and, for Mick, there could be no bigger humiliation. He'd been rolling around on the floor, desperately trying to rescue his kit – and his dignity. It got too much for him and he laid into me, hitting me as hard as he could. I'm told that I moved slightly to the side as Mick ran towards me, which probably saved my life. I shudder at the thought of what could have happened had the razor sharp edge of the cymbals, rather than the stand, sliced into my neck.

Ray screamed, convinced I was dead. Mick, too, thought he'd killed me and sprinted out of the theatre, into the street, as fast as he could. He was in a complete state of panic. The police were called – although how difficult could it have been to find a traumatised young guy running through the streets of Cardiff wearing a frilly white shirt and pink hunting jacket? It was our road manager, Sam, who eventually found Mick trying to blend into the background in a café. Sam reassured him I wasn't dead and told him to ditch his jacket and shirt, head to the train station, and get out of town as fast as he could – didn't matter where. I was taken to Cardiff Royal Infirmary, given a load of stitches, and then driven back to London where I spent a week or so recovering at my sister Joyce's place. At the police station, Ray found that the police were keen I press charges against Mick. For grievous bodily harm. But

I didn't want to land him in the shit, and, had I proceeded, what would that have meant for the future of The Kinks?

In the weeks following Cardiff, the future was far from certain. Concerts were cancelled for the foreseeable future. Mick moved back to his mother's place in East Mosley, never to set foot in Connaught Gardens again. Pete, Ray, me, Robert, Grenville, we were all walking around in a daze. We assumed it was all over. Certainly the music press were predicting as much. How could The Kinks continue after that? And yet nobody had actually discussed breaking up, or especially wanted to. Our next single, 'Set Me Free' and 'I Need You', was about to be released, and there was talk of a US tour starting in a few weeks' time. We were all licking our wounds, but The Kinks apparently had a life force of its own. Future plans had to be made, the management couldn't just drop everything, and there were frantic efforts to rescue the group, including releasing a cock-and-bull story to the press about how the incident had been a comedy routine that went wrong. Not that anyone believed it.

It was suggested at one point that Mick could be replaced by Mitch Mitchell, later of the Jimi Hendrix Experience, and what an adventure that would have been. But Larry Page and our management were trying desperately to get Mick and I back together. He rang each of us individually, inviting us to his office to talk about the future. We all assumed we were going for a one-to-one chat with Larry, and then sat together in his office in an awkward, shell-shocked silence when we realised what he'd done. Larry gave it to us straight. We were due to fly to America for our first US tour in a month's time and having to cancel might mean the end of the road for The Kinks. Three weeks after Cardiff we played a low-pressure concert in Lancaster, with everyone looking on anxiously in case Mick and I started knocking lumps out of each other again. Largely by keeping out of each other's way, we managed a veneer of civility. Mick later acknowledged that his reluctance to speak his mind had been a problem, while I had to concede that my habit of trying to get Mick to side with me over Ray was guaranteed to cause resentment. After a while we managed to move on, and work together, although our relationship never fully recovered.

Everything that had happened over the last few months had made me question where my life was going. My drinking and drug habit were raging out of control and damaging my relationships. I'd started going steady with a lovely girl called Marianne, but my repugnant, drunken behaviour scared her away. This had been my first serious relationship since Sue, and I blew it – and had nobody to blame but myself. The music we were making, and my absolute commitment to the band, felt very real, although so much else – the partying, the life on the road, constantly being in the public eye – felt like living in a bubble. The incident in Cardiff had presented the band with a moment of reckoning, a fork in the road. At that point we could have all walked away and got on with our lives, but we chose to come back. The music was great and getting better, and maybe that was enough to pull us through. And fate would look kindly upon me in another way: I was about to meet Lisbet again.

CHAPTER FOUR

WHERE HAVE ALL THE GOOD TIMES GONE?

We visited America for the first time in February 1965 as part of what became known as the British Invasion, when our contemporaries were also finding a keen new audience for innovative rock. This was the last leg of that tour during which we'd fried our nuts wearing hunting jackets on Bondi Beach. From Australia we travelled to New Zealand, and then to Hong Kong and Singapore, before flying to San Francisco. In New York we recorded a couple of numbers for the television show *Hullabaloo*, but didn't play live. This trip was all about raising our profile ahead of a proposed US tour that June. We did interviews and press for radio stations and tried to keep our noses clean. When we flew back to the UK in time to promote 'Ev'rybody's Gonna Be Happy', everything was set for us to take America by storm later in the year. Or so we thought.

Given how deeply Ray and I had immersed ourselves in American culture, back to when Rene brought us records from Canada when she came home to visit, and also to the world that opened up once we'd discovered *Jazz On A Summer's Day*, I was initially very disappointed with what we found there. In February none of us could have guessed that The Kinks would have hit such a crisis point onstage in Cardiff. The trauma still hadn't gone away, but touring America was crucial for the future of the band.

Flying into New York was, of course, jaw-dropping – the energy and sound of that city, with all those mythical buildings whizzing past the car window as we were driven to the hotel. Our first concerts were at the Academy of Music in Manhattan and we were given police escorts to gigs. The Dave Clark Five was also on the bill, but was our billing as 'The Kings' a portent for how this tour would turn out? After New York, we headed to Illinois, where we played in Chicago, then, via Denver, we headed to the West Coast: concerts in Sacramento, Stockton, Hollywood, Los Angeles, San Francisco – then onwards to places like Honolulu and Seattle, with a final date in Vancouver.

As soon as we left New York, weird shit started happening. The night we played Chicago was also Ray's twenty-first birthday and the audience couldn't have been nicer, and he was presented with a huge birthday cake. But the following day our concert in Louisville was cancelled because the promoter hadn't sold enough tickets. Stockton was also cancelled because not enough tickets had been sold; at other venues we refused to go on over arguments about money. Our concert in Springfield did go ahead, and the promoter was one John Wayne Gacy. He threw us a party after one show and I thought he was a really nice guy. Which shows what a good judge of character I was in those days – in 1980 he was arrested and became America's most notorious serial killer. It turns out things were even crankier than we realised at the time.

It was a perfect storm of chaos. My injuries had needed more time to heal before my doctor allowed me to fly, and a whole week of concerts in promising-sounding places like Boston, Rhode Island and New Haven were cancelled, and replacements were hastily slotted into the schedule without anyone thinking through the suitability of the venue or the travel practicalities. For reasons I can't fathom still, Robert and Grenville both decided to stay home, which left Larry Page to carry the entire burden of the tour on his own. Not that he minded at first – he had the opportunity to scout for new talent. Midway through, Larry bailed. 'Important stuff to do at home,' he said, and everything was left to our road manager Sam Curtis, who did his best, but was out of his depth in these very difficult circumstances. We'd show up to find the gig hadn't been advertised and that such a small crowd had turned up it was barely worth setting up our instruments.

On the coach between gigs, on a bad day, the atmosphere was strained and tense, even though we were excited to be visiting these places. Nothing would have pleased Ray more had the whole damn tour been called off. He would have gladly used Cardiff as an excuse. Most days he sat in the coach the absolute picture of misery, his teary eyes staring into the distance. Ray wanted to be home with Rasa and Louisa, not at a small-town theatre arguing the toss with some scumbag promoter who didn't want to pay us. And fair enough. Meanwhile Mick looked sullen and anxious, and Larry positioned himself between us in case our fragile truce fell apart. Poor Pete hardly dared speak, nervous that anything he said might be taken the wrong way and spark trouble. After leaving New York, we took a long flight and an endless coach journey to Peoria, Illinois, and found that once again the concert hadn't been properly promoted. The audience was tiny and glared at us like we were freaks. That was the moment, I think, when reality hit home and morale dropped through the floor – we had nearly three weeks of this crap to put up with, and it was no fun.

In Reno, Nevada, it transpired we had a clash: we'd been booked to play the same night as the local rodeo and we stared out into another deserted auditorium. The promoter sidled up nervously before we played: ticket sales had been low and would we accept half our agreed fee? We did, but played a twenty-minute set rather than forty, which was a purely symbolic victory – we'd still had to travel all day to get there. The next night, in Sacramento, more of the same shit with the same promoter and we exacted revenge by playing 'You Really Got Me' for the whole set, lopping bits off the structure and playing long improvised solos. Which was cathartic for us, but the promoter, incensed at our impertinence, lodged a complaint of 'unprofessional conduct' to a local musicians' union representative – which was the first in a long list of complaints we racked up by end of the tour which would come back to haunt us.

Like we needed reminding that this tour was jinxed, I handed my guitar over at the airport check-in in Stockton and they managed to lose it en route to Los Angeles. It was a Guild guitar originally custom-built for George Harrison and was on loan from the makers on the understanding that it came back in one piece. We waited and waited until all the bags rolled through on the conveyor belt – no guitar. I never saw the instrument again, and the most immediate problem was our appearance on various television shows, including the ever-popular *Shindig*. Someone from the television studio took me to a local guitar shop and, at last, fortune looked kindly at me. The guy behind the counter was giving me the hard-sell on expensive new guitars when my eyes were drawn towards a triangular guitar case that was leaning against the wall at the back of the shop. Turned out it was a Gibson Futuristic, the Flying V, with its distinctive three-sided headstock. By the end of the 1960s this was *the* must-have guitar; Gibson custom-made one for Hendrix and then manufactured a whole new run. But I had stumbled across one of the original 1950s instruments, of which only very few existed. I handed over $200 and ran out the shop before the owner could change his mind, and went on television looking as cool as fuck holding my new guitar.

Another cool thing about *Shindig* was the unexpected opportunity to play with a guitarist who only a few years earlier I had considered a hero. James Burton had played on a load of great records like Dale Hawkins' 'Susie Q' and he also worked with Rick Nelson. Now he was working with the *Shindig* house band, a group they called The Shindogs. The show ended with the spotlight on me. I sang 'Long Tall Shorty' and it was arranged that girls from the audience would 'spontaneously' dance towards the stage. The Kinks were surrounded by The Shindogs as I sang and it was a beautiful moment. Later, after we returned to the UK and recorded 'Till the End of the Day', I tried to channel something of James Burton's sound and energy into my solo as a tribute to the great man.

After the television shows we had a few days off, and this was the best bit of the tour. On 3 July we played at the Hollywood Bowl as part of The Beach Boys' Summer Spectacular. The Beach Boys headlined, and also on the bill were the likes of The Byrds, Sonny & Cher and The Righteous Brothers – and an oddball British group called The Liverpool Five, who were freeloading off The Beatles even though they were Londoners. We were living the LA fantasy, and stayed at the Beverly Hills Hotel. After the disappointments of small-town America this was more like it. America! The stuff of dreams! We even met Dean Martin who was on Reprise, the label that released our music in the US. Although years later I did become a big fan, back then there was so much going on, I'm not even sure I recognised him.

Playing the Hollywood Bowl as part of The Beach Boys' Summer Spectacular, I walked around in absolute awe. I couldn't believe that we were on the same bill as The Byrds. I'd admired their first couple of albums – *Mr. Tambourine Man* and *Turn! Turn! Turn!* – very much. Their music continued a vital thread of Americana, and the way they incorporated blues, folk, rock and ideas from the latest thinking in jazz, was incredible. They were at the vanguard and had developed a spacey, psychedelic sound all of their own, while their singer Roger McGuinn – wearing his trademark rose-coloured shades – was the very epitome of cool. I also liked hearing The Righteous Brothers. Their music was smooth, without a single rough corner, but their singing was gorgeous and I enjoyed their feel. Brian Wilson was around backstage at the Hollywood Bowl but lost in his own world of weirdness; his brother Dennis was more sociable. I much preferred the work The Beach Boys did later to the stuff we heard in 1965. This was the height of their pop surf phase, songs like 'California Girls' and 'Do You Wanna Dance?' And I was from Muswell Hill. What the fuck did I know about surfing?

If we hoped some of that Hollywood Bowl stardust might rub off on the rest of the tour, we were dragged back to harsh reality the next night. We flew to San Francisco to play Cow Palace, a sizeable arena where The Beatles had played a year earlier. The promoter was the same guy we'd crossed swords with in Reno and Sacramento. We asked to be paid up front and, when he refused, told him we weren't going on. The rest of the tour was spent playing slimmed-down versions of the Hollywood Bowl concert, without The Beach Boys. The final concert was in Seattle on 10 July, and then we couldn't wait to fly home. After all our adventures in New York and Los Angeles, our next concert was a week later – in Great Yarmouth. It felt great to be home.

America had proved infinitely more complex than I had realised. What was considered acceptable in New York City was not true for some of the smaller towns we visited. The British Invasion – if it meant anything in small-town America – had been led by The Beatles and The Rolling Stones, both of whom had huge teams of publicists and slick road managers who knew how to step clear of those banana skins we slipped over on. The well-groomed image of The Beatles was entirely non-threatening to conservative America. While it's true that The Rolling Stones projected an edgier image, they always behaved impeccably onstage and were dressed in their natty suits and ties, with neat haircuts like the first day back at school. And then The Kinks came along – with our long hair and pink hunting jackets, always arguing the toss with promoters and forever spinning into chaos. Had we been more experienced and worldly-wise, we'd have put up with a bit of shit to establish ourselves in the US, and reaped the rewards later. But our instinct was to fight back when people dicked around with the money, especially as Robert and Grenville weren't there to calm the waters.

Some things about the US had appealed to me. To breathe the same air as my musical heroes – Leadbelly, Chuck Berry, Little Richard, Big Bill Broonzy, Buddy Holly, Eddie Cochran, Sonny Boy Williamson and Hank Williams – was a thrill. Even in London in the mid-1960s it was impossible to buy pizza or pasta worthy of the name. To go into a restaurant in New York or Los Angeles and taste proper pizza was a treat, and I loved the burgers. The outgoing, sunny nature of the people – their 'have a nice day' attitude, the enterprising sense that anything was possible – was an eye-opener to anyone coming from London, where waiters prided themselves on being rude and cabbies wouldn't drive you south of the river. But there were sides of America that felt hopelessly backward-looking, afraid of dealing with the here and now. Ray and I had grown up mesmerised by American rock, blues and jazz, but American radio was obsessing over The Beatles and I could hear that music back in England. London in the 1960s was still scarred by the war, physically and emotionally, whereas life in America, assuming you had dollars in the bank, was privileged and comfortable. People felt very steadfast in their beliefs and were unwilling to bend, not unlike the British middle classes. Listening to Elvis Presley still represented rebellion, and the message of bands like The Kinks, The Rolling Stones, The Beatles – or a great American band like The Byrds – was apparently beyond them.

Some older American musicians felt resentful about young whippersnapper British musicians handing back a version of rock and roll to them. Americans had invented rock and roll, and now these scruffy Brits were showing them how to play it, and beating them at their own game by surging to the top of the charts. But it's undeniable that, for a period during the 1960s, all the energy of pop and youth revolution was with British music. The pendulum began to swing noticeably the other way when the horrors of Vietnam became obvious, and young people turned their fury on President Nixon.

I wonder how deeply British culture was understood and appreciated in America at that time. When Robert and Grenville tried to set up what would have been our second US tour for the next year, we learned that we were banned – without explanation. I've seen all kinds of crazy bollocks written about why we were barred. I've read that we were asked to leave the country because Mick hit me over the head with his hi-hat, or that we were busted for drugs. There are as many falsehoods churning around the internet as you care to look for, but the truth is far more mundane. Only years later did we realise that each time we cancelled a concert, or pulled one of our stunts, like playing a twenty-minute set, or driving everyone nuts with forty minutes of 'You Really Got Me', complaints were made to the union. Each time we had an altercation with a promoter or musicians' union representative, it was held in evidence against us. We were innocents abroad who had no idea about the power of these union people. The expectation was that US tours by British bands would tick along flawlessly. The Beatles had managed perfectly well before us, but they had Brian Epstein on their side: all they needed to do was show up and play. We had no such luck. Robert and Grenville stayed home, Larry didn't last the distance, we failed to keep our mouths shut when things didn't work out. In short, everyone connected with The Kinks, band and management, went wrong. We all fucked up big time.

What was going on with Larry Page? That's what we wanted to know. When he decided to fly back to London after the Hollywood

Bowl concert, Larry's casualness and tactlessness felt galling. He should have been working to make our tour run smoothly, but spent most of his time in Hollywood sniffing around Sonny & Cher, no doubt itching to sign them to Edward Kassner. Larry reckoned that the Hollywood Bowl gig would put The Kinks on the map in America. We'd be bigger than The Beatles, he thought, and he had tolerated the difficult earlier stages of the tour on that understanding. He hadn't counted on Ray's mood swings yo-yoing all over the place. Ray argued with a union guy a day or so before the Hollywood Bowl, after which his depression spiralled. So badly, in fact, that he didn't want to do the concert and Larry had to battle to make him see sense. The decision was taken to fly Rasa out to Los Angeles. Back in London, Robert and Grenville scrambled to book her a flight and magic up a passport. When all that was sorted, Larry flew home. He'd found the tensions and constant troubleshooting exhausting, fair enough, but now there were huge questions hanging over his commitment to The Kinks.

After our return, the full extent of Larry's antics became clearer. Grenville and Robert were pissed off that he exploited the trip for his own ends, and then left us in the lurch. A consensus emerged that Larry's position had become untenable, but nobody could see any easy, painless way to sever the ties. He tried to flex his muscles by insisting we release 'Ring The Bells' as our next single instead of 'See My Friends'. He had taken Ray into the Gold Star Studios in Hollywood before the Hollywood Bowl gig to record the song, and his only interest in using it now was to assert his influence, as publisher, over Pye Records. 'Ring The Bells' was solid enough and ended up on our next album, *The Kink Kontroversy*, but 'See My Friends' sounded completely fresh and was the obvious choice for our next single. Shel Talmy, acting for Pye, stood his ground and was adamant that 'Ring The Bells' was not to be released. He prevailed and was, of course, vindicated when 'See My Friends' was released.

In the very early days of The Kinks, when we were exceptionally naïve in the ways of business, we had signed separate agreements with Robert and Grenville's company, Boscobel, and with Denmark Productions, run by Larry. We paid percentages to both companies, and now a power-struggle erupted between our publisher and our management over control of The Kinks, which ended up in court. The whole process was expensive, stressful and tedious, but there was no doubt over which way we wanted it to go. We wanted Larry out of the picture.

Ray prevented Larry recording Sonny & Cher in a cover of his song 'I Go To Sleep' by withholding permission. Larry had also produced an album of lounge-room orchestral versions of Kinks hits he called *Kinky Music*, credited to the Larry Page Orchestra, which sounded overblown and absurd, like he didn't fully understand our music. The Larry Page Orchestra! I mean, talk about delusions of grandeur! When the legal letters started to fly backwards and forwards, Ray attempted to pre-empt the outcome by signing with a new publisher, Belinda Music, and then the shit hit the fan. Edward Kassner lashed out immediately by serving a writ on everyone: Ray, Robert and Grenville, Pye Records and Belinda Music. He also tried to derail our next single, 'Till the End of the Day' and 'Where Have All the Good Times Gone', by issuing an injunction that reasserted his, Kassner's, publishing rights to the songs. Pye Records, to their credit, released the record anyway, but none of the television programmes we would have usually played to promote a new record – *Thank Your Lucky Stars* and *Ready, Steady, Go!* – would go anywhere near the record until the case was resolved. They didn't want to be dragged into a mess not of their making.

Although attempts were made to break the impasse, the case

only came to court in May 1967 and, in the meantime, it felt like the legal wrangling would roll on for ever. Robert heard about a hot-shot manager from New York called Allen Klein who he thought might be able to help, and we agreed to hire him. Klein had built his reputation looking after Sam Cooke, before he turned his attention to British bands. He had managed to get a stack of cash for The Rolling Stones when their contract with Decca came up for renewal. A while after Brian Epstein's tragic death in 1967, Klein attached himself to The Beatles and ended up triggering friction within the band, and some thought his business practices were very questionable. But given the legal mess we were in, he still seemed like the right man for the job. Klein dealt with it all when our own contract with Pye came up for renewal – and unlocking the situation with Kassner and Page was part of the job.

As he grappled with it all, work on our next album, the record that became *Face To Face*, was put on ice, and Pye instead issued a budget-price compilation album called *Well Respected Kinks*, which ended up doing well, although I was much more interested in getting our latest music out there. Klein realised soon enough that there wasn't the same cash sloshing round The Kinks as The Rolling Stones – and more so when he saw the commercial potential of The Beatles. He failed to make any headway with Kassner, and his renegotiation of our contract with Pye in the UK, and with Warner-Reprise in the US, gave us better terms, although only marginally. When Klein turned his attention to The Beatles he ended up dividing McCartney against the rest of the group.

Throughout this period of uncertainty, I tried to stay focused on the music and remained optimistic. I was young and wide-eyed, and my attitude was that it'll all work out. But I could see the effect all this pressure was having on Ray. He was still feeling shaky after Cardiff and America, and the thought that Larry was using his position as publisher to freeload off his work churned him up inside. All Ray's techniques of self-preservation, familiar to me from childhood, came to the fore. He was depressed and I sympathised, but his dismissive attitude was causing resentment within the band. In particular, Ray's relationship with Pete started to become rocky.

Whatever the strains between me and Ray over the years, we'd be brothers always, we had that bond. But Ray's negativity was contributing towards Pete's disillusionment. Their rivalry reached back as far as their school days together at William Grimshaw, and Pete's sense that somehow he always ended up hanging off Ray's coat-tails. Years ago, I found an old photograph taken at a school sports day that summed up their relationship – Ray is edging ahead to cross the finishing line, while Pete is a few steps behind, disappointment and exasperation etched all over his face. Pete was a seriously gifted musician, and something else he had in common with Ray was his aptitude for graphic design and drawing cartoons. He had been happy in our very early days, when everything had seemed so new and exciting, but now that Ray was being difficult those earlier rivalries opened up again. Seeds of doubt were likely growing inside Pete's mind about his future in the band.

Since we returned from the US, our touring and recording schedule had been unrelenting, with too much opportunity for resentments to build. In August 1965, we finished off an EP that was due for release in the autumn as *Kwyet Kinks*, four tracks – 'Wait Till The Summer Comes Along', 'Such A Shame', 'A Well Respected Man', 'Don't You Fret' – designed to highlight the side of our music that came out of folk, country and balladry. The wordplay – 'Kwyet' meaning 'quiet' – was too subtle for some, perhaps, and the importance of *Kwyet Kinks* has often been overlooked. Although it would become part of our live sets only later, Ray's song 'A Well Respected Man' captured the popular imagination immediately and opened up a new side of his writing. Robert and Grenville had been long-term admirers of the English playwright, satirist and songwriter Noël Coward and encouraged us to listen to his work. Coward was indeed a master songwriter whose view of English culture resonated with us. Robert and Grenville recognised something of themselves in the character of the song: 'He's a well respected man about town/Doing the best things so conservatively.'

I was getting it together with my own songwriting too. 'Wait Till The Summer Comes Along' was my first solo songwriting credit on a Kinks record. The song had a country feel and slipped freely around different keys. I was proud of it and my confessional lyric, tied to my memories of Sue – 'I've been cryin' all the winter/I've been waiting for some good to come my way/But I'll wait till the summer comes along/Dear Lord, have I done so much wrong' – set the tone for other songs that were floating around in my imagination like 'Death of a Clown'. Our next album, *The Kink Kontroversy* – and single 'Till the End of the Day' with 'Where Have All the Good Times Gone' on the B-side – were far from 'kwyet' and I guess fans were getting used to the idea that the only thing to expect from The Kinks was the unexpected. Originally we were going to call the album *The Kinks Kontroversy*, but someone at the label thought *The Kink Kontroversy* sounded more enigmatic and mysterious. 'Kontroversy' was a playful reference to me and Mick's shenanigans in Cardiff and our less than angelic behaviour in the US.

'Till the End of the Day' belonged to the same stable as 'You Really Got Me' and 'All Day and All of the Night', and *The Kink Kontroversy* wound up as a smorgasbord of the styles and approaches that were obsessing us. We were much more studio-savvy by now, but the pressure to get songs in the can as quickly as possible was absolute, and the whole album was done and dusted within about a week in October 1965. I was listening to loads of blues records by the likes of John Lee Hooker, Howlin' Wolf and Muddy Waters at the time, and was really taken with an old Sleepy John Estes' track, 'Milk Cow Blues', from 1930. We decided to come up with our own take on the song, lending it a more contemporary feel. There was no time to overthink, trying lots and lots of takes, and I loved its daredevil spontaneity.

Ray's songwriting was moving well beyond the confines of what everybody understood a pop song to be, into areas of social commentary, and looking at the world, posing questions about it. 'Where Have All the Good Times Gone' was a song that operated on so many layers. 'Ma and Pa look back at the things they used to do/Didn't have much money but they always told the truth/Daddy didn't have no toys/Mommy didn't meet no boys.' That line, about Ma and Pa looking back on the things they used to do, contained actual truths and felt almost unbearably poignant to me. Ray mining the past for the emotions he wanted to convey, and a song like this, wasn't too far away from something like 'Picture Book' from *The Kinks Are The Village Green Preservation Society*. How could someone with such sensitive antennae, who used the art of songwriting to analyse emotions, also at times act so insensitively? That's the nature of art though. Sometimes in our eagerness to create, inevitably, feathers get ruffled – maybe that's just the nature of things. There's no rulebook. Sometimes people get hurt, even though that's not the intention. A little human understanding and forgiveness can go a long way.

CHAPTER FIVE

NEVER MET A GIRL LIKE YOU

Our constant touring did little to lift Ray's depressive moods, which made life hard going for everyone else. That autumn we performed in Germany, then in Sweden, Finland and Denmark, before heading back into Germany – and onwards to France, Switzerland and Iceland. The concert in Copenhagen was our first gig in Denmark since the riot at the Tivoli Theatre and this time we managed to play without any invasions from the police.

But in Berlin, the venue had managed to mess up the ticketing and the audience surged to the front to bagsy the best seats in the theatre. In the confusion everything got delayed and by the time we played the whole audience was pissed. Screaming Lord Sutch opened for us and his crazy theatrics whipped the crowd up into a frenzy. He set fire to a dummy he called Jack the Ripper, and pretended to stab someone in his band, then threw their innards into the crowd, a joke no doubt aimed at our antics in Cardiff. Beer bottles started flying when we took to the stage and security guards had a full-on stage invasion to deal with. We got through our set and were escorted away by the police afterwards and dumped inside what amounted to a cage for our own protection. Once again, the next day newspaper headlines put the blame squarely on us. Violence flared at other stops on the tour, and Sam Curtis was hospitalised after being struck by a flying piece of masonry. None of us wanted to live with this stress, and Ray was utterly despairing at the end of that tour. What future lay in singing thoughtful songs like 'Well Respected Man' and 'Where Have All the Good Times Gone' while people were chucking beer bottles at each other? As always I tried to remain optimistic and cheerful, but it was hard going.

A week earlier, in Copenhagen, I'd decided that I must find Lisbet again. Our last meeting had hardly ended romantically, and in all the pandemonium of being bundled into a police van, I hadn't taken down her phone number, and didn't even know her surname. I thought about contacting her through The Carousel Club, and as I was wandering the streets of Copenhagen trying to find the club, something remarkable happened. I saw a girl walking towards me. She was carrying schoolbooks, and she certainly looked like Lisbet. But the coincidence seemed too much. It couldn't be her, no way. But as she came nearer to me, I realised it *was* her! She was flabbergasted, and at first shy and bashful. As we started talking, though, the intensity we shared earlier that year fired up again; turns out, she had always hoped we would meet again, even though it seemed like an impossible fantasy.

We held each other tightly and kissed in my hotel room, and that was the moment I realised I was falling in love. She was so sweet and sensitive, and our mutual attraction was off the scale; her beauty was exquisitely delicate and I told her that she was my Little Chinese Doll. The couple of days after the concert in Copenhagen were free, and Lisbet and I spent them together, immersed in each other's company. My first visit to her city had hardly been a success, but now she showed me the best of Copenhagen – the Little Mermaid statue and Tivoli Gardens as the sun was setting. We had romantic dinners late into the night, and I discovered that Copenhagen was actually a very cool and fun city, full of the sound of young people laughing and enjoying themselves. And I acquired a taste for everything Danish: pastries, Danish beer – Elephant beer especially – Prince cigarettes and quality coffee that you couldn't find at home. We spent a magical couple of days together, and teared up when I left, promising that this would not be the last time.

Life was about to catch up with me big time, but for the moment, as Ray's moods see-sawed, I carried on partying and enjoying my excesses. I was living back at Denmark Terrace and had rented my house in Connaught Gardens to Mitch Mitchell, who had been briefly considered as a replacement for Mick in the panic following Cardiff. This was before Mitch played with Hendrix. He was then with a band called Riot Squad, but I had to kick him out. He was obsessed with pigeons, and kept a flock of them in the bedroom. The whole place stank of pigeon shit. He had to go.

Signs of Ray's distress were becoming impossible to ignore. There was a disturbing episode in, of all places, Cardiff, at the same theatre where Mick had hit me with his hi-hat. Returning there was unnerving enough and then Ray's microphone failed in the middle of our set. Technical screw-ups happen occasionally and you just have to laugh them off, but Ray's response was bizarrely out of proportion. He chucked his guitar down in frustration, then ran to the wings and brought the curtain down as the three of us continued to play. He was pacing backwards and forwards. Someone scrambled to fix the microphone and Ray was persuaded to continue – but this incident gave a window into his unease.

Even a song that beamed such a broad smile as 'Dedicated Follower of Fashion' did nothing to raise his spirits. I never thought that song would lead anywhere when he brought it along – it sounded overly frivolous to me, and we went through hell trying to finish a take. Ray couldn't find a way of realising the sound he had in his head, nor communicating what he wanted to the rest of us. We tried different combinations of guitars, and even a version with barrelhouse piano. But none of this satisfied Ray, and eventually we stumbled towards a solution through trial and error. The folksy mood of those earlier attempts did not necessarily make for a clean fit with Ray's sardonic lyric and it was decided that the guitars needed to be clanky and mechanistic, like George Formby's cheeky ukulele sound, then – bingo! – it worked. That air of put-on stiffness matched the humour of the lyric and we were able to finish the record.

It was issued as a single in February 1966, with 'Sittin' On My Sofa' on the B-side, a song that we'd thrown together in the studio. The record raced to the top of the charts, and 'Dedicated Follower of Fashion' became the nation's favourite catchy pop record, our biggest hit since 'Tired of Waiting'. Even though it was considered 'social commentary' and I thought it was based around Ray's humorous musings, we all had mixed feelings about the way it was received as the sound of the record and the tone of the song represented such a departure for us. It came about when Ray got into a scrap with some fashionistas at a party round at his place, and one designer in particular infuriated him by suggesting his trousers were too flared, like only people 'in the know' knew the exact measurements that were allowed before they could start ridiculing. Ray kicked them out of his house, and the song, he said subsequently, wrote itself: he sat at his typewriter and the words just poured out.

Even though The Kinks were riding a wave of popularity, how the song was received pressed all Ray's buttons about being an outsider. He hated when people ran up to him in the street and screamed, 'Oh yes, he is!', like a catchphrase from some lame sitcom. Mick took full advantage of the record's notoriety and, following our lead, camped it up shamelessly in a fancy jacket for a photo shoot in *Vanity Fair*. But whatever the fashion, being in The Kinks was about exploring who we were as individuals. We wanted to be popular and have a good laugh, but conforming to the latest fads and tastes was the kiss of death and this was a tough circle to square. Fashion could be so serious and up-itself. I loved wearing saucy, flamboyant clothes – but only ever to have fun. My friend Mike Quinn was always showing me the latest ostentatious, often downright silly, clothes that had arrived at his boutique on Carnaby Street. One day he showed me a fantastic coat that I snapped up: yellow velvet patches in the shape of flowers scattered irregularly over heavy fabric that seemed an off-cut from curtains, completed with massive lapels. I wore it forever, and then my kids used it for fancy dress. I loved hats too. I found a pink floppy hat in another shop on Carnaby Street, which could be moulded into all sorts of weird and wonderful shapes. I gave it a huge pointy top and put it on, like I was walking around with a massive question mark on my head.

I was comfortable only if people were noticing me and knew who I was; for Ray, though, that side of life was becoming increasingly difficult to negotiate. His crisis had been brewing for ages and finally careered out of control during another trip abroad. At the end of February 1966, when we set off for Switzerland, Ray looked extremely fragile to me. The first concert we were due to play was cancelled because of another riot, which did nothing to boost anyone's morale. There were six more concerts to play but Ray was so delicate that I felt he might crumble at any moment. A doctor was called and he was diagnosed with flu, aggravated by nerves and general fatigue. How shocking to see him brought so low. When we returned home, he collapsed into bed and Robert and Grenville had no option but to cancel everything.

But there was a problem. To alleviate some of the pressure on Ray, it had already been decided to dice up tours to Europe into shorter 'legs', allowing for rest time at home. Later that March we had nine dates to play in France and Belgium and, even under these circumstances, to have cancelled would have been expensive: we'd have been in breach of contract. Robert and Grenville hit upon the idea of doing the concerts anyway, with someone else deputising for Ray. Their plan was that I'd sing the lead parts, while Mick Grace, then with a band called The Cockneys, would play the rhythm parts. Grace happened to look a little like Ray, but surely Grenville and Robert were away with the fairies – this was insane. We'll never get away with it, I told them. 'But, David, none of the British pop journalists will be there – it'll be just fine,' came Grenville's response.

In today's world of social media and YouTube, pulling a fast one like that would be impossible. Whenever we appeared on a television show, Grenville had a quiet word with the director to ensure that the camera focused almost entirely on me, with cut-away shots only to Grace's hands, never his face. And all credit to him. We had a play-through before leaving for France and he was a fine musician, and had taken time to learn all the parts carefully, and he did very well. Keeping up the pretence for two weeks can't have been easy, with everyone staring at him constantly – although he shared Ray's slightly gloomy exterior. Shouldering so much responsibility myself was hard, but part of me relished the challenge, and a combination of nerves and alcohol pulled me through. And we did get away with it – just about. I began to notice one guy who came to every gig, always sitting in the front row. At one concert, as I was about to solo, he waved me over, pointed at Grace and said in broken English as he shook his head, 'Dave – he not Ray!' like he expected me to step back in amazement and say, 'My God, you're right – why did nobody tell me?'

Soon after we arrived back in London, I went to see Ray and he was in a bad way, agitated and slightly manic. Rasa was finding the situation increasingly hard going and she ended up at loggerheads with Mum and my sisters about the best way to cope, which made Ray's mood worse. Now he was fretting about his marriage going wrong too. One day he ran all the way from Muswell Hill to

Denmark Street in Soho – one hell of a long way – to have it out with Larry Page and The Kinks' publicist Brian Sommerville, who he hit. We were about to enter a glorious summer creatively. Ray's song 'Sunny Afternoon' would deliver us a number one, but his problems were a real worry.

When Ray played me 'Sunny Afternoon' on the piano in his front room at his house on Fortis Green, I was filled with heightened expectation of what was to come. I'd gone to see how Ray was doing. He ushered me towards his piano and for the first time I heard that hypnotic descending bass part we would come to know so well. Rasa looked on expectantly. I picked up my guitar and felt my way into the bass line as he sang the first verse, I just couldn't help myself. This was something exceptional. It was like when Ray played 'You Really Got Me' for me for the first time all over again.

The song was released as a single in June 1966, a few weeks after we'd recorded it, and it captured the public mood instantly. Its music, I think, helped pulled Ray out of his emotional torment. The summer of '66 was roaring hot, and the image his lyric painted of an upper-class toff on his uppers, but kicking back with a few beers, soaking up the heat, lazin' on a summer's day, was perfect. Ray's subplot – that this guy had been taxed to buggery by the government, had a 'big fat momma' he desperately wanted to escape, while knowing that a sunny afternoon in summertime was a pleasure money couldn't buy – this was like Noël Coward shaking hands with Monty Python. 'Big fat momma' was also a passing reference to our own mother. I marvelled at how Ray could create such a witty song while in the depths of depression. 'Sunny Afternoon' knocked The Beatles' 'Paperback Writer' off number one within a few weeks, which felt very gratifying, I have to say. A month later, England won the football World Cup and it was rumoured that the team sang 'Dedicated Follower of Fashion' in the changing rooms before they went on. That same day we had a gig and because the match went into extra time, we were late leaving London for the show. By the time we eventually arrived at the venue in Exeter, it was too late. The audience had mostly vanished and the promoter saw through our pathetic attempts at an apology. He was well pissed off and kicked Ray up the arse. But what did he expect! After all, England had won the World Cup.

This was truly The Kinks' summer, or so we thought, but we were only ever a sidestep away from calamity. A few days after the release of 'Sunny Afternoon' we were back on the road – Brighton to Sunderland, and then to the north-west. After a concert in Morecambe on 3 June, Pete decided to travel back in the van to the hotel in Manchester with Jonah, our roadie. Pete preferred to slip away quietly from gigs to escape the fans coming backstage – and Jonah's company was preferable to eavesdropping on whatever squabbles Ray and I might be having. As he told the story later, Quaife was having a snooze in the van when suddenly it was like the sky had fallen in. Glass shattered around him, and there was a deafening din, and he felt a sharp stabbing pain in his leg. Jonah had fallen asleep at the wheel, come off the road, and bashed into the back of a lorry. It was a miracle they survived at all. The windscreen was wrenched loose and Jonah took a direct hit to his face, the cut glass leaving the inside of his mouth in a bit of a state. Disoriented, Pete ran from the van as fast as he could – and straight into the dual carriageway. By the time the emergency services arrived, Jonah was in a critical state inside the van and Pete was found in a confused way at the side of the road.

When Grenville picked up the phone and heard there had been an accident, he apparently said, 'Oh, good good, is anybody dead?' That was his gallows humour. But it's never good news when the phone rings in the dead of night and, by the time he rang me, Grenville was so distressed he could barely get his words out. Pete and

Jonah had been taken to Warrington Hospital and Jonah was in intensive care with a fractured pelvis and ribs, and severe stomach lesions on top of the injuries to his face and mouth. Grenville and I visited the hospital the next morning, and it was painful to see Pete in such a traumatised state. He was propped up in a hospital bed, and looked like he'd been hollowed out from the inside. Never have I seen anyone look so terrified. Jonah was in such a bad way we weren't allowed to see him. Pete told us later that he'd listened all night to Jonah screaming in pain. It all felt so devastating. Pete and Jonah had been part of our lives since the very early days. In the aftermath of the accident, Jonah's relationship with the band fell away. His recovery in hospital and at home proved long and arduous, and he opted for a less frenetic pace of life, working at his dad's shop on Denmark Terrace. Later he moved to Canada and reinvented himself as a pop singer – he got himself signed to Decca in 1969.

Even before the accident, Pete had been questioning his role within the band, and that September handed in his notice. Following the crash, gigs were cancelled, and we hired John Dalton to deputise so that we could work again, and John would ultimately became our full-time bassist. Jonah was Pete's close mate, and Pete was haunted by what he'd witnessed that night, and by fears of what could have been. He floated in and out for a while. By November he was back and stayed for another couple of years: his final album with us was *The Kinks Are The Village Green Preservation Society* and he was around while we were piecing together the follow-up, *Arthur (Or the Decline and Fall of the British Empire)*, but left finally, never to return, before we recorded the album.

We had our loyalties to Pete, and it can't have been easy for John, never quite knowing whether he was in the band or not. John had been playing with The Mark Four, a band popular on the local circuit but whose records never quite cut through. Grenville brought him along to audition, and John already had all the bass parts under his fingers and played with a great feel. There was no question he was the right man for the job, and we also bonded over our shared love of football. He appeared with us on *Top of the Pops* only a few hours after his audition, and played his first gig with us a couple of days later. Our next album, *Face To Face* was released at the end of October, and John was included on one track, 'Little Miss Queen Of Darkness', a droll piece that included an overdubbed drum solo from Mick which Ray wanted to sound fragmented, with lots of space between the notes, like, he said, Joe Morello's famous drum solo on Dave Brubeck's 'Take Five'.

I remain extremely fond of *Face To Face*. This album was our first since the American tour debacle, and the first record in which we dealt with the reality that the US was off limits – so what, as a British band, could we say about Britain? One night after a concert, Pete and I were trying to call our girlfriends in Copenhagen, and the operator kept connecting us to wrong numbers. Frustration turned to hilarity, and the idea for a song was born. Its riff and its shuffle beat were inspired by an old Leadbelly record, but the first thing you hear is the sound of a phone ringing and Grenville's cutglass, English prep-school-master voice asking, 'Who's that speaking, please?' And that was how *Face To Face* opened.

Postponed because of the ongoing legal case, we'd actually had the time to hone and finesse an album, with its fourteen brand new songs. 'Sunny Afternoon' appeared in pride of place on the B-side, with songs like 'Dandy', 'House In The Country' and 'Most Exclusive Residence For Sale' baking extra layers into the satire. 'Dandy' was based on observations of Swinging London, and I always felt his lyric was in part an affectionate nod to me. The other two songs were portraits of shameless social climbers who had more money than sense, like 'Sunny Afternoon'. But there were personal sides to the album too. Ray poured his private emotions into 'Too Much On

My Mind', which has always been a personal favourite of mine, and 'Rosie Won't You Please Come Home' was about something that had affected the whole family. Our sister Rose was about to move to Adelaide in Australia. Neither she nor Terry, Rose's son and our cousin, wanted to go, but Rose's husband Arthur was determined to leave London. He wanted to kick-start a new life. Following Jonah's departure, Terry had started coming along on tours and we thought he might be our new roadie or become involved with management of some kind.

Arthur was a rather serious man who kept himself to himself, and I never got to know him well. Rose wrote an airmail letter to my mum about the difficult journey from Southampton. Terry and she had cried all the way, she said, and that was before they reached the awful immigration centre where they had to stay in Melbourne until the authorities could house them properly. Almost as soon as the three of them became Australian citizens, Terry was conscripted into the army just as the Vietnam War was starting – which was never part of their plan, and army life didn't suit Terry's temperament. He didn't see any action, but leaving London made him screamingly unhappy. A while later he developed heart problems and was in hospital more often than he wasn't. I don't think it any exaggeration to say that being taken away from everything he loved – his friends, family and his familiar surroundings – had maybe given him a broken heart. Arthur himself later died from cancer, and the whole Australian adventure backfired. Not that we knew any of this would happen, but the song expressed our deep unease about the move. It also seeded the idea for the album we would make after *The Kinks Are The Village Green Preservation Society* – which was *Arthur (Or the Decline and Fall of the British Empire)*.

A week before *Face To Face* was released, we were back in the studio and made a record that embodied what The Kinks had come to represent. 'Dead End Street', with 'Big Black Smoke' on the B-side, was the other side of the coin from 'Dedicated Follower of Fashion' – the frivolity of 1960s high-camp fashion bumping into a bleak vision of the brutal reality that poverty and slums were still part of British life. Ray had never been as seduced by the glamour of pop as me, and saw right through the worst of its excesses. While we'd had fun in the 1960s, many people were stuck in dead-end street with lives that hadn't much changed since the war. The lyric told of leaking ceilings, no jobs, and the knock on the door from the rent collector; the cold and the frost, a Sunday joint except all they had to eat was bread and honey: 'People are living on dead end street/Gonna die on dead end street.' There was no sugarcoating the past in the song. We had been working-class kids. Our mother had bought groceries on tick. We knew the world portrayed in that song. 'Dead End Street' was about family, about our tribe, about where we had really come from. But it was also a call to action: the song expressed a determination that the world didn't have to be like this, things could be different, *had* to be different. The troubles of the ordinary person mattered too.

As it was finally released, 'Dead End Street' sounded like nothing else we'd done. I had the idea of using two bass players. Pete played a Daneletro bass that sounded trebly, in a Duane Eddy way, and I thought the contrast with a regular bass would be fascinating: a deeper sound against something more twangy. By the time we came to record the song at the end of October, Quaife had left the band and Dalton played a Daneletro on the record and I played the other bass part, the two bass parts crossing over each other – the Daneletro descending as the other line ascended. Let's add a brass instrument into the mix, Ray thought, to evoke the memory of brass bands. We had included session musicians and backing vocals on our records from the very beginning that were never part of the live shows. On *The Kink Kontroversy* and *Face To Face*, we'd used Nicky Hopkins, an exceptional session pianist, who also played harpsichord – and he appeared again on *Something Else by The Kinks* and *The Kinks Are The Village Green Preservation Society*. But the brass part was more than an instrumental backing. It was integral to 'Dead End Street', and took a while to get right.

We'd hired a French horn player who played very nicely, but then Ray started having doubts, thinking that the French horn was too magisterial and triumphalist. Shel Talmy reckoned the track was fine and wanted to go home. So we pretended to leave the studio, walked around the block a few times until Shel had left, crept back in and started all over again. Ray decided the song needed an earthier, more melancholic trombone sound and Grenville was sent out into the night to find a suitable player, and he managed to find a trombonist, John Matthews, in a pub called The Mason's Arms near the Pye Studios – a well-known musicians' hang. And what a difference! The song was transformed instantly into something poignant and urgent, the gravelly trombone dirge adding hints of the blues as it ground against the two basses. When we played the new version to Shel, he claimed he couldn't tell the difference. Ray had all but produced this final version himself and seeds of doubt were sown about Shel's continuing involvement.

Not that the BBC understood 'Dead End Street' either. We made a film to promote the record, which the BBC refused to broadcast. Back in 1966, there was no understanding about 'the music video'. This was a whole decade and a bit before MTV arrived, and our film was more of a free-floating fantasy hooked off the song. It climaxed with pure slapstick as a corpse – one of our roadies, Stan, dressed up – jumped out of a coffin and chased us down the road. We filmed on Little Green Street, a mews between Kentish Town and Tufnell Park in north London, on the same day that Pete had returned to the band, and the first thing we made him do was dress as a pallbearer, who was knocking on doors, looking for the dead. I dressed up as a grieving widow, my huge black sideburns rather giving the game away, and I cartoon-cried into the camera. When we were chased by the corpse at the end, with the film sped up for added comic effect, it was pure Keystone Kops. Oasis made a similar film years later around their song 'The Importance of Being Idle' and got away with it. But the BBC took a very dim view and thought we were ridiculing death, and the film wasn't seen until many years later.

'Big Black Smoke' never caught on, but was the perfect B-side and companion piece to 'Dead End Street'. The song was about a young girl from the country who thinks she might find a more exciting life in the city. You think the setting is Victorian, but somehow she ends up in 1960s Soho surrounded by coffee bars and temptations like drugs and fags. She realises she prefers home, and the song ends with me as a town crier yelling 'Oyez, oyez!' The 'Dead End Street' single went to number five in the charts, and turned out to be very influential, inspiring 'London Calling' by The Clash, as well as Oasis. *Face To Face* ended up competing alongside The Beatles' *Revolver* and The Rolling Stones' *Aftermath* in the album charts, and bounced around the Top 20 for over ten weeks.

The summer of 1966 had been long and hot. Despite the creative highs, all the problems we'd encountered had left everyone feeling jittery, like the next catastrophe might be just around the corner. That autumn, though, everything changed. I'd heard that Lisbet was moving to London to learn English at a college near Tottenham Court Road and I couldn't have been happier. Then one day we bumped into each other on Fortis Green: as a Dane, she'd remembered my family lived on 'Denmark' Terrace and she was curious to see where I'd grown up. We hadn't seen each other since those magical few days in Copenhagen, and once she arrived in London we picked up exactly where we'd left off. Now it was my turn to show her my city.

As 1966 rolled into 1967, Lisbet's arrival coincided with a decisive shift in my mood. The partying was wearing thin. I was tired, physically and emotionally, and overwhelmed with depression. Early one morning, after a long night of partying, I looked around the room and the fog lifted from my eyes. What the fuck was I doing? People were sprawled everywhere over the floor and, yes, I'd had a good time. But I didn't really know anyone. They weren't my friends. They were hangers-on, attracted to pop stars like flies buzzing around shit. I'd spent all night talking, but had said nothing of consequence. It was all fake and meaningless. Ray's depression acted as a warning – I knew I had to find a way around this weird shit.

In 1967 I turned twenty. Maybe it was time to grow up, and one day, shortly after that party, Lisbet gave me good reason. We were driving around London when she told me that she was pregnant. She assumed that the prospect of having children, and the commitment, might have terrified me. We don't have to marry, she said; she would have the baby anyway. I took a long hard look at myself. Here was my chance to have a wife and children; to make a home and move on. Part of me pondered about what life might have been had my time with Sue not been snatched away, but Lisbet and I got engaged and were married the following April in Frederiksberg in Denmark, in a small town hall. Once we came back to London, we found a house in East Barnet, a ten-minute drive from Ray's place in Muswell Hill. Our son Martin was born in September, and what a joyful day that was. My dad welled up with emotion – he loved Ray's daughters, Louisa and Victoria deeply – and now the first male grandchild had arrived who could carry the family name forwards.

Seeking solace from depression also heightened my interest in the psychic world, also in alternative practices like astrology and Tarot. I took it very seriously, read a load of books on the subject of astrology, and also went to lectures. The irony was not lost on me that I had been completely hopeless at school and now I was studying hard. Astrology actually interested me, that was the difference. But as I learned how to cast a horoscope and draw up a progressed chart (an extension of your birth chart which reflects your potential growth and development) how I wished I was better at maths, as it was integral to the whole process. Within this ancient science I was finding all the tools I needed to comprehend so many things that felt beyond my understanding. I also began to fully appreciate the wealth of information contained within Tarot cards, and my lifelong intrigue with mysticism and the occult had taken hold. Was I was cracking into the DNA of life itself?

Another consequence of slowing down and taking life seriously was that I carved out space to think about my own songwriting again. One morning shortly after our wedding, I was feeling reflective and melancholic. My life as a raver was over, no question about that. At a party I couldn't just be Dave; I was 'Dave Davies of The Kinks' and people expected me to switch on cheerfulness like a tap and be a 'personality' whether I felt like it or not; and increasingly I did not. But embarking on this new life as a husband and father also felt very scary. I went to Denmark Terrace and sat at the old upright piano, the same instrument on which Ray had demonstrated 'You Really Got Me' all those years earlier. It had been bashed around at parties for so many years that it was barely in tune with itself, but I felt very comfortable sitting there – the familiarity was exactly what I needed. 'My make-up is dry and it cracks around my chin/I'm drowning my sorrows in whisky and gin.' Those words came into my head as my fingers plucked out a little earworm melody. As a kid, clowns had always terrified me, and this was the beginning of my song

'Death of a Clown' – a song about facing my fears. Clowns were never what they seemed.

I'd been walking around with a big stupid smile painted on my face for years, while on the inside I was cracking up. Having to be creatively honest in a business that felt so artificial and fickle, surrounded by insincere people feeding off our talents . . . I was a bundle of insecurities. 'Death of a Clown' was about those confusing and conflicting feelings. A few days later we were in the studio and the rest happened remarkably quickly. Ray helped fix the bridge and I added a couple more lines. I wanted the intro to lead listeners directly inside the emotional heart of the song, and to hear an instrumental sound that was vulnerable, like it could crack at any moment. Ray reached inside the Steinway grand piano, took a guitar plectrum out of his pocket and picked out my melody on the strings inside of the piano. What a brilliant idea. We added some studio magic, overdubbing and echo, and there it was – a haunted, disembodied introduction that set up the song perfectly.

Robert adored the song and decided 'Death of a Clown' should be a single. It was a huge hit in Europe, and reached number three in the British charts. This was a song in which I had revealed a lot about myself and the attention it received was both humbling and terrifying. Robert put its success down to its expressive purity; it said what it needed to, he said, and no more. I was booked to sing it on *Top of the Pops* solo and the night before was as nervous as hell. My dad suggested we all go down the pub for a stiff drink to calm my nerves. Ray had been very enthusiastic when we were recording 'Death of a Clown', but in the pub got a bit prickly. Cancel *Top of the Pops* if my nerves were not up to it – 'Everyone will understand,' he kept saying. He even offered to call Robert himself, like he was doing me a favour. But Lisbet saw through Ray's game and caught his eye. 'Oh no, Dave must do it,' she said, 'it'll be huge fun.' Behind all the camaraderie, Ray was pulled two ways: he wanted the song to do well, but I sensed he felt uneasy because I'd pulled this off on my own. The next day I turned up at the studio wearing a fantastic Charles II-style coat that I'd found at Berman's in the West End. It had gold braid and was so long its bell-shaped bottom seemed to leak into the floor. What a look! Alan Freeman introduced me as 'Ray Davies' and I screamed, '*Dave* Davies – you did that on purpose!' Then I sang the song and guess what? Lisbet was proved right and, in the end, everyone willed me on, and I had a fantastic, fun time despite my nerves.

'Death of a Clown' changed the dynamic. Suddenly Pye wanted more solo records and also a new Kinks album, and Robert suggested I should go solo. I gave it serious thought, but realistically any solo career would have meant the end of The Kinks. Despite the problems and tensions, the band had become central to my life and the comradeship was very important to me. Whenever The Kinks ends, I thought, I still want to be on board. Shortly after the release of 'Death of a Clown', an article in *Melody Maker* reported that Warner Brothers had made me an offer to star in what was described as 'one of their major films'. I was to be cast as 'a tearaway' and would be heading to Hollywood early the following year. I was going to be promoted as a big star in America, Robert was quoted as saying, but nothing came of it. Robert and Grenville somehow thought they could wave a magic wand and it would all happen – I'd be making films and solo albums while The Kinks continued recording albums and touring. Ray wrote a song called 'Groovy Movies' about our aspirations to work in film.

That next Kinks album turned out to be *Something Else by The Kinks*, while my solo album ended up being put aside for a while. Robert had booked a tiny studio at Polydor, but the space felt more like a box room than a proper studio. Complete with cheap and nasty Electrostatic speakers, which had rough wire mesh wrapped around the front, the whole set-up sounded absolutely atrocious.

After a day of attempting to make it work, all my insecurities flooded back. Robert and Polydor were trying to capitalise on the success of 'Death of a Clown' by forcing a solo album out of me on a shoestring budget – that's how it felt. So the next day's session was cancelled and I wouldn't make a proper stab at a solo album until a year later.

Something Else by The Kinks, released in September 1966, included another two songs by me – 'Funny Face' and 'Love Me Till The Sun Shines' – both about my complicated and unresolved feelings for Sue. Yes, I was married, and loved Lisbet very much, but the manner in which my relationship with Sue was severed hurt, and I still felt anguish, like the grief that had never gone away entirely, and this also fed my depression. Despite the solo album leading nowhere, Pye were keen to have a follow-up to 'Death of a Clown' and that November I hit upon something promising. I'd been messing with some patterns from a Lead Belly song, and out popped a chromatic riff that I couldn't stop playing. This became the starting point of 'Suzanah's Still Alive', another song about Sue. Released as a single in late November, with 'Funny Face' as the B-side, it wasn't the immediate success of 'Death of a Clown' but it did enter the charts – and whenever I play a gig it's a song people still want to hear.

Wit, whimsy, wistfulness, humour, irony, cynicism – *Something Else by The Kinks* had all these qualities in spades. Pye miscalculated by releasing a lot of the best material as singles first, which meant the album didn't sell as we'd hoped. 'Death of a Clown' had already been out for months, alongside a song of Ray's that had been a massive hit earlier in the year. 'Waterloo Sunset' had been released that May and raced to number two in the charts. The first time I heard any of it, Ray hadn't yet worked out the bridge and even the chorus was work-in-progress. But it opened with another of Ray's entrancing descending bass lines that seemed to coil into the inside of your very being. Immediately he demonstrated it, I couldn't help but improvise some vocal backings. And what a treat to work it up in the studio. We ended up feeding the guitars through a tape delay, so they sounded like watery ripples of sound.

Something Else by The Kinks opened with 'David Watts', a song inspired by one of the weirdest evenings in the history of The Kinks, and we'd had a few of those. In the summer of 1966, shortly after the release of 'Sunny Afternoon' and before Pete rejoined the band, we played an outdoor concert in Rutland, at the Big Beat Festival. Girls screamed, lots of beer was consumed and the cheering hit such decibels that we could barely hear ourselves over the sound system. The gig had been promoted by David Watts, a local bigwig who loved music. When we met him before the concert he was charm itself, but serious, with a slight military air, and very well tailored.

David came backstage afterwards and suggested we went back to his place, which turned out to be a lavish Georgian manor house deep in the countryside, with perfectly manicured gardens and gravel that scrunched underfoot when you walked up the drive. We were made to feel very welcome. There was food to eat, hash to smoke and more bottles of pink champagne – *pink* champagne, never drunk that before – than we could ever have consumed. Part way through the evening, there was a knock at the door and a bunch of heavy-set, burly blokes marched into the room. They were dressed in suits and long raincoats, and couldn't have looked more like coppers had they said 'Evenin' all.' Shit, what was this? A drugs bust? Soon enough it became clear they were good friends of David's, and I relaxed.

But perhaps too much. The pink champagne was moreish and was starting to go to my head. We had noticed already that there did not appear to be a Mrs Watts, but there were some women around, and laughter bounced off the walls as Mick and I started camping it up by doing an effeminate dance, our hips wiggling, our arses waving in the air. The women melted away at that point, and I was amazed to see the plainclothes policemen start hugging and kissing each other, and join in with the dancing. Then Mick took all his clothes off and started prancing bollock naked around the room. Watts's hard-as-nails, sergeant-major exterior evaporated and he started dancing too, his jazz hands flapping uncontrollably as he pinched kisses from the policemen and rubbed himself up against them. Never in all my born days had I seen anyone shed inhibitions with such complete abandonment, like he'd transformed from General Montgomery into Kenneth Williams before our very eyes. The gay police started egging Mick on as he waltzed around the room. Believe it or not though, all that turned out to be a mere prelude for the main action of the evening.

David walked over to me, placed his arm around my shoulder, and ushered me into a quiet corner. As he looked at me with his big doe eyes, it was clear he was as randy as a goat, and I empathised with how young women must feel when being leered at by a dirty old man. He coaxed me upstairs and took me into his gym which was, er, conveniently situated next to his bedroom; his intentions could not have been clearer. I was horrified, although part of me was, I must admit, fascinated by this psychological power game. Being a prick-tease, having control over this man's sexual desire, was exciting. But David didn't guide me towards his bedroom as I was expecting. Instead he asked me to sit on his exercise bike and work out while he watched. As I started to sweat, my muscular legs moving up and down on the pedals, his excitement grew. When the inevitable pass came, he didn't hold back. He wrapped his arms around me, pulling me into a bear-hug embrace, and his hands went everywhere, like an octopus on heat.

Finally he'd crossed a line. He was pissed and emotional, and although I didn't want to upset him, I desperately wanted to be anywhere else. The raucous laughter and high-jinks wafted up from downstairs and I gently moved David towards the door and suggested we rejoin everybody else. I didn't expect it to work, but it did, and I started dancing with the others, and there was safety in numbers. As I was dancing I noticed that David had fallen into a deep conversation with Ray, who looked deadly serious. I assumed Ray was protecting the family honour, explaining to him that I was a married man, with a son, and very much unavailable. When David came to find me, I thought he was about to apologise for misreading the signals and for letting things go too far. But no. He put his arm around me again, and took me for a walk in the garden and sat me on a swing next to some willow trees – the ideal romantic spot. Then he told me how he loved and cared for me, and that he had a proposition.

'I'd like you to come and live with me,' he stuttered, his face blushing like a lovesick teenager. My stomach churned with the shock, and when I made up some excuse like 'Well, it's all a bit sudden, I need to think it over,' he seemed very put out and genuinely puzzled: 'But Ray said that he's concerned about your prospects and suggested a solution. You live with me, and Ray gets this house.' I was gobsmacked and started boiling with rage. What an arsehole Ray was. I rounded everyone up as quickly as I could and ran for the front door.

Ray transformed this whole incident into a riotously funny satirical song. On *Something Else by The Kinks*, the David Watts of the song 'David Watts' is that kid at school that everybody else in his class aspires to be. 'He is the head boy at the school/He is the captain of the team/He is so gay and fancy free/And I wish I could have all that he's got.' The narrator of the song sings of himself, 'I am a dull and simple lad/Cannot tell water from champagne/And I have never met the Queen/And I wish I could be like David Watts.' An old music-hall ditty, 'The Galloping Major', also fed into Ray's song. We'd heard this song when we were kids, probably sung by Uncle Frank at parties, and we'd always sung it within the band as an in-joke. You can hear the spirit – and perhaps even a hint of the melody and its self-important oom-pah bass – in 'David Watts'. The gay innuendo and inside jokes were all perfectly judged, especially if you happened to know the real David Watts, who we encountered again a while after the release of *Something Else by The Kinks* and found to be a good sport. He got the joke, was flattered by the hat-tip even. True enough, he also said we were utter bastards to send him up that way, but we talked through what had happened that strange evening and managed to laugh the whole thing off.

So Ray had written a great song – but at what cost? This incident showed a lot about the state of his mind. Ray and I had been through so much together and I felt protective of him and looked up to him as an older brother. We had made great music together and I had always been supportive of his work. And then I find he was prepared to trade me in for a house in the country. Talk about putting the cunt into *count*ry house.

CHAPTER SIX

ONE DAY WE'LL BE FREE

Never one to name-drop, me, as I said one day to Jimi Hendrix as we were flying together to Stockholm on a small plane. We'd seen each other around the place before, normally at parties or at drinking spots like The Scotch of St James club. Although his reputation onstage was as a hellraiser who was prone to trashing his guitar, in real life he was thoughtful, quiet and softly spoken. Jimi was a natural introvert and in that sense reminded me of Ray. We'd both been booked to play on the same television programme in Stockholm, the Swedish equivalent of *Top of the Pops*, around the time I was promoting either 'Death of a Clown' or 'Suzanah's Still Alive'. If you think we sat on that flight talking theories of harmony, or about how to change the world through the power of music, you'd be mistaken. Jimi then was not the legend that he became. He was highly respected by us all, but *Are You Experienced?* had only just been released, and he was another musician on the scene. So we had a beer and chewed the cud. But he did ask about 'You Really Got Me' and how I'd achieved my guitar sound. When I explained about using a razor blade to slash the speaker cone inside the amplifier, he told me he considered it a landmark record and that he loved the gravel and the roughness of my sound – high praise indeed coming from a musician of his calibre.

Looking back from a distance of over fifty years, it's noticeable that Hendrix, The Who and The Doors latched on to our early rock and R&B influenced songs, whereas the generations that followed – like The Clash, The Jam, Ian Dury, Madness, Blur – mostly gravitated towards the music we released later on *Something Else by The Kinks* and *The Kinks Are The Village Green Preservation Society*. A few years ago, an early demo of The Doors' 'Hello, I Love You' came to light and I realised that their version of my guitar sound had obviously been triggered by 'All Day and All of the Night'. The sound was so close they must have realised that they couldn't get away with it – the final record used a keyboard instead. When we heard 'Hello, I Love You' back in 1967, Ray and I thought it had been nicked. The riff, the melodic line, the chord sequence – all too close to be a coincidence. Ray's publisher wanted to sue because it was such a shameless rip-off. Perhaps they could have acknowledged the connection. But Ray and I thought, It's a bit of fun, it's a compliment, we'll let it go. And anyway I loved Jim Morrison's voice – what an original.

An early version of The Who – when they were still called The High Numbers – opened for us a few times, and their song 'I Can't Explain' was obviously inspired by 'You Really Got Me'. They even had Shel Talmy producing. I was always pleased to hear Pete Townshend say in interviews how big an impact The Kinks had made on him. Back then they all looked deathly stern when performing – apart from their kickass drummer Keith Moon who thrived on creating mayhem.

As 1967 moved into 1968, our music was going through its most radical period of change so far. Just before Christmas '67, Robert and Grenville had made a concerted effort to get The Kinks back to the US, but it was a lost cause. Their application for working visas was turned down, a commercial blow for sure, but one which confirmed that we needed to follow the direction *Something Else* had set. In October 1967 the single of 'Autumn Almanac' and 'Mr Pleasant' did very well. 'Autumn Almanac' was one of Ray's poetic and uniquely English-sounding songs. But our next single, released in April '68, of 'Wonderboy' and 'Pretty Polly' flopped badly. Our management and Pye were still keen on pursuing singles and the three-minute rock song, whereas Ray was edging towards thinking on a grander scale. Singles versus albums, and the commercial implications of that decision, threw up all sorts of deep questions for us to ponder, especially as *Something Else* hadn't been the big seller we'd hoped.

I was, of course, very supportive of Ray's work, and the directions he wanted to pursue. Conversations were happening between Ray and Grenville about Englishness – what it was, what it meant, and the whole idea of preservation of English culture. The Kinks weren't alone. This was the period of John Betjeman, and of a general discussion about what it meant to be English in a world that was changing at such a rapid pace. Grenville was dispatched to do research into English oddities: flea societies in Surrey, badminton clubs in Roehampton, stamp-collecting circles in Basingstoke, tea and crumpets on the village green while listening to Schubert. All those things were very much part of our culture, and experimenting musically was an exercise in testing where we could go with our ideas. People thought that they knew what The Kinks were all about. Truth is, after playing songs like 'You Really Got Me' and 'All Day and All of the Night' for years, we wanted to integrate other sounds and moods in our work, always with a view to keeping our music moving forwards. The best was yet to come. I didn't want to be known for creating only loud R&B riffs. And Ray was of a similar mind.

Hearing Ray sing 'Autumn Almanac' and 'Wonderboy' was always a tonic, and I admired how his songwriting had become more exploratory, existential even. Those songs and the material that would become *The Village Green Preservation Society* never seemed phoney and were very original for the time. We weren't occupying the same territory as The Who or The Rolling Stones. Ray had hit on realism. We'd always been known as upstarts, but we were also becoming rock exiles. I felt that The Kinks could so easily have been called The Misfits.

Baked inside 'Autumn Almanac' was a musical sleight-of-hand. There had been a very nice song of Ray's left over from the *Something Else* sessions called 'My Street' that we couldn't fit in anywhere on the album, nor was it suitable for a single. So we took it apart, then Ray turned it backwards and, hidden inside, was what became the middle section of 'Autumn Almanac'. Ray went away and wrote the rest, and slotted the whole thing together like a mosaic. Before *The Village Green Preservation Society* existed, here was a song which could easily have been part of that album – a new, alternative fantasy world. The song was about our childhood. Roast beef on Sundays, tea and toasted buttered currant buns, holidays in Blackpool, going to the match on Saturday afternoon. But the season was also changing. The song opens deep in the earth, with a caterpillar crawling out of a hedge that is soaked with dew at dawn. We hear about the leaves changing colour, also about a gardener with a 'rheumatic back' – what a fantastic rhyme for 'almanac'! I'm sure the song was inspired in part by our dad's love of gardening. 'Autumn Almanac' went to number three in the charts and, like 'Dedicated Follower of Fashion', became a football chant, at Arsenal and other clubs.

But even with our recent run of 'Death of a Clown', 'Waterloo Sunset' and 'Autumn Almanac', 'Wonderboy' demonstrated the impossibility of second-guessing chart success. Rasa was pregnant again and Ray sang to his unborn child – which he foresaw, wrongly as it turned out, would be a boy. It was an utterly charming song, I thought, melodically catchy and poignant, and we recorded it in March 1968, alongside the first songs we made for *The Village Green Preservation Society*. Pete turned his nose up at it. It was certainly a long way from 'You Really Got Me' or 'All Day and All of the Night', but then again we'd all changed as people; we'd grown up. Years later we heard that John Lennon loved 'Wonderboy' and would play the record again and again. But, sadly, the public disagreed with him, and us. We promoted it on every radio and television show that would have us, but the record surfaced only briefly in the charts, then sank without trace. It was our only single not to have made the Top 20 since our first two, back before 'You Really Got Me' was released. So dire were the sales that, for a while at least, we seriously wondered whether it would ever be possible to recover. The thought was definitely hanging in the air when we went into the studio to record *The Kinks Are The Village Green Preservation Society* – this could be our lap of honour, our last ever record.

The months leading up to *The Village Green Preservation Society* were filled with uncertainty as we inched our way into making the album. But one important thing went our way: at the end of May 1967 our legal case against Larry Page and Edward Kassner was heard in the High Court of Justice. We were all on our best behaviour in court, wanting to make a good impression on the judge, although I was told off by our barrister when I pointed in utter disbelief at some bullshit of Larry's and belly-laughed; he said, 'Never do that again.' Ray didn't hold back on the witness stand, telling the judge how Larry had behaved in the US: making deals to benefit himself, then leaving us in the lurch. How could he behave like that and still expect to exploit Kinks songs for his own ends, setting up recording sessions with Sonny & Cher and making tasteless orchestral versions of our music? The case boiled down to questions of trust and we found the judge – Judge Widgery – to be more sympathetic than any of us had dared hope. We won! The judge accepted our legal argument that I had been a minor when the original contracts were signed, and they were therefore null and void. He accepted that Larry's actions had diminished trust between Kassner and The Kinks.

Page lodged an appeal a year later and managed to claw back some cash, but otherwise he was out of our hair, and it would be many years before we'd see him again. We had a new booking agent, Barry Dickins, who was enthusiastic. Earlier in the year he'd got us a series of engagements in Sweden, which sounded good on paper except, once we arrived, we discovered that we were due to play a string of amusement parks and holiday camps. Performing 'Dead End Street' and 'Autumn Almanac' to kids sucking on their ice creams was soul destroying. We were furious.

Around the time of the court case, we also found ourselves up in the north-east of England playing cabaret dates in Durham, Stockton-on-Tees and Spennymoor, near Sunderland. Only a year earlier we'd been playing the Hollywood Bowl on the same bill as The Beach Boys, and that summer 'Death of a Clown' had seemed like it might push my career in a new direction. How far we'd fallen in such a short space of time. I was afraid that The Kinks were destined to fade away. A scary prospect. I would regularly have a few drinks before going onstage for those cabaret gigs. Drinking took the edge off. I'd played those songs so often I could run on instinct anyway. But I always lovingly remember performing Ray's song 'Don't You Fret', which had come out as a track on an EP around this time. It touched me deeply and reminded me of our family when we were growing up.

'Wonderboy', however, had become an albatross commercially, although strangely it has always been a favourite of mine. Keith Moon, never one to spare anyone's sensitivities, ripped the piss out of it in *Melody Maker*, and said we sounded dated. We watched as younger bands played the rock festivals that had once been ours, while we were relegated to the cabaret circuit. Problem was, the direction of our recent singles – 'Death of a Clown', 'Autumn Alma-nac', 'Waterloo Sunset', 'Wonderboy' – was towards more introverted and thoughtful pop, which hardly lent itself to cabaret.

The beginning of 1968 was quiet. Ray had signed up to a satirical television show called *The Eleventh Hour*, which required he write a new topical song every week, and only occasionally did we play a show. We'd worked full throttle since 1964 and now the sense of drift was palpable. Pete turned up and played whenever we did a concert, but was becoming increasingly withdrawn. His hunch that 'Wonderboy' would prove a disaster had more than been justified. He thought of the song as an overindulgence, and Ray's increasing tendency towards playing his cards close to his chest – rarely discussing his songs, just telling people what to play – was driving him nuts.

An ugly argument erupted in the studio between Ray and Pete when we were recording 'Days'. Ray had been fiddling with some tiny, no doubt insignificant detail for hours, and I noticed Pete messing around with tape boxes. To fill the time, he began doodling on the side: a cartoon man wearing a raincoat. This left Ray feeling disgruntled by Pete's offhand manner and I was taken aback by it too. Ray accused Pete of sitting on his arse drawing dumb pictures, while he – Ray – was slogging a gut to perfect the song. Pete was furious and left the room mumbling sarcastically under his breath, and nothing anyone could say was enough to bring him back. A few days later we were due to play a concert in Bray, near Dublin, but we realised Pete hadn't boarded the flight; he'd come to the airport in London then melted away. Robert and Grenville managed to book him onto the next flight and he did the same thing again. Pete's days with The Kinks were clearly numbered.

This was the atmosphere against which *The Village Green*

Preservation Society was pieced together over several sessions during 1968, along with many other songs which – like 'Days' – could have been included on the album but didn't make the final cut. We also recorded some curiosities, including the theme song for a film spin-off of the television series *Till Death Us Do Part*, which it was hoped Warren Mitchell, the actor who played Alf Garnett, would sing. Looking back at all the music we made, I'm staggered that we managed to overcome the tensions to record anything – let alone the record many people consider to be a signature album, even if it didn't seem so at the time. But when things weren't going well it brought a different excitement, there was another energy to feed off. So I tried to remain philosophical about it.

I remember hearing Ray in his front room messing with the riffs and phrases that would end up in *The Village Green Preservation Society*, but one track was already in the can. 'Village Green' had been recorded as long ago as November 1966, shortly after we'd finished 'Dead End Street'. When Ray brought it along we had no clue that this song was the key that would unlock something bigger, but I loved the newness of it, and Pete and Mick did too. Ray was writing like a keen-eyed chronicler. He was writing about people's lives. But I couldn't write songs in that way myself. I had to feel inspired by an emotion or feeling.

Our relationship with Shel Talmy hadn't ended in tears, rather a mutual understanding emerged that his time with us had run its course. Nobody knew how The Kinks needed to sound better than The Kinks – especially now that our songs had such a distinctive and personal sound. Despite the tensions, our time in the studio was actually better than usual; working without a producer encouraged Ray and me to be open with each other about what was working musically and what was not. The songs were Ray's ideas, but they'd be complete only once we had worked on them in the studio. We cultivated the sense of an arrangement, a collective feeling through which we could develop a piece of music. It would sadden me when later Ray would turn up on radio and television programmes and minimise my input in developing the music. Ray was always so protective of everything. To be fair, the business side of the music business can be cut-throat, and we were still reeling after the legal fight against Larry Page. Ray had certainly learned more about his craft as a songwriter, but the business changes people, often making them ruthless. The effect of money on people can be weird. Someone gets 10 per cent, somebody else gets 10 per cent of someone's 5 per cent. Writing music is hard enough. If something worked, use it. Doesn't matter who thought of it. That was my mindset.

We used Nicky Hopkins on keyboards again and the sound of the album – Nicky playing harpsichord sounds on the opening track, 'The Village Green Preservation Society' – evolved in the studio, as did my realisation that each track presented a portrait of a local character. Monica, Wicked Annabella, Johnny Thunder – these were people I either knew, or felt like I did. Ray had a knack for choosing a character, creating a backstory, then giving the song substance by basing that character on somebody real. 'Johnny Thunder' was based on a biker from Muswell Hill. He'd been at William Grimshaw around the same time as us, and his real name was Johnny, although he thought of himself as a James Dean character, all mean and moody on his motorbike. He was a loner and, although he had a girlfriend, I always thought she terrified him. One day we heard that he'd died in a motorcycle accident on the big roundabout in Muswell Hill, near the cinema. His footrest had caught the kerb and knocked him off his bike. 'Wicked Annabella' was more of a composite character, a tribute to crabby old spinsters everywhere: the crotchety old lady who lives in a corner house who, as a kid, you're terrified to walk past in case she whacks you with her walking stick. I volunteered to sing 'Wicked Annabella' because I could relate to weird shit like witchcraft, and I could make it funny and leery. Mick's drumming was fantastic, and I loved the overall feel of it, the unique strangeness of that song.

'Picture Book' was an occasion when the whole band gelled. The song was based on a slow hypnotic boogie riff. It was about the family photo album, which contained the most rooted memories of childhood, and the idea of using basic musical patterns fit the concept like a glove: the basic scales of music, the basic scales of life. *The Village Green Preservation Society*, and some of the songs we recorded around it, were connected musically. Crashing through the middle of 'Last of the Steam-Powered Trains' was a chromatically rising scale – the same pattern that ended 'Days'. We recorded 'Days' a few months earlier, and I consider them both 'end of days' songs. 'Days' acknowledges that once again the season was changing: the life we'd all been leading was about to end. 'Steam-Powered Trains' looked both ways at once. The rhythm of a train is relentless, always moving forwards. Reminiscent of Howlin' Wolf's 'Smokestack Lightning', the song revived the spirit of the early R&B Kinks sound while it also asked the question directly: could this be the end of the track for The Kinks? Was this our last album?

'Big Sky' has long been one of my favourites and in the song we created a real-imaginary world. In the middle Ray and I sing in harmony, 'One day we'll be free.' This is the bridge section, but it is also an emotional bridge towards another dimension. 'Big Sky' zooms outwards, looking from the heavens down on the rest of the album, down at the village green. Ray and I were connected musically, but also as brothers, as family. Even had this been our last album, those feelings would have been eternal, without a beginning or an end. *The Village Green Preservation Society* was about an England that did exist or never existed, or may exist in the future. When I was chucked out of school, I took it as an invitation to create a world of my own. Living inside my imagination immediately lifted me out of the doldrums of everyday life, lifting me towards a higher consciousness, towards journeys that have no beginning or end and which can be joined at any moment. 'Big Sky' spoke to me about all those feelings. The magnetism of that song never wears thin.

Around the time we were rehearsing the *Village Green* songs, I wrote a playful song called 'Donkey and the Kangaroo'. It was a parable really – about not knowing what the song was about, then finding out only through the process of writing it; it was a song about writing songs. Ray was disinterested, but Pete saw its potential and supported me as we tried to make it work. Then Ray started playing something of his own instead, and Pete went off in a huff, upset that Ray was wrapped up in his own ideas. I had of course seen this mean-spirited side of Ray previously, but Pete was stunned at his disparaging comments and self-obsessed behaviour. Maybe 'Donkey and the Kangaroo' might have sat nicely as a companion to 'Phenomenal Cat', which I thought was fantastically psychedelic. Maybe one day I'll finish my song, but who knows what it could have become.

Thankfully, *The Village Green Preservation Society* was not our last album. Soon we'd regroup to record *Arthur*, but the doors firmly closed on that first incarnation of The Kinks. As soon as *Village Green* was finished and released, Pete left the band – this time for good, and our internal split ran alongside irreversible change all around us.

By the end of the 1960s, the London my parents had known seemed over. The community spirit we had experienced as kids in East Finchley and Muswell Hill – my mum leaving the front door on the latch in case anyone wanted to drop by for a cuppa – was of the past. The country was a harsher place suddenly. On the title track, 'The Village Green Preservation Society', Ray sang about

'God save little shops, china cups and virginity' – this line always amused me; the virginity part was tongue-in-cheek, not to be taken literally. As poetic licence for an innocence that once lost could never be regained, it was the perfect analogy. Handsome Victorian terraced houses, the backbone of families across London, were getting pulled down in favour of harsh, unfriendly tower blocks, unlovely and often threatening places to live. Whole stretches of idyllic countryside were destroyed to accommodate road-building schemes. Planners and architects dreamed their dreams, but they too often forgot that *people* are always at the heart of any community – and what about their needs and dreams? Fast forward a decade or so into the 1980s and we saw the result of this social experiment. A society not rooted in the warmth of community can breed only self-interest and social climbing. People had forgotten about their roots and what truly mattered in life.

With Pete gone we reached out again to John Dalton, who finally took his place as a full-time Kink. Pete's last few outings with us had been in the north-east playing those cabaret evenings. At the end of one gig, he jammed his foot down on his amp and smothered what we were playing with atonal squeaks and bangs, a clear message that he was feeling creatively boxed-in. In the end I respected his honesty; Pete always had integrity. The situation was unlikely to improve and it was better for everyone concerned that he move on. Dalton – we called him Nobby, a nickname he inherited from his football mates – arrived into the middle of a fractious situation, with a load of new music to learn, and I take my hat off to him – he picked up the baton from Pete without stumbling or ever dropping it.

In an early sign of how our music would ultimately develop during the early 1970s, Ray was itching to turn *The Village Green Preservation Society* into a stage show weaving a story around the characters he'd created for the album. Pye were lukewarm on the idea, to put it mildly, and never came up with any extra cash to make it happen. One reason might have been that the album was reviewed respectfully, if never lavishly, but didn't sell anywhere near the number of copies we'd hoped. Also Pye couldn't see anything obvious to extract as a single, which did nothing to persuade them to throw good money after what they assumed was bad on an album with limited commercial appeal. Our previous single, 'Days', had been released the previous summer, and the decision to put out 'Plastic Man' with 'King Kong' on the B-side was another badly flawed decision. The lyric contained the word 'bum' and, following the 'Dead End Street' debacle, the BBC again declined to broadcast the promotional video we'd made to accompany the song. People had waited months for a Kinks single they could love like 'Waterloo Sunset' or 'Days', but 'Plastic Man' turned out to be another commercial failure – especially after we'd just released an album in which every track would become a classic over time.

What a disorientating yet productive period it was. The 1968 Eurovision Song Contest, held that April at the Royal Albert Hall, was won by a singer from Spain who traded under the name Massiel. She was up against Cliff Richard, whose song 'Congratulations' was favourite. When I listened to Massiel's 'La La La' I recognised the source straight away – it was the chorus of 'Death of a Clown' stretched into being *the whole bloody song*. It was abysmal bollocks and I couldn't help but feel like I'd been taken for a ride.

At that time Ray and I also played for a pro-celebrity football team called the Showbiz Eleven. Sharing a football pitch with great players of the past like Danny Blanchflower, Bobby Moore, Jon Charles and Billy Wright was a dream made real. I played inside-left and Ray was right mid-field. Tommy Steele was a very effective winger and Jess Conrad was a pretty useful goalkeeper and a very funny guy. He was very amused by my brother's stinginess and nicknamed him Ray 'I Spent a Pound' Davies; he called me Dave 'We can't make it without you' Davies. Tom Courtenay played and, it turned out, was a very good footballer too. Bobby Smith, who had played for Chelsea, Spurs and England, sometimes played with us and always arrived with a bottle of scotch. To warm up, he'd drink half, then massage the rest into his legs, always with a big smile on his face. The professional careers of these players were, of course, long in the past, but I was amazed at how much strength and ability they had embedded in their muscles. Blanchflower was getting on but, watching him close-up on the field, I was astonished to see how dexterous and agile he remained; and I realised how much nuance of body movement is missed when we watch from the terraces.

It was similar to music really. Blanchflower took charge during one match at Leeds United football ground and his authority trickled down to every player on the field; he unified the team, gave it purpose. He told me off for looking for the ball, which, he said, slowed everything down. 'Just run towards the goal and the ball will find you,' he explained. And he was as good as his word. Whenever I ran into the six-yard box and an opportunity to score opened up, the ball would appear magically at my feet. Blanchflower would flip the thing over my shoulder and land it in front of my feet, his aim and pacing immaculate always. It was like duetting with a virtuosic violinist; never did he drop a beat or miss a note. I also found his lack of ego very refreshing. He was on the field to make other players look great, to help them score, and that for him was satisfaction enough.

Moments in the celebrity spotlight like these were still a regular part of life, but I was learning that pop music was a fickle business. By the time 'Plastic Man' was released we'd not had a hit single for nine months, since 'Waterloo Sunset', and people were taking notice. When I walked into Lord Jim, a boutique on Carnaby Street, the owner was all smiles. I picked out some jackets as I had done many times before. I was about to leave the shop when the owner said, 'Sorry, Dave, you'll have to pay cash or put them back.' I looked at him with surprise, because normally I'd take what I wanted and he'd send an invoice to the office, sometimes he wouldn't bother. Me spreading the word by wearing his stuff on television was payment enough. Then he said, 'Come back when you've had a hit record again,' and I lost my cool. I threw the jackets back at him and stormed out the shop, knocking over a load of clothes as I left. Not my best moment, I'll admit, and he was perfectly entitled to ask for payment. But a few months earlier he had been begging me to take clothes away, his tongue rammed firmly up my arse. Now he had behaved like this, and he prodded a raw nerve. A while later his shop closed down and I saw him manning a market stall on Berwick Street in Soho. I ignored him but couldn't help feeling a tinge of *Schadenfreude*.

The paradox was, of course, that I'd spent most of the last year or so desperately trying to escape the fakeness and the phoney smiles; all the hangers-on and people trying to feather their own nests. But the Lord Jim guy had left me with my ego around my ankles. I was depressed and part of me would have been happy to call it a day, yet walking away would have been harder. My third solo single, 'Lincoln County', had been released a couple of months after 'Days' but didn't chart nearly as well as 'Death of a Clown' or 'Suzanah's Still Alive'. Despite the setback I was giving serious thought again to my own songs.

After the false start when I'd tried to record my solo album eighteen months earlier, I cautiously went back into the studio before Christmas 1968, just after the *Village Green* album was released, to record some demos. 'Hold My Hand'/'Creeping Jean' was issued as a single in January 1969, and I felt that either song could have kick-started ideas for a solo album. The material I recorded around this time has appeared in various forms over the years, as *The Album That Never Was* and later under the title *Hidden Treasures*; and it all appeared again as a bonus disc to a reissue of the *Arthur* album in 2019. Ray told an interviewer, as a joke, that my album would be released as *A Hole In The Sock Of Dave Davies*, and the title kind of stuck. Fans kept asking when *A Hole In The Sock* would be released, but nothing about the project felt right and taking responsibility for a solo album was weighing me down. There's a song on there called 'I'm Crying' – and I was. After 'Hold My Hand' I had thought maybe I can do this, because I knew how to write a decent ballad and all kinds of other stuff. But writing songs made me feel morose, and I found it impossible to write to order; I needed to feel inspired. Eventually Pye suggested an album release in the summer of 1969 under the title *Lincoln County*, but I willed the idea to go away.

Which was a pity because when I listen back to those songs now, I can hear all sorts of interesting stuff going on. 'Lincoln County' itself had a country vibe inspired by Eddie Cochran – with a backstory based around something that had happened in Muswell Hill. My mum had been walking along Princes Avenue when she saw a scarf in a little paper bag that someone had stuffed into a crack in the wall. She brought it home and draped it over her shoulders and around her head, and decided to keep it. No chance of tracing the owner, she said, and she looked very glam in it. But she didn't know that the person who'd hidden the scarf in the wall was sitting next to her – it was me! I'd bought it as a birthday present for Sue. It was dark purple and I thought it would suit her perfectly. On the way home, though, I had doubts. What about if she thought the scarf was a stupid present? So I hid it, never suspecting I'd see it again. And certainly not wrapped around my mother's shoulders, and that triggered the idea for the song and gave me the lyric: 'I got a head scarf, fair, I got for my momma that she won't wear.' Later, though,

I suspected Mum had seen me put it in the wall. 'Hold My Hand' was released after 'Lincoln County' and uses the same punctuating phrase – dah-da-daa-da-daa – as 'The Village Green Preservation Society', which is an intriguing chicken-and-egg story. My memory is that phrase had been bouncing around between Ray and me for a while. He put it in his song, and I put it in mine. It was a tiny riff, but very useful as a link. Something like that becomes a musical tool which can allow you to stop one thing and start another, tricks that move ears to a different part of the song.

'Lincoln County' was a hit in Holland, 'Hold My Hand' in Germany, and in early 1969 I was booked to perform 'Hold My Hand' live on *Beat Club*, which was a popular television programme in Germany at the time, broadcast from Bremen. It was important I go to help promote the record, but its failure to chart at home tipped my already fragile state into a major depression. I would have done anything to avoid getting on that plane and I invited a friend, I think the singer Leapy Lee – real name Lee Graham – along for company. We started drinking at the airport and ended up laughing all the way to Germany. Lee was a party animal, and rubbed shoulders with showbiz folks. He knew the actress Diana Dors and went to parties at her place in Chelsea which sometimes, he said, ended in her bedroom, with various people frolicking around naked under a mirrored ceiling. All very entertaining to hear – but I was in such a pitiful state by the time we arrived at the studio, I couldn't walk in a straight line.

As I staggered and swayed, the floor manager invited me onto the studio floor to show me around the set and explain how they envisaged my song working. I was supposed to appear on a rotating stage, then walk down a flight of stairs to another stage below, where a young girl would be waiting for me. I would look deep into her eyes, take her by the hand, and walk along another very narrow catwalk platform that led to the other side of the studio. All while lip-synching to the backing track. Given I couldn't stand up, I had no clue about how I was meant to follow this complex choreography and made my excuses. I told him I wasn't feeling great and that I needed to rest in the dressing room – 'no need for a rehearsal, the show will be fine, I promise you,' I said.

I tottered back to the dressing room and Lee was sitting on a sofa wearing a big, silly smile with his arms around two call girls. Arranged on the table in front of them were bottles of wine and some strongly scented pot waiting to be rolled into joints. I knew I shouldn't because I was about to perform, but I grabbed a bottle of wine and rolled a joint anyway, and whatever I was smoking wasn't the pot I was used to from home. After a few puffs I was in another world, all dreamy and serene, like I was dancing among the clouds. Then one of the girls gently moved me to a couch, peeled off my shirt and started giving me a massage. Her touch, as she kneaded my back and shoulders, soothing every muscle she brushed against, was exquisite. She knew exactly which buttons to press, and I blissed out. Next thing I knew, she had undressed me and was kissing my stomach. As she continued to lick and probe, it was like her tongue was inside my brain, soothing my frazzled state and caressing all my sensory centres.

There was a loud knock on the door and I woke up with a thump. I'd fallen into a deep, near-hypnotic sleep, and this was my stage call – I was on in five minutes. I could have slept for hours longer but I dragged myself up from the couch, tripping over the wine glasses and ashtrays that were littering the floor, and thought, shit, I'd better put some clothes on. I don't know how I managed to walk to the studio. I felt nauseous, and my legs and arms felt like they had been set inside concrete. I was worrying about all the alcohol I'd consumed and wondering what the fuck had been in those smokes.

Then I saw the rotating platform, the long staircase and the girl waiting at the bottom, and the reality dawned – I could no more do what they wanted than I could suddenly speak Chinese. I wasn't a wholesome Perry Como-type crooner in a neatly tailored suit beaming fake smiles. Moreover, I knew I'd topple over, and the girl was a no-no; either she'd make me laugh or I'd throw up into her lap. The producer was hovering anxiously, sensing that his plans were unravelling. I used all my powers of persuasion: 'I *must* sing sitting on a stool,' I reasoned. 'It'll be much more intimate and emotionally true if I'm sitting, just me and no girl.' I got away with it only because the clock was ticking down to show time and there was no time to argue. A stool appeared, I perched on top of it, and more through luck than anything else managed to stay upright. All the way through I was praying hard – 'Sweet Jesus! Please let this end' – as I could hear the floor manager and cameramen sniggering at my predicament. The desire to sleep was all-consuming. The second the last note sounded, I slipped off the stool and was helped back to the dressing room. While I slept, Lee went to the bar with the two call girls and later that day, somehow, I found myself back in my own bed at home – but I have no recall of how I made it there.

My addictions were running seriously out of control. Looking back now I realise I was a hardcore alcoholic and drug addict, and my behaviour was putting my marriage to Lisbet under considerable strain. One night I staggered home very late to find that she had made dinner and lovingly set the table, while all I wanted to do was sleep off my drug-induced hangover. I wasn't hungry, but to keep the peace, I thought I should try to eat something. As Lisbet was bringing the food, I collapsed, and my fall knocked over the dining table and sent the plates smashing to the floor. I cut my arms badly and blood poured everywhere. Lisbet burst into tears and was furious, quite rightly. She looked at me in disgust as she helped me over to the couch and then she tried to mop up the damage. When I came to, I saw that she'd gone through the pockets of my jacket and was pouring my drugs down the sink. I grabbed her hands and we tussled with each other: in my fucked-up state, I had to rescue my precious drugs at all costs. That was my main priority. I tried to scoop out the drugs as they gurgled down the plughole. In desperation, I ran to the garage and came back with my toolbox and took the plumbing apart in a frantic attempt to retrieve some pills. I succeeded, but what a pitiful state I was in. Lisbet was distraught and, she told me later on, had reservations about getting into a marriage with someone who treated her so clumsily at times. I felt suitably chastened and ashamed, and realised I was in a mess – and that I'd be in an even bigger mess had I not been married to Lisbet.

Around me, friends had started dying from their addictions. The incident with the kitchen sink occurred after I'd spent the day in the Trident Studios, next to The Marquee Club in Soho, working with Ewin Stephens, an old friend from Muswell Hill. Lisbet was instinctively suspicious of Ewin, and with good reason. He was a hardcore junkie who lived a carefree life funded by money left to him by his mother, which he spent like cash was about to go out of fashion. Ewin's young wife was very pretty and very shy on the surface, but she was in fact very open-minded and we'd all get stoned together. Ewin wanted to be a rock singer at all costs. He had spent a fortune on booking studio time and buying instruments, but one thing he could never buy was a convincing singing voice and, truth be told, he wasn't very good. One night when we got stoned together and my defences were down, I said I'd write him a batch of songs and produce them in the studio. Which seemed like a good idea at the time.

Ewin hired the Trident, never cheap, and Elton John's bass player and drummer, and also the guitarist Albert Lee, a gifted player who'd later work with Emmylou Harris. It was a fantastic band, and the only problem was Ewin's obsession with trying to 'be' Bob Dylan. The day started well enough. With a band of that calibre, routining the songs was no sweat, and soon enough we were taking a break in the pub. Ewin got some beers, then produced amphetamines which we knocked back with whisky chasers. Back in the studio, he kept rolling joints and handing out pills and beer. I'd decided it was best to get the backing tracks down first. That way the musicians could finish for the day, and then we'd try to make Ewin sound halfway decent. I sang the songs first to give the players something to bounce off, and Albert started laying in his parts. The first solo he played was a killer, but I kept asking him for more. One more, Albert, let's try again! I was so far gone I thought that the best solo would always be the next one. Also Albert sounded so great that I could have listened to him all day; I was getting off on making him play. Eventually his patience snapped, and I let him go.

It was time to record Ewin's vocal tracks. He staggered towards the microphone but there was no way he could sing. He made a few hapless attempts, grunting into the microphone like a flatulent pig. Horrendous. I was long past the point of caring, and summoning up any authority I had left, I called it a day. 'See you tomorrow,' I said from behind the mixing desk, trying to look like a cool record producer. Ewin had spent a fortune, with virtually nothing to show for it. He was a crumpled heap on the floor when I left the studio, and he waved at me pathetically. In my mind, I was still George Martin or Quincy Jones and I walked out with a flourish. Suddenly it went dark and I started thrashing around in the darkness and yelled for help as stuff started crashing around me. Then a door opened and I saw the engineer. I'd walked into the broom cupboard and had been hit on the head by a mop. Which I suspect never happened to Quincy. The engineer led me out to the street, keeping watch like he was my nanny, and somehow I found my way home – and collapsed over the dining table, ruining the meal Lisbet had cooked.

A while later I received a phone call out of the blue to tell me that Ewin had OD'd on heroin and died. The last time I'd seen him, he'd pleaded with me to borrow a fancy pair of thigh-length boots, handmade by Anello & Davide. How could boots have possibly looked cooler? They were fashioned out of tan leather, and had a large Cuban heel and were skintight, stretching right up my crotch – where there were loops through which I could thread a belt. They were stunning and irreplaceable, and hugely expensive. Having splashed out on studio time but not finishing his record, Ewin had organised a photo shoot for the front cover of the album, and he reckoned my boots would make him look like a rock god. Now he was dead. I was stunned and my heart went out to his wife, especially as she had a child from a previous relationship. It was heartbreaking and should have served as a warning to me. But all I worried about was my boots. How callous it would have been to ask for them back; I never saw them again.

A year or so later my friend from the William Grimshaw days, George Harris, was found dead, lying in the street somewhere around Soho, after overdosing on a lethal cocktail of heroin and methedrine. He was twenty-one and life had never been easy for him; after getting expelled from school he had never found a purpose. It was so tragic. I heard about George's death from his mother in very bizarre circumstances. At that time when my mental health was so fragile, I wanted to reconnect with my past as a way of finding myself again. I'd walked along Fortis Green Avenue to find the street where George lived with his mother and brother. It had been a long time since I'd seen him, and I was filled with the anticipation of seeing an old friend again and catching up about old times. I found the house and rang the doorbell, but nobody was home. A pity, but I thought I'd come back later and I went for a walk around Muswell Hill. When I saw that the El Toro coffee bar, where I hung out with Sue, and where Ray and I had played little gigs, was now a Chinese restaurant, I felt regretful.

Also gone was the Athenaeum Ballroom, where we'd met Robert and Grenville for the first time and played shows as The Ravens. That splendid building had been ripped down and in its place was a branch of Sainsbury's. I walked in to buy a can of lemonade and, standing waiting to pay, I saw George's mother – and I half expected to see George standing beside her. I told her that I'd just called on them but Mrs Harris told me they had moved to a smaller flat. Since George had died, they didn't need such a large house and had moved. What? George had *died*? I was shaken to my core. Earlier that day, as it happened, my mum had told me that George had been taken into hospital a few weeks earlier. He needed a kidney transplant and I knew why immediately. His drug addiction had obviously taken its toll, causing him massive internal damage. The last time I'd seen him, some years earlier, he was already heavily addicted and his life was governed around getting his next fix. His mum told me that after coming out of hospital he'd turned over a new leaf and was recovering well. But one night she had a call from the police who told her that George had been found dead. The supermarket was crowded and noisy, and rather than carry on this emotional conversation I took her telephone number and told her I'd ring. But I never called. Every time I picked up the phone, the prospect felt too painful.

After telling me about George's kidney operation, Mum dropped another piece of news that made my heart race. She had seen Sue. I would often visit Mum hoping that she might have news about Sue and Tracey, and she told me that Tracey was seven and doing really well. I was desperate to see a photo and Mum reached into her bag – and there was Tracey, the first time I'd seen a picture of her.

Those slightly forlorn Davies eyes were unmistakable, but what a beauty she was with her cute cubby cheeks. I couldn't take my eyes off the photograph – until Mum eventually, very gently, lifted it out of my hands and placed it back into her bag. What happened in the past should stay in the past, she thought. I had a wife and a family of my own now – my second son, Simon, would be born in June 1970 – and they should be my priority. Especially as Sue had made a new life. She had got married and was living in Hatfield in Hertfordshire, although Mum didn't have an address. What a day this was turning out to be. It had felt good being back in the familiar surroundings of Denmark Terrace, sitting in the living room again and looking at the family photographs on the mantelpiece, feeling the warmth of the relationships that Ray and I had shared with our sisters. Mum had been to Wylie's the bakers, on Fortis Green, and bought a fresh white loaf, which she cut up into doorstopper slices and served with cheese and pickle. And she made a pot of fresh tea, all served up in her best china.

Ever since I'd been very little, cheese and pickle had been my favourite, and for all the weirdness I had experienced on the road, and all the destructive stuff I was pumping into my body, here was a reminder of a more nourishing way of living, like Mum knew exactly what I needed. When she told me about George going into hospital, I told her that I hoped one day we'd release a record together. He had turned into a shit-hot guitarist and after the early successes with The Kinks, when I had some cash in the bank, I'd hired a studio in Soho and we recorded some demos together. When we were younger, we'd spend hours listening to blues records, and now we recorded some of those same songs, also a couple of things by Spider John Koerner. It never went any further, partly because I was so occupied with The Kinks. My afternoon with Mum turned tearful, like she could feel the pain I was in. She held back her own tears as she watched me looking longingly at that photograph of Tracey. Typically, she tried to make light of it. 'You were such a beautiful little boy, David,' she said, 'but what an absolute sod you were. Gorgeous, but naughty all the bloody time.' We laughed. 'When the sun shone on your blond hair, you looked like an angel with a halo. But one day, I thought, that halo's gonna slip around your bloody neck and strangle you, you little sod.'

After the news about Sue, I was already feeling reflective and despondent when I left Denmark Terrace – then I walked straight into hearing the news about George. I drove away from Muswell Hill with sadness in my soul. Instead of driving home to Lisbet in Barnet, I diverted to the A1 and headed for Hatfield. If only I could see Sue and Tracey – that would mean everything to me. Once I arrived, I drove around the streets like I was in a trance, around the same streets again, again, again: Sue, Tracey, *where are you?* Then the realisation hit me like a ton of bricks. George had died. I was never going to see him again, he was gone and wasn't coming back. He was a purist and had taken the piss out of The Kinks mercilessly. Hit records and *Top of the Pops*? 'You've sold out!' he'd tell me. Always in a humorous way, albeit with an undertone of jealousy because he wanted to be a musician too. Ray and I had managed to make something out of our lives with music. George had not, and I had loved him, and I should have been there for him. I had lost my best friend, and I couldn't help but think about Ewin too. Two friends lost to drugs – a tragic and needless waste of young lives that had been filled with promise.

I turned the car around and headed back to my home in East Barnet. I was in a glum and sombre mood, but as soon as I walked through the door something changed. I was home. I had a family. I was alive. Lisbet greeted me warmly and Martin ran into my arms, and I picked him up and gave him a bear hug as tears rolled down my cheeks. Actually, my life was in a good place. I was married to a beautiful woman who really cared about me; maybe Mum was right, I should stop raking over the coals of the past and be grateful for how my life was now. Later I channelled all my feelings about George into a grieving love song for a fallen friend that I called 'Georgie Was'. It was recorded, but I couldn't bring myself to release it and wouldn't even now. The song was a mournful tribute in which I sang of the horrors of drug addiction. This was one for me; it was too personal to be out there in the world.

Meantime I tried to be rational and realistic about Tracey. Sue was married to a man who Tracey thought of as her dad. I couldn't blunder into the middle of that; it would not have been fair. Many years later, though, I found out that Sue would regularly visit Rasa when The Kinks were away on tour. She wanted to know how I was coping with life, and apparently a part of her hadn't moved on either. The situation was always going to be complicated, but just maybe I could have had some relationship with Tracey had both sets of parents not interfered. Seeing my daughter would have gone a long way to soothing the ache I felt inside.

CHAPTER SEVEN

SO WHERE DO I GO, WHAT DO I SEE?

Despite the chaos swirling around daily life, I was feeling good about The Kinks. We'd taken a battering following the release of 'Wonderboy' and while *The Kinks Are The Village Green Preservation Society* had hardly set the album charts on fire, the record had gained us respect. A lot of creative people recognised what we had attempted to do, that we had set off on a direction of our own. Knowing this helped us salvage our confidence and find a sense of purpose again. After being a bass player who covered Pete's parts, John Dalton had become more integral to the band, which helped. The nature of touring is that people get on each other's tits, and John and I certainly had our moments, but without any of the dramas that coloured Pete's later time with the band. John was a rhythmically earthy musician who formed a solid rhythm section with Mick. I felt good about our self-assurance and creative tenacity, and that's there for all to hear in *Arthur (Or the Decline and Fall of the British Empire)*.

Arthur himself was cock-a-hoop that we'd based an album loosely around his character and his life. Before he died, he told Ray how much he loved the record and that he played it all the time. But the album was, I have to say, something of an ironic but loving tribute. Originally the idea had been to do *Arthur* as a television play, a so-called 'pop opera', and Ray worked up a script with the writer Julian Mitchell that we all really liked. Then Granada Television delayed putting the thing into production and everyone got very frustrated – especially after The Who released their own rock opera *Tommy* and stole our thunder; not that they meant to. By that point we'd recorded the music and Pye was desperate to release the album, which they did anyway on 10 October 1969 after the television people stalled again. Ray and Pete Townshend had a mutual friend, Barry Fantoni. I couldn't help but wonder if Barry had dropped a few hints about *Arthur*. Pete always seemed interested in what Ray and The Kinks were up to. Some reviews made inevitable comparisons with *Tommy*, but were generally very positive. With the album out, Granada finally decided to pull the plug and blamed the budget; too expensive or whatever. In the end we just had to deal with it.

In 2019, the BBC produced a radio version of *Arthur* which gave an idea of what could have been. The drama all happens on the day before (the fictional) Arthur and his family leave for Australia, and everyone reflects on the state of England and what, with the Empire gone and the old certainties evaporating, it meant to be British – it was following on from *The Village Green Preservation Society* in that sense. The character of the actual Arthur hangs over everything. He had assumed that life was inevitably going to be better in Australia – and at least he'd tried. But he ended up as dissatisfied over there as in London. At home he'd had a good job in a plastics factory and earned very good money. The good times had, he felt, passed him by. He had taken a punt at Australia and it didn't work out. Those mixed emotions, of hope and disappointment, of searching for a better life, are all inside *Arthur*.

Recording the album was a joy. Pye let us use their larger No. 1 studio and the speakers were state-of-the-art: powerful and muscular, with rich, sonorous bass, and it's obvious, I think, the difference they made to the beefed-up sound of the finished record. We knew we were putting together an album of fantastic new music. Before the album appeared, 'Shangri-La' was issued as a single and its message ended up confusing people. The idea of 'a Shangri-La' had become a bit of joke at the time. The ultimate middle-class dream was to buy a cosy semi-detached house in suburbia which you would call 'Shangri-La'. Ha ha ha. Some people missed the point and thought the song was a piss-take of middle-class aspirations, but it was more nuanced than that: 'Here's your reward for working so hard/Gone are the lavatories in the back yard/Gone all the days when you dreamed of that car/You just want to sit in your Shangri-la.' The song was entirely sympathetic to the middle class. Perhaps some of these people had escaped dead end street.

We had developed the knack for choosing precisely the wrong song to put out as a commercial single. 'Shangri-La' was over five minutes long and had a complex multi-sectional structure – in hindsight not ideal to release as a single. 'Drivin'', a funny song, was the first single we released from the album. It was based around the day trips we took as kids in Dad's car to places like Southend and Ramsgate. The in-joke was that the car was Dad's, but Arthur was the only person in our family who had a driving licence. So we all impatiently crammed into Dad's car – which he called Betsy – behind Arthur. But 'Drivin'' didn't do great business either. With a third single, though, we struck gold. 'Victoria' was the opening song on the album and set the scene. Victoria was on the throne. The Empire was crumbling, 'Sex was bad, called obscene, and the rich were so mean' and the working class held the monarchy in tremendous esteem, even as prudish Victorian puritan attitudes kept them in their place. 'Victoria' was backed by a funky rock riff and sounded in many ways like an old-fashioned Kinks song from the very early days. Lew Warburton turned in some fantastic arrangements for brass and strings that sounded like Count Basie bumping into James Brown, and the combination proved irresistible. We headed back into the singles charts.

On the album, 'Yes Sir, No Sir' followed right on with a song about a clueless young conscript – working class, of course – encouraged into a battle by a public-school officer twerp who couldn't have cared less about his fate, but promises to send a medal to his wife on his inevitable demise in battle. *Arthur* touched profound emotional truths. 'Some Mother's Son' did something pop hadn't done before. It took listeners inside the terror of war. Arthur's brother is killed during the Battle of the Somme, and the song tells of meaningless brutality and anguish. We felt the weight of the subject and worked incredibly hard to get every aspect of that song nailed: the arrangements, the voice parts, the balance of the band. One thing I've learned over the years: it's worth spending time getting the arrangement right, polishing every detail, before starting to record. You want the record to capture the impact of a song as you're discovering what it is. Record too many times and the performance can become a matter of routine. The danger is you kill it stone dead.

'Australia' was pretty much recorded in one take and this track was The Kinks at our most audacious. This song was powered by Ray's twisted, cynical sense of humour. 'Opportunities are available in all walks of life in Australia/So if you're young and you're healthy/Why not get a boat and come to Australia,' he sang – which sounds good until you consider what happened to Arthur and his family. This was our opportunity to express that our family had been tempted by this promise and that it had all blown up in their faces. The middle section of the song opened up into a free jam and I played an extended guitar solo, with all kinds of interesting bits of harmony and instrumental textures emerging underneath my feet to improvise against. It was like surfing over waveforms of pure sound, improvising off pure feeling. As I geared myself up to solo I thought about the jazz guitarist Jim Hall, whose playing I revered and who had worked with so many great players like Sonny Rollins, Paul Desmond and Bill Evans. I liked the rhythmic power and crunch of his playing as he soloed. Which brought me full circle: Jim had played as part of Jimmy Giuffre's trio on the *Jazz on a Summer's Day* film.

Ray and I both had tears in our eyes as we recorded the poignant title track, the last song on the album. This song answered some of the questions left hanging by 'Australia': 'Arthur we like you and want to help you/Somebody loves you, don't you know it?' Then just a week later, on 17 October 1969, we were playing at the Fillmore East in New York City, the opening night of our first US tour since the great disaster of 1965. To this day, nobody connected with The Kinks completely understands why the ban was lifted as quickly and unexpectedly as it had been imposed. Ray flew to Los Angeles to talk to some union people, and offered apologies for our behaviour, but he didn't return in an especially positive frame of mind. But suddenly we got the green light – and those visas. It's difficult to know how the fate of the group would have been different had we never been banned. Would we have recorded *Village Green* and *Arthur* had we been eyeing a career in America? Likely not. Our exile didn't do us any permanent damage, although it was clearly a problem that had needed to be resolved.

We had still been playing the occasional odd gig. Our agent had even booked us to play in Beirut, where we set up with the sound of tanks and gunshots in the background. When it became clear that the promoter couldn't pay us, we ran for the airport as quickly as we could. The Fillmore East in New York – now that was more like it! This was where Miles Davis, Janis Joplin, Hendrix, Frank Zappa and Crosby, Stills, Nash & Young performed. We played hits like 'You Really Got Me' and 'Till the End of the Day', but also new material from *Arthur*, the album we were promoting. Warner Brothers had repackaged *Village Green* for the tour, complete with 'God Save The Kinks' badges and little bags stuffed, apparently, with grass harvested from an English village green. We had rejected other bonkers promotional ideas – like 'fake' arrests to increase our notoriety and paying a load of teenage fans to turn up at John F. Kennedy airport to manufacture 'Kinks-mania'. Can you imagine?

I immediately became aware of how much our fanbase had changed since our first visit three years earlier. The screaming teenagers had been replaced by blokes with long beards, stoned out of their skulls, who nodded their heads wisely in time with the music. Some of these same guys presumably got hold of the wrong end of the stick and tried to smoke the village green grass, not that it was ever going to open any doors of perception. In many ways, though, a stoned audience would have worked in our favour. We played a haphazard show at the Fillmore. We were jetlagged and overtired, and also under-rehearsed and extremely tense. Opening for us that night were the Bonzo Dog Doo-Dah Band, and also Spirit, a psychedelic rock band visiting from the West Coast, whose members favoured overbearing solos that felt like they'd never bloody end.

Spirit came closer to the type of music normally heard at the Fillmore, and God knows what the audience would have made of us – and the Bonzos – had they not been so out of it. The Bonzos were like Monty Python with a music degree. Roger Spear would leap up to solo, then blow jazz through a plastic doll's leg, and their sets were full of English in-jokes about Princess Anne and Harold Wilson. Perhaps some of the potheads tried to find serious meaning beyond the absurdity, but anyone else would likely have been baffled, especially as Python hadn't yet made it over the Atlantic. We followed, and performed songs like 'Mr. Churchill Says', 'Yes Sir, No Sir', 'Victoria' and 'Well Respected Man' and I wonder if the audiences – who were hardly professors of English at Oxford – found us overly quaint. Some Americans can be quite literal and admire how the English take pride in our dysfunctional culture, that we don't mind taking the mickey out of ourselves. We have an ability to turn our eccentricities back on themselves. From Spike Milligan and The Goons, via Tony Hancock and Python, to Harry Hill, that is the foundation of the English sense of humour and comedy.

As the tour gathered momentum we slowly found our dynamism again, but it was a slow and laborious process. In Chicago, at the Kinetic Playground, we played on the same bill as The Who, and it was good to see Townshend again. The Who had been touring the US solidly throughout the time we were banned and had built a large and loyal fanbase. They were fresh from their unreal success playing the 1969 Woodstock Festival and we were reduced to opening for them. At the time this was a sour pill to swallow, and gave us a sense of how hard we needed to work to claw our way back in America. The *Arthur* versus *Tommy* situation hung unspoken in the air and it was awkward backstage. But these days I can appreciate what incredible music The Who were making, and how they deserved their status.

Incidents like that added to my unending homesickness, and not for the first time on the road I felt the black cloud of depression descending. Drugs were very easy to acquire, either from shady-looking guys hanging around outside gigs, knowing they could do great business, or from well-supplied groupies willing to help in one way or another. After one of the Fillmore gigs I went in search of English beer and found myself in The Haymarket, a rough-and-ready bar on 8th Avenue, near Times Square when it was far seedier than it is these days. There was an interesting crowd there: drunk bums mixed with dancers working on Broadway, and it was also a gay pick-up joint. It was here that I met Diana, who was an absolute ball of energy and very sexy. We started drinking wine at the bar and fell into a long conversation. Because we were so out of it, we ended up back in my hotel room, but the evening followed a path I wasn't expecting. She opened her bag and took out a drug called Angel Dust, and we rolled a joint or two which did the trick. I smoked it and my limbs went so wobbly I had to lie down. What a weird substance.

Did I ever tell you about the glamorous life of a rock star on tour? This first tour since the ban was all about re-establishing The Kinks in the US and we had to consider the budget. That meant staying at Holiday Inns – and sharing rooms. In New York, Grenville and I doubled up at the Holiday Inn on 42nd Street, and what a sorry shithole it was, grim and depressing. Diana and I had just had sex when we heard a key opening the bedroom door and Grenville tumbled in looking like he'd been enjoying a night of overindulgence and making-merry himself. In his pinstripe suit and black tie, he was the very definition of the posh Englishman abroad. Clearly pissed and with his tie skewwhiff, he had a look of glazed amusement in his eyes – which widened noticeably once he saw Diana lying next to me. Being the perfect English gentleman, he shook her hand and greeted her with a plummy 'Hello, dear': he might as well have said 'Enchanted, I'm sure.' He poured himself a glass of wine and perched on the end of his bed – then suddenly it was like we were in a bedroom farce.

I gestured towards Grenville to join us in bed. Diana glowered at me in utter disbelief and Grenville's demeanour changed totally. Gone was that dashing Terry-Thomas charm. Instead he became a hornball of lust and took his trousers off to reveal a pair of saggy, baggy white underpants which hung around his bollocks like a marquee. Sexy they were not. As Grenville tried to get into bed, Diana shot out the other end. She grabbed her clothes and got dressed, and I realised how unfair I'd been. I'd genuinely wanted to test the situation, but I should have been more considerate and thoughtful. I put her in a cab home and we met for lunch the next day and tried to see the funny side of it.

In Chicago, following a gig at the Kinetic Playground, I went back to the hotel with a girl I didn't even fancy. I was overwhelmed by feelings of self-loathing and felt conflicted – I had a wife at home. But I was so out of it, I couldn't have had sex even had I wanted to. So I flipped. The girl and that fucking awful hotel room, it was all too much. I trashed the room, pulling the lampshades down and overturning the beds and tables – and using whatever I could lay my hands on to smash the mirrors. I looked round at my handiwork, but it wasn't enough. So I darted into the corridor, screaming at the top of my voice, and ran up and down like a maniac. Then I came to the lift and punched the glass exit sign as hard as I could with my right hand. I staggered around with tears in my eyes and with blood spurting from the gash. I was in the midst of a catastrophic breakdown and I was convinced I was going crazy.

At the hospital, the doctor who sewed me up was very nice. Luckily I hadn't ripped through any ligaments, which might have affected my guitar-playing, I'd merely shredded the skin around my knuckles. He told me to rest my injury for a week and a load of concerts had to be cancelled. I took advantage of the enforced break to fly to Copenhagen, where Lisbet and the kids were visiting my mother-in-law. My physical injuries had largely healed by the time I flew back to the US to pick up the tour again, but the mental scars were oozing out of control.

We played in Detroit on the same bill as Joe Cocker, then wound our way towards Los Angeles via Cincinnati. And I just couldn't shake my patterns of addictive behaviour. The last time we'd been in Hollywood we'd lived the life, staying at the Beverly Hills Hotel and playing at the Hollywood Bowl. This time we were staying in a cheap hotel near Hollywood Boulevard called The Hollywood Hawaiian, and the schedule allowed us a week to settle in, before playing a gig at The Factory in LA and a run of shows at the Whisky a Go Go on Sunset Boulevard. Ray was the public face of the band and did the press interviews and took care of any business matters, while Dalton and Mick more than filled their boots with booze. For me, though, getting my next drink, and the usual excesses, was all I could think about. Since our last visit, LA had become awash with drugs, and anything anyone could have wanted – pot, cocaine, acid, speed, you name it – was on tap. It was a fun and exciting place to be.

That free week became a vacuum into which I poured everything that was bad for me. I was lonely and missing my family terribly, and things would have been different had they been along for the trip. In a nightclub I met Norma, who was up for pretty much anything. We hit it off immediately and got plastered together, then screwed our way into the early morning back at the hotel. She became my companion during our time in LA, and after a gig, back at the hotel, my world was shaken as I experienced my first acid trip. Norma had acquired some tiny white pills, and I went along with her suggestion that we take them. Would have been impolite not to and I was too pissed to care. She'd tripped herself a few times and these pills, she said, were the best around. And I mustn't worry – she'd be there to babysit me through if anything went wrong or it became too weird.

We glugged down a couple of pills each with a glass of wine, and I puffed expectantly on a Marlboro as we lay on the bed waiting for something to happen. Nothing for ages . . . then wooo OOOO oooah. I'd poured a second big glass of wine and as I inhaled on another cigarette there were two Daves suddenly. We were both smoking separate cigarettes and were experiencing different sensations. The classic first stage of an acid awakening. Norma held me close and soothed me with her calming words, although quite honestly, when you're high like that you feel superhuman and impervious to any fear or danger. The universe, and everything within it, opened up before my eyes and I was travelling, faster than the speed of light, straight for its core. In reality I was lying immobile in a cheap hotel room in Los Angeles, but inside my head I was racing towards what felt like eternal bliss. As Norma spoke, I heard many voices coiling around themselves like the branches of a vine. Banal objects – chairs, the wine glass I was holding in my hand – became objects of overwhelming wonder and beauty. Atoms and molecules danced before me. I was swept along by the pulsating force field of the chair that was next to the bed. It breathed. It had life – I witnessed a relentless slipstream of energy beyond what humans are usually privileged to witness. Walls were melting away from the ceiling and took on abstract forms.

The Captain – *my* Captain – was speaking to me. He was a mental being on a mission to explain what I was experiencing, to help me make sense of these enlightening, exhilarating mysteries. At the height of the ecstasy the great riddles of existence were stripped down to an understandable essence – profound questions were answered in a language that expressed itself, not in words, but as pure waves of energy. I looked to where Norma had been lying on the bed and, instead of a woman, I saw an alien being that looked like a reptile. But there was no terror, no sense of loss. The drug had reconnected me to primeval energies, connecting the present back to ancient truths. There was nothing to fear, my Captain told me. He showed me everything, like dreams and reality were one and the same. Everything I saw was wonderful, everything I saw was overwhelming. My Captain told me that I had been granted a rare view of the world and, to return to normal, I must unlearn all my preconceptions of life.

During the trip, along with the highs, came moments of the most acute, excruciating melancholy. As I came to, sadness pervaded everything. I took a walk around the hotel and nothing felt rooted in reality. Other guests, the receptionist at the front desk, looked like hollowed-out mannequins, which compounded my sensations of loneliness, like I was the last person left on earth. Back in the room, Norma told me that she had never experienced a trip like it: those pills must have been exceptionally potent. But I desperately wanted the effects to go away. 'Please, when will they end?' I pleaded again and again and again. And again. I grabbed a bottle of wine and gulped it down like water, but it did nothing to calm me and my paranoia spiralled. I ranted and screamed like an animal in distress. Norma gave me a sleeping pill and I slipped into a deep but very uneasy sleep.

When it was time to start playing our gigs, I felt terrible foreboding and anxiety. The previous couple of days had been terrifying and I was existing on a cocktail of sleeping pills, so I could rest, and alcohol to dim the pain, and everything felt alien to me. Ray acted oblivious, but Dalton cottoned on quickly that something strange was going on. 'It's like you're here in body,' he said, 'but your soul is some other place.' Which was very perceptive. I forced myself onstage and I tried my best, but the music sounded dislocated, like it might fall apart at any moment. So I walked out. I put my guitar into its case, found the nearest exit and, between the club and the hotel, I made a serious decision. This life was no longer for me. I decided to be on the next flight back to London and start life over again.

Back at the hotel, Grenville frantically tried to persuade me to reconsider, but I'd made up my mind and there was no going back now. The rest of our week at the Whisky was postponed and I took a couple of sleeping pills, and didn't get out of bed for two days. When I woke up the sense of loneliness was crushing; emotionally, physically and spiritually I was hanging on by a thread. I went to see Ray in his room. I needed my brother at a time like this; I needed my family. But Ray didn't need me. Perhaps he was pissed off because of the cancelled shows, but I might as well have been talking to a stranger I'd met on the street. He was cold, unfeeling and utterly indifferent. I told him that all I wanted to do was go home. I was in a crisis and needed my own brother to empathise. But no. He told me about some bullshit dream he'd had about an old man walking down the street, who had glanced at Ray then slammed the door to his house. 'Don't close the door on the world, Dave,' Ray said. Then he told me I should see the tour out: 'We have another week of shows to play at the Fillmore in San Francisco and a few one-nighters, then we can head home, have a rest, and a rethink about the future.'

The promised heart-to-heart about the future direction of The Kinks never materialised, nor did I expect it would. Almost as soon as we were home, plans were afoot for other US tours the following year and there was a new album to think about, that would become *Lola Versus Powerman and the Moneygoround*. I was absorbed still by my personal torment and a couple of years would pass before I found a convincing way through what felt like an emotional maze. Whenever I saw the exit, and ran there, it was blocked. I kept my problems from Lisbet. Telling her everything that had gone on in the US would have been impossible, obviously, but I couldn't have made it through the crisis without her love and sunniness. It was becoming clear that I had to rebuild my inner life, brick by brick. Abusing my body with drugs and booze came with very serious consequences. I was riddled with self-hatred and paranoia. I couldn't shake the fear that I was being controlled by 'Them' – by dark, malevolent forces toying with us like we were puppets. They pulled our strings, and we danced, and they mocked our sheer ignorance and stupidity. This was The Big Truth. I had survived the 1960s, and the 1970s would be about examining *who am I* and piecing myself back together.

A US tour that kicked off at the end of January 1970 unravelled after a handful of shows because Mick contracted hepatitis, and all the remaining dates were cancelled. By the time we went back in the summer, opening in Minneapolis on 22 May, we were in a better place as a band. Earlier that month we'd recorded 'Lola' and, once again, in my gut, I knew it was destined to do very well for us. And I shudder to think what might have happened to The Kinks had we not managed to turn the tide of unsuccessful singles. Ray pinned his words around a chord sequence which we had jammed together a week or so before we recorded. We didn't know it at the time but *Lola Versus Powerman and the Moneygoround* would be our last album for Pye, and it was a very strong record. After the concept-album vibe of both *Village Green* and *Arthur, Lola* was a more conventionally arranged sequence of songs – or looked like it might be. Typically for The Kinks, the album looked two ways at once, with a lyricism that floated like a butterfly and a 'fuck you' attitude that stung like a bee. Ray's songs 'Denmark Street', 'Top of the Pops' and 'Moneygoround' satirised the more disreputable elements of the music business. His 'Get Back in Line' belonged to the same stable as 'Dead End Street' as an expression of the working-class experience. My contribution to the album was a heartfelt, to me, ballad I called 'Strangers'. This was a song about everything currently spinning around my exhausted brain: about paranoia, about unconditional love and reconciliation – about learning that sometimes you need to give up a part of who you are to become part of something greater.

'Lola' landed at just the right moment, when the public were one hundred per cent ready for the record. It was typical of Ray to observe quietly, then write a song that captured a particular moment in time. Since the very early days, when we were christened 'The Kinks' by Arthur Howes in the Lotus House Chinese restaurant on the Edgware Road, we appealed to people who refused to fit in, who found The Beatles' halo was not for them. With our hunting uniforms and boots we were kinky and, touring the US the previous year, we'd attracted cross-dressers and trans-vestites; in New York, the Warhol people loved us. After one gig, Ray fell into a deep conversation with the actress Candy Darling, famous for her work on Warhol's films, and they went for dinner – then he noticed her five o'clock shadow, although he'd claim later that he knew she was transgender all along. On another occasion Robert Wace spent an evening drinking champagne and dancing all night with a girl before the same penny dropped. Way back when we recorded 'Party Line' on *Face To Face* there was a line about 'Who's on the other end [of the phone]?/Is she big, is she small?/Is she a she at all?' 'Lola' was a track we were destined to release somehow.

The single had been scheduled for release during our US tour, and we played the song onstage before anyone heard the record. But out of nowhere came a problem. News reached us that the BBC were refusing to play 'Lola' because Ray's lyric contained a refer-ence to Coca Cola, which might have rhymed with Lola but contravened their strict policies on advertising and what today they call 'product placement'. Could we come up with a solution? Our concert at the University of Minnesota was cancelled to allow Ray to fly back to London. After all the flops and bans, we couldn't risk anything spoiling the chances of 'Lola' being a success. So Ray dubbed in 'cherry cola' to save the BBC's blushes, and flew back to the US in time to play the Aragon Ballroom in Chicago. Then the punchline: the engineers couldn't get the splice to fit, so Ray had to fly back again and redo the whole thing, forcing us to cancel a show in New York.

Just before the US tour, The Kinks had become a five-piece band. After Nicky Hopkins stopped working with us following the *Village Green* album, Ray had played keyboards himself on *Arthur* – but Grenville figured having a keyboard player as a permanent band member, who played live, could freshen things up a bit. He had in mind John Gosling, who was then studying at the Royal Academy of Music, and the second we met him, I knew he was right. He was a funny guy who quickly became known as 'The Baptist' because, with his pointy beard, he looked like everyone's idea of what John the Baptist should look like – like we'd been sent 'a John the Baptist' from Central Casting. The first time he performed with the band live was on *Top of the Pops* when we played 'Apeman', another song from the *Lola* album. It was suggested, semi-jokingly, that John dress up in a gorilla costume for our appearance – and suddenly there he was, all six foot three of him, stuffed inside a gorilla costume, looking like he'd escaped from the set of *King Kong*. Between rehearsals we all took full advantage of the BBC bar and by the time came for us to play, our gorilla was pissed. It was show time and John's debut with The Kinks was less than auspicious. By the time the camera zoomed round to him, he'd tripped over a cable – and all viewers saw was a close-up of an empty piano stool against a wall. I bit my tongue and desperately tried not to catch anyone's eye as I carried on playing – then we ran offstage and shrieked with laughter.

John was generally clumsy and endearingly gullible – more than once he fell for the old trick of 'John, have you got the time?', then he'd look at his wristwatch and pour his pint down his front. He was totally the right personality for us; and, more importantly, musically John made a decisive difference and Grenville's intuition had proved spot on. The band felt like a cohesive unit again for the first time since Quaife had left. Dalton and Gosling, together, played like they were on fire, and I could hear how much their deep grooves and rhythmic drive were inspiring Mick. A joy that had been missing for a while returned to the band and that's exactly what you want – the collective energy of everyone inspiring everybody else to new heights.

The first time John played with us live onstage was during that summer tour of the US, and he quickly learned the extent to which The Kinks were fuelled by alcohol – not for nothing did American fans nickname us 'The Juicers'. Although we had cottoned on to the fact that upsetting union people in the US was a really bad idea, our conduct offstage was as unruly as ever and was doing real damage to our relationship with Grenville and Robert. Grenville looked on in horror and disbelief a little while later when, during a flight back from Reykjavik, we behaved like drunken louts. I'd splashed out on a sheepskin coat at the airport and thought it would be *hilarious* to go on all fours up and down the aisle of the plane, doing an impression of a wild animal and biting people's legs. The cabin crew, not wanting to escalate the situation, moved us all to the back of the plane and watched over us like hawks. The captain gave us a stern dressing-down, telling us our behaviour was reckless and unacceptable; if we couldn't control ourselves, he'd divert the plane to Glasgow and have us arrested.

We managed to rein it in until about an hour or so before landing, when Dalton started to get restless. He was annoyed because the plane had been late taking off from Reykjavik and he was going to miss playing for his local football team. Suddenly he ran towards the cockpit and demanded the pilot made an emergency landing in Cheshunt, where he was due to play. John thought he was being funny – but nobody in the cabin crew laughed. He was dragged back to his seat, and this was the final straw. The bar was closed and when we arrived at Heathrow all the other passengers were let off the plane first – and we were escorted away by armed police. Grenville was mortified and I'd never seen him so upset. In my wisdom I decided to pick a fight with one of the officers, and Grenville, deploying all his upper-class charm, cooled the situation down. But he had reached his limit – that was the point he decided, enough, this can't go on.

We reached a crossroads during another tour of the US that

November – our third of the year. Once again it was time off that got me, and everybody else, into trouble. We had a day to ourselves in Los Angeles. Ray stayed behind at the hotel to do interviews, and the rest of us hit the shops on Hollywood Boulevard. Among the goodies we acquired, I found a gangster suit and replica pistol and walked around like I was in *The Godfather*. Mick found a clown costume; Baptist made a very convincing Viking and Dalton was dressed to the nines in a 1950s suit. We had a fun night at Filthy McNasty's, then we moved to the Whisky a Go Go, where things went from bad to worse. I saw some record executives I recognised sitting in one of the booths and I playfully waved my replica pistol in their direction. But this wasn't Muswell Hill, this was LA, and they went apeshit. Until I assured them it was a replica, they assumed they were all about to breathe their last.

It was an unfortunate faux pas but I didn't think anything of it until the next morning, when Grenville called a meeting. Mick had hurt his back dancing and hobbled into Grenville's hotel room and we were all hung-over and no doubt stank of booze. Grenville was puce with fury. Apparently the record executives I'd inadvertently threatened had been from our own label. They'd genuinely feared for their lives and had lodged a complaint, which got back to our management. Grenville let rip, and all the frustration of the last couple of months poured out of his mouth, words spurting like water from a fire hydrant. We were behaving like a spoilt bunch of kids, and he wasn't going to put up with it any longer. We needed to grow *the fuck* up. If we carried on with this reckless behaviour we'd ruin everything – 'You'll destroy your careers. Do you really want that?'

We were suitably chastened, and mumbled our apologies. Ray piped up and said we'd think over his words, and Grenville nodded with relief: he felt he'd been listened to and that we understood. Just then the door of his room was flung open and there was

Baptist in full Viking costume. He'd found a Viking horn and, excited to show us, blew it at full blast. It was so ear-splitting it felt like the foundations of the building were shaking under our feet. Baptist had unwittingly cut through the tension in the room and we all roared with laughter. All apart from Grenville, who was horrified and dumbfounded by this prank. He stormed out of the room, whispering angrily under his breath. And within a few weeks we were, for the first time since 1963, without management. Grenville and Robert had decided to call it a day.

Needless to say, our behaviour didn't improve. Touring anywhere – the US, UK or Europe – became agony for me and alcohol was the prop that got me through. Before one concert at Philharmonic Hall in New York at the end of March 1971 we'd had plenty to drink to fortify our nerves – it's a big, imposing hall. Once we were onstage Ray started behaving weirdly, staggering from side to side, and looking like he was about to throw up. In the middle of 'Apeman' he took a step back and it was like a trapdoor had opened up on the stage. He stumbled and fell, crashing into my bank of speakers and amps, which all took a tumble. He tried to right himself and a roadie appeared to help him to the wings. What to do? Somebody had already run onstage and snatched Ray's microphone and made away with it. So I thought, sod it, let's bring the whole audience onstage. I invited them up and all hell broke loose. A sea of humanity rushed towards me. Some kids started whacking Baptist's piano, while others tried to make off with Mick's cymbals. Dalton, meanwhile, was doing his best to shield his instruments. I stood in the middle of the chaos and shrugged. This was The Kinks, misbehaving better every time, like we were doing our best to get banned once again from the US. Later Ray claimed someone had spiked his drink . . . hmm, likely story . . .

Rebecca, me, Jonathan Lea, Tom Currier and Teddy Freese, on tour USA November 2013.

Me on tour in the US, 2014.

Back to where it all started. Me at the Clissold Arms, April 2014.

Me with good friend and great musician Jim Sclavunos,
Bethlehem, Pennsylvania, November 2014.

Me and Steven Van Zandt backstage at the
City Winery, New York, 2014.

Me with my long-time friend Bob
Frank, New York, 2014, at the launch
of my *Ripping Up Time* album.

Me with my son Daniel, August 9, 2015, in Malibu.

My young actor son Eddie,
taken in Los Angeles.

Me and Rebecca onstage at City Winery, October 23, 2015.

Jonathan Lea, Dennis Diken, me and Tom Currier playing a soundcheck, November 2015.

Backstage at the Roxy, Los Angeles, November 3, 2015. Great to see Shel Talmy again and chat about the old days.

Me goofing around backstage with my old friend Mark Hamill, 2016.

Dennis Diken, me and David Nolte, at Suffolk Theatre, Riverhead, New York, April 2017.

Mick Foley and me, discussing his love of The Kinks and my mother's love of wrestling. City Winery, New York, April 2017.

Dolly and me taking a nostalgic walk in North Finchley, May 2017.

Me and my son Russell, in a recording studio in Portugal while we were making the album *Open Road*, 2017. Russ is an established musician, producer and composer – with various aliases including Abakus, Cinnamon Chasers and Aiiso.

Me and Russell, promo photo for the *Open Road* album.

Before a show, Paramount Theatre, Peekskill, New York, March 2018.

Me and my niece Jackie in the US, 2019.

Me with my son Christian, February 3 2019, North London.

Me with my son Simon in Manhattan – with Robert Johnson keeping his beady eye on us.

Me and old mate Billy J. Kramer backstage in Long Island, New York, 2019.

CHAPTER EIGHT

WAIT TILL THE SUMMER COMES ALONG

. . . jump, Dave, jump, do it now, jump, go on, jump, do this thing, you've reached the end, no way back now, Dave, jump, jump, it's all over, no way back, *jump*, you might as well jump, hit the sidewalk, it'll all be over for sure then, it's too late for anything else, jump, no way back, Dave, jump, jump, jump . . . Ray, Ray . . . Mick . . . John . . . voices in my head, help me, please help me with these voices in my head . . . it's over, Dave, jump . . . the voices in my head, they're running out of control, guys, help me, this cunting hotel room, can't do it any more . . . here's a joke you'll like – jump jump, who's there? Dave, it's Dave, wondering how you're doing – jump, do it now, jump, jump – I'm not doing badly actually, oh, apart from *losing my fucking mind* and taking a one-way trip down down down to oblivion, apart from that I'm dandy, dandy, dandy, where you going to go now, who you going to run to . . . give me some gin, I'm not an alcoholic, just need something to dim the . . . oh, you think I am an alcoholic, Dave? you're probably right, but this city, New York, don't want to be here, too far from home, it's fucking manic – me calling something else manic though, ha, ha, ha, ha, that's funny – no sleep, nobody ever fucking sleeps in this city, jump, jump, Dave, do it, it's all over . . . no sleep, must fucking sleep, so noisy here, people everywhere, never any peace . . . help me, Ray, Mick, it's the voices, you see, doing *my fucking head in* . . . I'm not paranoid, though, because they THEM they THEM they really are after me, THEM voices are getting louder, all the time, by the hour, by the minute, by the second, louder, louder, jump jump, who's there? NOT YOU, DAVE, ha ha ha ha ha . . . the voices, louder, the torment, can't go on, can't do this shit, that guitarist I met, Johnny, nice guy, played in Sha Na Na, 'wherever you go, that's where you are', nice words, Johnny, deep, like some poem from a fucking Christmas cracker – is that why you killed yourself a few weeks later? Must be . . . jump, jump, jump, the voices louder, by the minute, by the second, need to talk to someone, oh God, help . . . me . . . who's me though? . . . can't, can't. Go. On, can't, not a moment longer, please, please . . . help . . .

I put my head in my hands, rolled onto the floor and burst into tears. It was August 1972, and the same Holiday Inn, on 42nd Street and 8th Avenue in Manhattan where I'd taken Angel Dust a couple of years earlier, was where everything came dangerously close to reaching an abrupt end. We'd been playing a string of shows opening for The Beach Boys, and on one amazing night in Hartford, Connecticut, with The Doors and Dr John. But however great the music, coming back to that miserable hotel room, with its lurid orange carpet and fake smiles, felt like being banged up in a prison camp. I was in a vulnerable state and my paranoia, which I'd spent years keeping at bay, suddenly engulfed me. The black clouds of depression devoured my soul. Rain was lashing against the window; nature was crying fierce and determined tears too. How had life come to this? Who could rescue me? I'd been perched on the brink of this calamity since that acid trip in LA and had desperately tried to hold the consequences at bay. I should have sought professional help, but now it was hopeless. 'They' had won. I reached for a bottle of scotch and staggered towards the window, a gazillion floors up from where the dark, damp, unforgiving city glared back at me, completely unmoved by my predicament. I slugged the drink back and reasoned that my addictions had inflicted damage that no doctor could ever fix. I knocked frantically against the furniture, trying to get my own attention; to warn myself, because nobody else would listen, that I was about to jump. Panic surged through my veins. I closed my eyes, edged closer to the window, and began to count and to pray hard.

Then a loud knock at the door gave me a jolt. I jumped back into the room and ran to see who was there. It was Linda, an old girlfriend I'd met during one of our previous trips to New York. She'd noticed that The Kinks were in town and had come to see if I wanted a drink. I couldn't pretend that I was OK, nor did I have to. Linda saw what was going on right away. We hugged and her presence, and her gentle, caring voice, started to ease my anxiety. She had been a regular at Kinks shows, but had been training to become a nurse, she explained, and her studies had taken all her spare time. Recently she had been shadowing the nurses at a psychiatric hospital, and the spirits weren't messing around. They not only sent a nurse, they sent a nurse who'd been caring for people with mental illness. The spirits instigated my rescue by dispatching an angel.

My two sons saved me too. I could have taken the easy route and jumped, but how could I have done that to Simon and Martin? Having kids meant everything to me. I don't think people realise until kids come into their lives how children can be a deep support in many ways – a spiritual and emotional survival kit. I tearfully explained to Linda about the state I'd got myself into. The words tumbled out in breathless, panicky splutters, and she put her hands on mine to calm me. Had she not showed up at that precise moment, who knows what could have happened. At least I'd hit my lowest point. I needed to choose whether my life had a future or not – and at that point I chose to live. The idea that Linda just happened to knock on my hotel room door at that moment by chance was unbelievable. The gods had aligned, and from that moment on everything in my life changed. I stopped – immediately – doing acid and taking drugs, and slowly weaned myself off the booze, and thought carefully about my diet and I became a vegetarian. Back in London I got into yoga and explored mysticism and the psychic world. I shed my old skin and started to grow a new one, and slowly a whole other world revealed itself.

I lived parts of my life in secret. These days, when everyone posts endlessly on social media, the tendency is to over-explain every emotion and thought, but I believe that it's not always necessary to explain every feeling in your head. When you're undergoing rehab, the self-loathing and shame is so painful you don't want to talk about it – but moving through the shame is the only way out. Of course Lisbet knew I was doing drugs and drinking too much, and no doubt she suspected that I was having affairs, although it was never discussed. Danish people are savvy and tough-minded. They don't feel the need to explain everything; therefore what happened in New York stayed in the deeper recesses of my mind. I needed to devise ways to deal with this change in my life; with my spiritual psychic death and rebirth. The Kinks and all the touring were the constant scenery of my life, and I had to find a new way of positioning myself inside that landscape. It was a deeply emotional process and actually it's OK to be lost because I believe that there is ultimate good. When despair devours you, hope springs eternal. Even the smallest act of kindness can put you on a new path.

I wasn't equipped, or feeling any necessity, to embark on any new career. The Kinks weren't done yet, there was still more work to do. But entering the psychic world was something I could do to help myself. Every time I went into central London I visited Foyles bookshop on Charing Cross Road and also Watkins Books in Cecil Court, a shop that specialises in books about the occult and mysticism, which is still there today. I read everything I could lay my hands on and three books spoke to me in particular – *The Middle Pillar* by Israel Regardie, *Hatha Yoga* by Theos Bernard and Swami

Vivekananda's *Raja Yoga*. Vivekananda's book made me realise that it's perfectly legitimate to feel lost. His book offered advice on how to navigate the mind for people whose emotional life had left them feeling disoriented.

Regardie had worked as Aleister Crowley's secretary, before developing his own independent ideas about the occult, which he documented in a series of books. Towards the end of his life Regardie gave psychological readings and I contacted him when we were playing in Los Angeles. I got to know him a little and he was an exceptionally impressive individual. His voice carried the power within him. *The Middle Pillar* was his brilliant analysis of these inner spiritual systems that were familiar to me from studying yoga. What he called 'The Middle Pillar' was a Western set of practices that correlated to the yoga system, using sacred words from the Kabbalah. Yoga is based around the symbolism of the lotus in a pond. The roots extend down into the earth and grow into a flower, through the water and towards the light, which correlates to the emotional, spiritual and physical part of your being. That analogy aligns with psychic centres of the human body, the symbol of the seed in the mud inside the pond, which you have to release and nurture so that it can be warmed by the sun, which is like spiritual light.

I realised Regardie's work had questioned many of Crowley's ideas and his techniques. I can't dismiss Crowley's work though. He was a vital cultural influence on so many creative people, and his *Book of Thoth* is one of the most brilliant books ever written about interpreting the Tarot. At the end he went a bit mad, but then who am I to talk? We all go a bit mad. Madness is part of our mind. We can't shut it behind a door. It must be allowed to express itself. We're all mad on some level, and madness is dangerous only when it devours you. In a way, the human mind and psyche is divided between extreme madness and a more orderly side, and creative people need to learn to embrace both and to channel these energies harmoniously.

I found Karl Jung inspiring because he tried to understand what was going on in this crazy inner world and how that interacted psychologically with art and music. No mean feat. I was also very intrigued by Rudolf Steiner who was both a clairvoyant and an academic. Steiner had an interesting sense of artistry and he wrote about how the soul is intimately affected by colour and music. The most important thing I learned: through the hard work and study of spiritual investigation you can learn how to learn. We may not ever know all there is to know but we should never give up trying to know more. Humility and trust is the key.

Ray knew I was dealing with so much shit he didn't want to worry me with business matters. Is that why, when he was negotiating to move The Kinks to a new record label, he didn't consult me? Or was he just being secretive and a manipulative sod? Or just taking the initiative? Either way, our next album, *Muswell Hillbillies*, appeared on RCA at the end of November 1971. If the plan was to further our career in the US, then moving to RCA was a very wise move. We toured the album in the US during February and March '72, supported by another band founded on Fortis Green, Fairport Convention, and we came back that summer to promote *Everybody's In Show-Biz*, a live album recorded mostly at Carnegie Hall earlier that year. The album ended with a chunk of *Muswell Hillbillies* given the live treatment, then revisited earlier stuff like 'Lola' and 'Brainwashed'. 'Celluloid Heroes' from the album was issued as a single and promptly disappeared, although became popular later – how many times had that happened to us? RCA threw all their resources behind us and made a fuss wherever we went. In New York they threw a launch party for *Muswell Hillbillies* and I looked round the room and saw the likes of Lou Reed, Andy Warhol and

Alice Cooper. In LA they threw another party for us in Holly-wood, but some sod spiked the butter with acid, and the food was fucked up, and I can't remember anything about it. It was during the *Everybody's In Show-Biz* tour that my life changed for ever in that New York hotel room.

I missed Robert and Grenville; Grenville in particular had become a close confidant. Without management, and a new record deal, Ray had more control over The Kinks than ever. He was forever the enigma. As his songwriting probed ever deeper into the human condition, he had become more business savvy. His song 'Moneygoround' from *Lola Versus Powerman and the Moneygoround* tried to exorcise the ghosts of how we'd been treated in the past, but with an edgy streak of reality, telling it like it was. Robert and Grenville must have been upset at Ray's unflattering portrayal of them in his lyric, which implied shady financial dealings with Larry Page. The song was Ray's commentary on the transition as we moved to RCA, but he was unfair to Grenville and Robert I felt. They had a management company and were thinking beyond only managing The Kinks. They were in business and wanted to make money, although never in the way Ray suggested. I believe they were good and decent men.

I always loved *Muswell Hillbillies*, but I had mixed feelings about the direction The Kinks followed next, with two volumes of *Preservation* and the album *Soap Opera*. Someone like Ray is never going to fall below a certain level, but these albums displayed just how self-involved he had become – but he was a writer and very prolific. It was Ray's world now and we all had to live in it, and it was unnerving to see how quickly someone could disappear up their own arse. *Muswell Hillbillies* had been a brilliantly observed and conceived record. What a set of songs! '20th Century Man', 'Holiday', 'Skin and Bone', 'Uncle Son'. Like *Village Green* and *Arthur*, it was a heartfelt portrait of characters and situations we knew. Decent working-class folk, who had worked hard all their lives, were being priced out of their own communities and forced to live in newly, cheaply built suburban 'New Towns'. Ray's idea of building musical bridges between our working class and the dispossessed of America was super-smart. Culturally our two countries were very different, but American blues and folk music had asked similar questions. People like Johnny Cash and Pete Seeger were great songwriters, and also inspirational geniuses and social commentators.

The setting was north London, but the music was steeped in references to folk, blues, ragtime and boogie. 'Uncle Son' was the emotional heart of the album. Uncle Son had been my mum's brother. He was known as Sonny although his real name was Albert, and he died when Ray and I were kids. He'd seen active service during the war and then worked on the railway and contracted an illness. He was an archetypal hard-working, good-looking, vibrant young man of his time. He wasn't a genius at anything, but he led an authentic and ethical life based around sound principles that were open to abuse from exploitative politicians. This song opened up another angle on the ideas we had explored in 'Yes Sir, No Sir' on *Arthur*. 'Oklahoma USA' had lots of different layers. On one level it was a song about how you could lose yourself in the fantasy world of songs – and especially of the Hollywood musicals which we all loved as a family. But at the time Ray had a girlfriend from Oklahoma. She was very sweet and they were fond of each other, so it was also wrapped up in his feelings about her.

Muswell Hillbillies would be the last album in the vein of earlier Kinks records for a few years we would make for a while. When the creativity is flowing and the door gets slammed in your face it messes with your mind and I never wanted to do that to Ray. But we were moving too far in the direction of The Kinks existing only as Ray Davies' backing band. Was Ray's megalomania feeding his narcissism? Or the other way round? He'd tease me onstage, calling me his 'annoying little brother', or 'Here's Dave "Death of a Clown" Davies'. Anything to patronise me and keep me in my place. It was like he thought suddenly he was James Joyce, James Cagney, James Bond and James Dean all rolled into one. When Ray told me about *Preservation*, it wasn't without interest, I thought, but surely more suited to the stage or film than to a Kinks album. Ray had devised a whole dystopian drama based around an opposition leader's efforts to establish an authoritarian government by turning the army against the incumbent leader. Mr Black and Mr Flash, he called them. Flash was a loveable rogue, a populist leader who, although a charlatan and cheat, at least had a sense of humour: like Max Miller gone astray. Flash is deposed by Mr Black, which leads to a period of soul-searching. Could he have behaved better? Thought more carefully about his citizens? Especially as the new Black regime is ruthless in enforcing complete observance of its draconian laws.

Maybe Ray's ideas were ahead of his time, but I had to laugh because working with Ray was part pleasure, part pain. By then I was emotionally more secure, but was still prone to self-doubt, and the days I felt wobbly, it seemed like he didn't care. He would splutter with disdain when I proposed we should work on some of the songs together. I wouldn't have suggested the idea had I not felt I had something positive to bring. At the same time his antennae were always sharp. An alternative guitar tuning I'd been working at on my own at home, that sounded like the blues filtered through a sitar raga, appealed to him. Next thing I know, Ray had maybe borrowed it for his song 'Daylight', which was part of the first *Preservation* album.

But he was my brother and I was always there for him. The day of his twenty-ninth birthday, on 21 June 1973, Ray called me out the blue with some devastating news. Rasa had taken the kids to Bradford and left him. He had no idea what she'd been planning and was utterly distraught. I'll never forget walking up the gravel path to his front door and looking in through the window. Ray was slumped in an armchair in his living room, looking deflated and beaten. His tears flowed and I thought back to only a few weeks earlier when we'd been working on music in this same room, when it had been filled with the joy of creation. Now it was an empty box, as though the house, and Ray, had been hollowed out from the inside. Ray was no angel and hadn't always treated Rasa well. His meanness and control-freakery; his inability to cope when Rasa aspired to be more than 'Mrs Ray Davies'. I can only imagine. But the way she left him, without warning and on his birthday, was needlessly vindictive.

My family, and other members of the band, rallied round. We all wanted to console Ray and reassure him. My sister Joyce and I even schlepped up to Bradford in an attempt to reason with Rasa. But it soon became clear that their marriage was a lost cause; it was over. Her family had never particularly approved of Ray, or cared much for the Davieses, and I realised that they – and Rasa's elder sister in particular – had cooked up the scheme between them; Rasa would leave, on Ray's birthday for maximum impact. I'd never hit it off with Rasa's sister. She always looked at me as though I was a piece of shit, and this was the action of a cruel mind. I knew that Rasa had been manipulated, and although I'd always loved her, I found forgiveness difficult. Nobody has to stay in an unhappy marriage, but we're all human beings with vulnerabilities and feelings, and Rasa could have handled matters more humanely.

A week or so later, during a concert at the White City Stadium near Shepherd's Bush in London, Ray broke down onstage and, to my astonishment, announced his retirement. Choked with tears, he walked to the microphone and yelled: 'I'm sick of the whole fucking business, sick up to here with it. It's over.' Ray can have a weird sense of humour which delights in the perverse, and I thought he was joking. But I didn't get the chance to ask him: as soon as the show was over, Ray legged it out the building and I drove home feeling mystified by his behaviour.

In the small hours of the morning, I had a call from the Whittington Hospital in Archway telling me that Ray was seriously ill. Before the concert that night, he'd necked a whole bottle of pills and was suffering the effects of a drugs overdose. The nurse explained that they'd pumped his stomach and that he was in the recovery area. Lisbet and I raced down there and we found Ray looking afraid and helpless. He came home with us, and Lisbet's sunny and optimistic nature proved the best medicine. She cooked delicious food and was always around when he wanted to talk. He took refuge in music and listened to Mahler's 'Resurrection' Symphony on a loop; he'd get to the end, then immediately flip it back to the start. I hadn't spent so much time one-on-one with Ray for some years. We started jamming on our guitars and the last decade or so melted away, like The Kinks had never happened: we were two brothers once again, enjoying making music together, like at Denmark Terrace all those years ago.

We picked up the pieces on the *Preservation* album when he was stronger and this was the first record we made at our new studio. Helped along by the advance we received from RCA, we bought a shell of a building in Hornsey and worked hard to transform it into a studio which we christened Konk. Mick and I pulled together and took control of the building works, then I focused on acquiring the recording equipment. Ray was a massive pain when it came to countersigning the cheques – I'd put a down payment on a Neve mixing console and I practically had to move Ray's hand for him to sign off the rest of the money – but one day, at long last, we finished the building works and started using the studio. Konk was a big thumbs up to the future, a financial investment but also an emotional investment in The Kinks. Property in that part of London in those days was reasonable. It cost us something like thirty thousand quid, but it was *ours* and we came to love it.

Since Shel Talmy's departure we had developed our own method of operating without a producer, with Ray taking over as producer while still using studio engineers and technicians. Now it was all down to us. Nobody else knew how to use the equipment when we were recording *Preservation*. So I immersed myself in the engineering side of producing a record. Developing my interest in how to record deepened my understanding of what music could be, handing me newfound insights into the nuances of sound, and this new fascination of mine took on a direction I couldn't have foreseen. We decided to start our own production company and record label – called Konk – and scouted for promising new bands with which we could work. If this idea took off, I thought, I wouldn't need to devote so much time to Ray's eccentricities and there'd be more me-time at home with my kids – and more time to write and paint.

We signed a distribution deal with ABC in the US and hired Tony Dimitriades to manage the label day-to-day. Tony, also from Muswell Hill, proved a very effective business manager and went on to manage Tom Petty and Billy Idol. Claire Hamill released her third album, *Stage Door Johnnies*, on Konk, while Andy Desmond's album, *Living On A Shoestring*, had John Gosling on keyboards, and I played on one track – and John and I produced the album. One night at The Troubadour Club in South Kensington, Ray heard a folk-rock band called Café Society which he reckoned had bags of potential. It was led by the singer and guitarist Tom Robinson, to whom Alexis Korner had taken a shine. Tom had also obviously immersed himself in The Kinks, especially the *Face To Face* and *Village Green* era, and learned a lot from Ray's songwriting. Café Society was a natural fit on our label. Unfortunately the band also knew a thing or two about how to fall out among themselves, and the sessions weren't always happy affairs. But the album was really good, I thought – although it sold only a few hundred copies.

Tom blamed us. Too overproduced, he said, and the relationship ended abruptly when Ray kept him waiting for too long at Konk one afternoon. Ray the control freak used to get off on keeping people hanging around and waiting for his grand entrance – Ladies and Gentlemen, Ray Davies is in the house! But Tom's ego was just as bulbous as Ray's. When he finally strolled in, Tom ran to the piano and teased him with a sardonic, Mrs Mills honkytonk busk-through of 'Tired of Waiting'. Ray didn't see the funny side at all and that was the last we saw of Tom. A few years later he saw the Sex Pistols live and moved into another mode as a punky gay activist and broke through with his song 'Glad To Be Gay'. Ray and Tom then traded veiled insults via songs. 'Prince of the Punks', the B-side of The Kinks' 'Father Christmas', took a sideways swipe at Tom, who then fired back later on with 'Don't Take No For An Answer'. Couple of twats, but I love them both.

Partly because the Konk albums didn't sell especially well, but also because The Kinks had built up such a fanbase in the US, the idea I might ease off a little came to nothing. By March 1974 we were back in the US touring *Preservation*. Despite poor record sales, the audiences kept coming, which was just as well – since the *Everybody's In Show-Biz* tour we had carried alongside the basic Kinks line-up a jazz brass and wind section, with two female singers. The brass section looked back to the fundamental truths of where rock music came from, while allowing us to touch on other areas of culture – brass bands playing hymns, vaudeville trombone farts, they could do it all.

The jazz players were led by the trumpeter Mike Cotton who had been an old-school trad jazzer in the mould of a Humphrey Lyttelton or Ken Colyer. He'd always had a side-interest in pop and around the time we were still performing as The Ravens, 'The

Mike Cotton Jazzmen' became 'The Mike Cotton Sound' and started working with pop material. Our history with Mike started with our first ever package tour in 1964, when Mike's 'Sound' shared the bill with us, and Gerry and the Pacemakers, Marianne Faithfull, Gene Pitney and the rest. He was great company and his musicians were always very quick at picking up any idea we presented and stamping it with their own mark: 'You sing it, we'll play it' was their motto. Most of the arrangements for *Preservation* were worked out in the studio, then the jazzers would write stuff out as a reminder. They were funny guys too, who helped lighten the mood during those long journeys from city to city. We ended up calling John Beecham, who played trombone and tuba, 'Freakout Boat'. His nickname had been 'Jazz Boat', a reference to the early Dixieland days, but we thought it needed updating, to reflect our crazy times. One night, Ray banged his head during a concert and had to be carried offstage. Mike calmly saved the day by walking to Ray's microphone and playing 'You Really Got Me' on harmonica – before Ray reappeared with a bandaged head to finish the gig.

We were backwards and forwards to the US throughout 1974, touring *Preservation*. I'd come to terms with touring and at last found it manageable, sometimes even fun. One night in New York I called up my friend Linda, who had nursed me through that awful night at the Holiday Inn, and feeling merry after a few drinks, we decided to try something new. We swapped clothes! It wasn't the first time I'd dressed in women's clothes, but this was the first time I'd done it so publicly; but New York makes you see life in a different way. Linda did a great job with my make-up then we found a wig somewhere, and at about three o'clock in the morning we hit town. I loved a club called Nobody's on Bleecker Street where once I'd chatted with Janis Joplin, and everything they say about how she could drink any guy under the table is true. But that was all part of her natural *joie de vivre*. She was generous of heart and super-friendly. When I heard she'd died, I couldn't help thinking she'd been devoured by the worst excesses of the music business.

Nobody's was a place musicians loved to hang. As soon as we walked through the door, I saw Baptist and Mick up to their usual tricks, both pissed. I tried to look as sexy as I could, and Linda could easily have passed for a butch bloke. Girls will be boys, and boys will be girls. It was a turn-on seeing Linda like that but, best thing of all, I walked in that room and nobody knew who I was or anything about me. Men were perving at me, and observing the world from this new perspective was an education. After everything I'd been through worrying about people's reactions to me, this was very cathartic, like the best free therapy I could have. I walked over to Mick and sat next to the girl he was chatting up and gazed deeply into his eyes. The dirty old sod started giving me the eye back. I was amazed he didn't recognise me. It was very late and the bar was dark, but really! Then I stood next to him, lifted up my dress and started rubbing myself through my underwear and gyrating. When the realisation of who I was hit Mick, it hit him hard. Gobsmacked is the only word. He spat his beer everywhere. I'd loved every moment of teasing him, and the look on his face was absolutely priceless.

During my spare time back at home, I had been delving ever deeper into mysticism. I started taking classes from a trance medium in Wood Green, north London, who channelled information, she said, from an ancient Egyptian child king. Lisbet was concerned about the stuff I was getting into, and Ray was somewhat unsure about my interest in spiritualism. But who cares what other people thought? I'd nearly jumped out of a New York hotel window and what's crazier? Taking acid and ending up dead on the sidewalk? Or reaching further inside my inner self? I was insatiably hungry for any information about mysticism, metaphysics and astrology. I also studied Zen Buddhism. Absorbing all I could was like a rebirth.

I was discovering more the essence of who I was. As far as The Kinks was concerned, though, I felt like Ray was requiring less and less of me. He had all those brass and woodwind instruments to play with now. It felt like he was sidelining me, while I was finding his concept album ideas increasingly uncomfortable. I wanted to play honest-to-goodness rock and roll again, which didn't seem too much to ask. We'd indulged Ray enough. I might have felt differently had the records actually been selling, but they weren't. We were very lucky that audiences wanted to see our live shows, but taking their loyalty for granted was a mistake. I worried desperately about the future.

Everything leads to something else and all around us rock and pop was radically changing. Bands like The Sex Pistols, The Jam, The Clash, The Damned and Generation X – and great American bands like The Ramones – had all put a bomb under a self-satisfied music industry that was failing to offer anything fresh or that had anything relevant to say. How invigorating and bracing to switch on the radio and hear these bands! Their howls of defiance, the acidic snarl of their humour, the visceral physicality of their records – it was liberating, bold and as exciting as fuck. The punk scene was born, just like The Kinks, out of the working-class experience, from young people with their laser-vision cutting through the crap of a system that allowed the wealthy to trouser wads of cash at the expense of those less fortunate. These bands, each in their own way, lashed out at a world that was feeling increasingly heartless and cruel.

I couldn't help feeling a kinship in the music; I always felt these bands and The Kinks to be on a similar wavelength. Their in-yer-face attitude was belligerent and unforgiving. Punk followed up on themes questioning society that bands like The Kinks had posed;

the lineage was clear. Its call to action had been fired up by the same discontent and weariness with the system that had motivated us; the certainty that there was no rosy future for anyone unless we grabbed it for ourselves.

We all know what happened to the punk dream ultimately but, just for a moment, it felt like an authentic rebellion against the prevailing mood in the 1980s of self-interest, privilege and greed. I've always been a fan of Johnny Rotten. Building a style of music from scratch; I love that approach and The Sex Pistols felt connected to our world. The band was, of course, an artificial creation in some respects; then again someone had to create *something* to make people stand up and take notice. Rhyming 'queen' with 'fascist regime'. Naked aggression or hilarious pisstake? Could it have been both? Their music had guts – and could also laugh at itself. I loved The Clash too. Evidently Mick Jones and Joe Strummer decided to start their band after coming to a Kinks gig, and later, when Mick formed Big Audio Dynamite, that group recorded at Konk.

When I was making my first solo album, *AFL1-3603*, at our studio, the receptionist knocked on the door and told me that Paul Weller had dropped by to say hello. Somehow he'd heard I was making a solo album and he wanted to wish me luck. I always felt Weller's writing for The Jam was tuned into Ray's writing. The band covered 'David Watts' on their album *All Mod Cons*, which also included 'Down in the Tube Station at Midnight'. Paul had brought along with him the single of 'Suzanah's Still Alive' that he'd bought back in the day and I signed it for him. I did wonder if The Jam properly understood what 'David Watts' was really about!

One night in New York I told Ray of my concerns. Typically for Ray, he deflected everything I was telling him. 'Let's talk about it when we're home,' he said. But far from taking anything we'd discussed on the chin, Ray led us towards *Soap Opera*. It had developed out of another project called *Starmaker*, a thirty-minute drama made for Granada Television in 1974 that cast Ray as an exaggerated caricature of himself. The story was not without potential. An ageing rock star, realising his best days are behind him, decides to become 'Norman', by swapping lives with an ordinary man. Was Ray choosing *at last* to purge his own demons through the character of Norman? Then we could get back to being a rock band?

But no. In the television version, the rock star genuinely comes to believe that he is Norman. He settles down with Norman's wife and admires the songs he once sang from a distance. Rock music endures, even when the talents behind the songs fade into the distance. That was the message of the final song, 'You Can't Stop the Music'. But once we started touring *Soap Opera*, Ray, in character as Norman, started referring to himself as Ray. Knowing that people wanted to hear some of our classic material, he would put songs like 'You Really Got Me' and 'Sunny Afternoon' into the show.

I felt lost during the filming of the television version, and also during the making of the album, and my certainty that Ray was leading The Kinks towards a disaster of his own making festered. The message when we turned up at the Granada Studios couldn't have been clearer. This was Ray's show. We were no better than his backing band. We were shunted into a small corner of the studio where there was barely room to set up. The sound was tinny and clearly nobody cared about that aspect of the show – we were never shown on screen, apart from occasionally in the background. The show opened with Ray, wearing a gleaming white suit, hugging a television camera as he sang, surrounded by the live audience. It was hilarious and pathetic at the same time, and that evening to me sounded like the end of The Kinks. I drove back to London that night feeling certain it was time for Ray and me to part company. I wanted to play rock music. Surely his ideas could be better served by some other format than The Kinks? I couldn't have known that there was still so much great Kinks music to come, over the next twenty years. But like the mystics say, a part of you has to die before you can be reborn.

Had Ray not been my brother it would have been far easier to walk away. There was unspoken pressure from within the family to stick together, to be respectful to my elder brother. And this coincided with a very sad time for us all. In July 1975 my dad died suddenly. A few weeks before his death, he'd come to our house for Sunday lunch and somehow I could sense that he was nearing his last days. His breathing was very laboured and he'd slowed down considerably; more than that, though, he looked lost in his own thoughts. He was pottering around the garden and performing his trick of listening to the birds chirping, then whistling their songs back at them. He looked happy, but suddenly I was filled with fear. I knew he was going to die. When he asked if I wanted to go down the pub, I was too afraid and made up some excuse about having a lot to do that afternoon. And that was the last time I saw him. The next day my parents went to stay at Ray's house in Surrey while Ray was away working, and a few days later Dad collapsed in the kitchen and died. For years afterwards I regretted not having that last pint with my dear old dad. How could I have been such a coward?

The process of grieving brought Ray and I closer together. As he dealt with his own sense of loss, I felt him reflecting on our relationship as brothers in The Kinks' next album, *Schoolboys in Disgrace*, which was hooked around our experiences at school, and in particular me getting expelled. After feeling that Ray had pushed me into the background on *Preservation* and *Soap Opera*, in this album he gave me something back. The record felt like a proper

Kinks record again, more guitar-based, and our sense of rebellious mischief had returned. So mustn't grumble. Ray worked up a story about a 'naughty little schoolboy' who had 'got himself into very serious trouble with a naughty schoolgirl and he was sent to the headmaster'. You didn't need to be Sherlock Holmes to work out who that was about. We assembled ideas for songs in Ray's music room at home, the same way we'd put together albums like *Something Else by The Kinks* and *Village Green*. It felt good.

The brass guys were still involved in some of the arrangements, but the album rocked. Setting the project during our schooldays in the late fifties gave us a reason to reflect on the music of that era, and to carve something fresh out of it. 'The First Time We Fall In Love' sounds like the best Elvis song that Elvis never sang: the verse slips in some harmonies as though Elvis is hanging out with The Beach Boys. I adored putting down some hardcore guitar riffs again. 'Education' proved to be a real showstopper that ended up in a deep gospel groove, but my favourite track on the whole album remains 'Headmaster'. It's an introspective song in which the main character looks back and wishes he'd had more sense: 'I feel like an innocent victim/I feel that I just can't win/Headmaster please give me one more chance.' My guitar solo on that track came straight from the heart. The spirit of regret and loss that Ray conjured up moved me deeply.

This was the final album we'd record for RCA and, following *Soap Opera*, I was relieved we'd managed to find a way out of the creative cul-de-sac. The final track we recorded for the album, 'No More Looking Back', had a searching quality, as if the lyric suggested that we were looking only to the future now. Our next album, *Sleepwalker*, was a long time coming. It did away with any theatrical trappings and *Schoolboys in Disgrace* was the last occasion we'd use a horn section. We were about to be reborn as a rock band, and not before time. An unexpected consequence of *Schoolboys in Disgrace*, though, as I mulled over school again, was that I was overwhelmed by my feelings for Sue. Time had done nothing to dim the pain and yearning. Could this torment ever end? Would I ever see Sue again, and meet Tracey?

Clive Davis saved The Kinks, I feel, helped give us back our centre. He had almost signed us when we left Pye, but RCA beat him to it. Clive taking an interest in any musician or group was a big deal. Until 1973, he'd been president of Columbia Records and the musicians he'd scouted for, and worked with, during his long career – Janis Joplin, Bruce Springsteen, Bob Dylan, Miles Davis, Whitney Houston, Aretha Franklin, Billy Joel, Earth Wind & Fire – represented an elite of popular music. He'd formed Arista, his own label, in 1974 and signed The Kinks in 1976. Earlier that year Ray had dropped one of his characteristic bombshells. He and his new wife, Yvonne, would be moving to New York City. Actually I was fine with it. Putting space – the whole Atlantic Ocean – between us was not the worst thing that could happen. I'd have time to work on material of my own at Konk without anyone peering over my shoulder. Meanwhile Ray would use his base in America to open up big opportunities for The Kinks. Getting Clive involved was a stroke of genius on Ray's part. Clive had been a Kinks fan for years and was happy to give us all the support we needed. About one thing he was insistent: our next album needed to cut through commercially and ditch all the theatrical paraphernalia. It must be a proper rock record.

By June '76 our new contract was signed and Clive flew over for a press launch at the Dorchester Hotel in London. I remember Clive telling everyone at the launch that The Kinks had a great future. He also told me that to move forward creatively it's sometimes necessary to take a couple of steps back to take stock. Then the hard work began. It took a while to get the measure of the album that became *Sleepwalker*. Progress, difficult anyway, got derailed when Dalton announced he was leaving the band. He was a homebody and the prospect of spending even more time in the US held no appeal for him. We could be in Boston or Chicago and John would suddenly become anxious about the football scores at home; he'd keep his watch fixed on English time in case he missed anything. He had arrived during a difficult time for the group and I had nothing but admiration for how he'd always brought his best to the band, with the minimum level of fuss. And now he was leaving on the cusp of this new adventure. Tragically John would likely have been forced to quit anyway. His youngest son became terminally ill with leukaemia and John helped nurse him through to the end.

We fished around for a replacement bass player and the pick of the bunch appeared to be Andy Pyle. He played on one track from *Sleepwalker*, 'Mr Big', a song I've always loved, and we all thought he was a decent guy. But slowly it became clear that Pyle was exploiting The Kinks as a means to launch his own band. We could never fault his bass playing and he was a very professional musician, but all the time he was on manoeuvres behind our backs. These days I think of him as a guy who played in The Kinks for a while, rather than ever being a fully fledged Kink.

The *Sleepwalker* tour in 1977 was memorable for a whole load of reasons. We had a new manager from Chicago, Elliot Abbott, who helped keep things ticking along smoothly, while the album itself had some truly powerful material. The title song was Ray expressing his difficulties with insomnia. It's a song spooked by the night. 'When midnight comes around, I start to lose my mind/When the sun puts out the light I join the creatures of the night.' What a line! 'Sleepless Nights' was a hilarious thing that Ray handed me to sing, about a guy who lives next door to a woman he fancies, but she never pays him attention. So he lies awake all night listening to her next door screwing her boyfriend: 'Once they start, they never stop/Through this sleepless night.' Often I've wondered if Ray gave me that character to play because he felt the song was too close to home. Other songs like 'Full Moon' and 'Stormy Sky' also existed in the twilight. 'Brother' was a general plea for brotherhood and harmony across the world. 'Juke Box Music' contained a heartrending line that has always cut me to the quick: 'It's all because of that music/That we slowly drifted apart/But it's only there to dance to, you shouldn't take it to heart.' That said it all. I loved Ray because he was my brother – but perhaps we'd have loved each other even more had we not been blood brothers.

One night, somewhere in Massachusetts, a whole troop of folks who had taken *Sleepwalker* too literally and convinced themselves that Ray and I were vampires turned up at a concert. Be careful what you wish for, it might come true. You may think you're summoning a demon to extract dastardly revenge on your nemesis, but once dark forces have been released they are just as likely to come back and bite you. Magic also cast its spell on that tour in a more positive way. I became good pals with one of our backing singers, Shirlie Roden. She had an interest in many similar ideas about metaphysics and the psychic world as me and, after shows, often we'd talk long into the night about spirituality and magic. Why not put those words into action, I thought, and I asked Shirlie if she'd be up for trying an experiment.

Shirlie was game, so I let her in on a few techniques. The basis of the experiment was a mental visualisation technique I'd read about in which energy is drawn into the body, illuminated with light, and projected outwards. During a concert tidal waves of very concentrated energy flow from the audience towards the musicians, but what if that energy could be harvested? Would it be possible to transform its emotional and psychic power, turning it into light and positive energy, and redirect it back to the audience as healing?

One night in Seattle, Ray was having to work unusually hard to fire the audience up. The house was only about half full, but even with a full audience some nights that can happen. During one song I nodded at Shirlie, and we did our thing, and the audience was immediately transformed. We'd pumped them full of energy and people started dancing in the aisles and chanting. Ray couldn't believe his eyes. We hadn't said a word to him before the show. And I understand you might be thinking this all sounds like weird shit, but we needed to believe sincerely that it *would* happen, and any scepticism would have spoilt the energy and interfered with our plan. What happened spoke for itself and throughout that tour, Shirlie and I continued to pull our trick. Filling people with joy and energy night after night filled us with energy and joy – so we had boundless energy to give back. What a great buzz it was.

Before we left New York, we played 'Sleepwalker' on *Saturday Night Live* alongside some other Kinks hits. Steve Martin was hosting and we were also invited to take part in one of the very first Coneheads sketches, which would have meant acting with Dan Aykroyd, Jan Curtin and Laraine Newman. I so wanted to do it, but Elliot Abbott, our manager, reckoned it would have trivialised our image and that was the end of that. To this day I regret that I didn't become a Conehead. When the tour reached Los Angeles and we had a few days off, Shirlie and I decided to hang out at the Whisky a Go Go one night. Blondie were playing and I always enjoyed hearing Debbie Harry and their cool drummer Clem Burke. As we were walking to our seats I noticed a young woman sitting in the next booth, and I was transfixed by her beauty. Long brown hair flowed down her back and when our eyes met, I felt strangely drawn to her. I walked up to where she was sitting, more because I couldn't help myself than intentionally. She said her name was Nancy, and we arranged to meet for a drink the next day at my hotel. All the way through Blondie's set and back in my room when

I was trying to sleep, I couldn't help but think about Nancy's deep dark-brown eyes beckoning me closer, ever closer. She turned up as arranged the next afternoon, and we clicked immediately. Her insights into psychic concerns and metaphysics were profound for someone of her age, and I adored the gentle lilt and silky contours of her voice. We held each other close and we kissed. The next morning I had to leave LA to continue our tour, but I promised to call Nancy when we circled back to LA.

A couple of months later, The Kinks played the Anaheim Stadium in LA on the same bill as Alice Cooper. Nancy and I couldn't get enough of each other. We spent the next couple of days going for long walks and talking; we kissed, cuddled and ate together. This relationship was obviously something special and I didn't want it to be focused around sex; I wanted us to discover each other properly first.

We were staying at the Continental Hyatt House Hotel on Sunset Boulevard, and lots of rock bands stayed there because the Whisky a Go Go was nearby. Rock stars chucked a load of televisions out of windows, and it was rumoured that John Bonham rode his motorbike down the corridors when Led Zeppelin played LA. One night Nancy and I were sitting in the bar when Keith Moon walked in. I hadn't seen him for a while. He was uncharacteristically subdued and introspective, his usual bonhomie nowhere to be seen. His jokes were forced and, looking into his eyes, I sensed someone who was unusually troubled, like he wanted someone to take all his pain away. How sad to see him in that state. We were due to leave LA the next day and every minute with Nancy was precious, so we made our apologies and left. A couple of months later he had died. When I heard the news, I thought back to my last sighting of him in that bar in LA, looking lost and alone. I knew only too well how easy it was to spiral into the sort of despair from which you might never re-emerge. It was like his soul had been pleading for help, but he couldn't express the gravity of his situation. The one word he couldn't say was 'help'. I wish now I'd done more for him.

The tour was almost finished, and Nancy ended up coming along for the rest of the trip. We had tried to say goodbye in LA, but the loss was just too darn painful. After the tour Nancy returned to LA and I flew home to London – to face some seismic decisions. I was utterly smitten with Nancy, but I already had a wife and kids. What was I going to say to Lisbet? How to explain? Let's just say that when I made Lisbet aware of the situation, she didn't take it well and the atmosphere in our house in Southgate became caked with tension; minor disagreements escalated. Lisbet was a good person who had put up with so much shit from me over so many years. Our fourth son Russell would come along in May 1979 and I loved my family passionately. Nancy, though, was constantly in my thoughts and I wanted to spend my life with her. Being tugged in two different directions, and for so long, was deeply unsettling.

All through the period that my personal life was changing, it was all change in The Kinks too. Following *Sleepwalker*, we started to work up new material in the studio, most of which ended up on our next album, *Misfits*. We also recorded a single called 'Father Christmas' that was released in December 1977 which bombed, but which I always loved: nobody wanted to hear Ray singing about Father Christmas giving people jobs rather than kids presents. If the idea had been to win over a public who liked their Christmas songs draped in tinsel and sugar, it was a brilliant song but not terribly well judged. That year we performed a Christmas show at the Rainbow Theatre in Finsbury Park to promote the single and it ended up being the most fun I'd had in ages.

We breathed new life into songs we hadn't performed for years and also dressed up in silly Christmas outfits. The plan was to perform 'Father Christmas' as an encore and that Ray would appear onstage in a Santa costume, long white beard, with a pillow stuffed up his coat, the full festive works. From the wings, I watched Ray hurriedly changing into his costume and a mischievous thought crossed my mind. When we walked back onstage, and before Ray could do anything about it, I launched into 'You Really Got Me' instead of 'Father Christmas'. The sheer look of horror on Ray's face as the crowd roared and the penny dropped that he was going to have to sing 'You Really Got Me' dressed like a prat. This was all my Christmases come at once. Every so often he glared at me through his plastic white beard and I cheerfully smiled back. He was trapped. Afterwards he tore off his costume and chucked it at me. The vision of Santa charging round the room and screaming 'You're a fucking cunt!' is imprinted on my memory.

Perhaps those words might have been better aimed at Andy Pyle, who was scheming to poach John Gosling for a new band of his own. Pyle pursued his own self-interest throughout the period he played with The Kinks. Eventually I saw through his habit of fawning around Ray and me, while plotting behind our backs. When he told us he was leaving – and taking John with him – I wasn't in the least bit surprised. In fact, I wondered what had taken him so long. Gosling's departure saddened Ray, and he was irritated because their departure kicked a hole through our progress on *Misfits*, and ended up delaying the album for a good few months. I'd sensed Gosling's dissatisfaction for a while and was philosophical about it. John's time with us had long since run its course and likely he would have left soon anyway, Pyle or no Pyle.

Ray took over keyboard duties in the studio and his pared-down style made me think that Gosling's playing had become overly fancy. Many of the songs were written on Ray's piano, and his keyboard-playing somehow got to the heart of the matter in a way Gosling never could. Ray would show Gosling what to play in the studio anyway; and now Ray's own touch, and the way he emotionally leaned into certain phrases within a song, made it much easier for everyone to pick up on the mood he was trying to convey. Still, I missed Baptist. He had contributed so much to the band over the years. After his last day working with us at Konk we parted on friendly terms, although John said, semi-jokingly, he hoped I wasn't going to cast an evil spell on him. I told him, of course not, we're mates – and besides, Pyle has already worked some sort of magic on you . . .

In addition to Gosling leaving, relations with Mick, never straightforward, started to become tense again and perhaps it would have been better had he left too. Mick was listless and exuded an air of boredom in the studio, like he couldn't be arsed. He never played badly. Then again his playing lacked any spark or imagination. There was a long history of that, stretching right back to the early days. Inevitably this created bad feeling with me. I suppose it was difficult being caught in the middle of Ray and me. His smiles could often be a façade and I was becoming peeved by his aloofness in the studio. We brought in a couple of other drummers to help us out while we finished *Misfits*. Clem Cattini, a fantastic session drummer, surely the only musician to have worked with Ken Dodd *and* Lou Reed, saved a track on the album called 'Live Life' from ending up on the cutting-room floor. He found a way of locking into the guitar track I'd already laid down and the whole thing sprang to life. His ears were bat-sharp. We also tried Nick Trevisick, who I'd been using on some material of my own.

Ray channelled all the insecurity surrounding the band into another Ray gem of a song he called a 'A Rock 'n' Roll Fantasy', which I considered the standout track on *Misfits*. It's a song about the frustrations of the rock and roll business, about wanting to break up the band and find some sort of new life altogether, but how meeting a fan called Dan – 'a guy in my block, he lives for rock' – with a passion for the music revives the idealism that got us started in rock in the first place. Elvis Presley died while Ray was writing the song, which helped set the mood too. My song, 'Trust Your Heart', which appeared later on the album, was an answer to Ray's song. It suggested, whatever you do in life, you've got to keep going – and trust your heart. The single of 'A Rock 'n' Roll Fantasy' went into the Top 30 in the US, our biggest hit since 'Lola' in America, which was a big relief given that *Sleepwalker* hadn't done the business that we, and Arista, had hoped.

Following that period of uncertainty, the gods smiled on us and the band didn't break up, and a new line-up snapped into place without too much trouble. A few days after we finished *Misfits* the bass player Jim Rodford, who we'd met way back in 1965 when he was working with Mike Cotton, happened to drop by the studio. Whether he was looking for a job that day I'm not sure, but we ended up hiring him and he stayed with the group for the next eighteen years, until the very end. Jim was warm and affable, and approached everything with a 'can do' attitude. I liked him very much. His death, in 2018, after he fell down the stairs at home, came as a bolt from the blue. What a tragedy and a sad end for someone who had been such an essential member of The Kinks for so many years. Jim's sassy rock and roll energy also made Mick up his game, and we were operating once again with a crack rhythm section. By the time we took *Misfits* on the road in May 1978 we'd also acquired a new keyboard player. Gordon Edwards brought joy and the excitement of being involved in the music, and made me realise how disinterested Baptist had been recently. He also played very good guitar and we'd jam together. Problem was, though, he was a junkie and sometimes he'd turn up at gigs out of his mind and made it through only by the seat of his pants. But I liked him very much and understood the emotions behind his addiction.

*

The summer of 1979 we all decamped to Manhattan to record our next album, at the Power Station and Blue Rock studios. The music was released later that year as *Low Budget* and I have especially fond memories of this period. We'd already prepped bits and bobs at Konk and our engineer, John Rollo, came with us and brought along his canny ears for gnarly guitar sounds and heavy rock drums. Producing the album quickly in New York would give it a spontaneous edge. Working against the constraint of studio time again focused our minds. We were booked into the studio for two weeks and the basics of each track had to be sewn up within that time. You gotta love a deadline.

Not that things got off to a promising start. Gordon failed to show up on the first day and we had no option but to sack him. He'd messed up – and on very expensive studio time. Ray returned to keyboard duties, which in the end streamlined the whole process. I felt sad about Gordon, but he had started to behave too much like an arsehole. There was no taking anything away from his musicianship, but the whole 'rock star' thing had gone to his head. I remember looking on in bemusement as he took a couple of lines and downed a bottle of whisky . . . just for a soundcheck. He'd missed out on the 1960s rock and roll high life first time round and was trying to live it too late. He was constantly stoned and would ring me in the dead of night to discuss song ideas. I humoured him, then rolled over and went back to sleep. It was hard not to like the guy, but we were serious about knuckling down to hard work and securing the future of the band on Arista. There was no room for a loose cannon. Ultimately Gordon would turn into another rock and roll casualty. He was found dead in his flat in 2003, a suicide. He was apparently never able to shake his addictions and, when the news came through, we were all shocked and saddened.

Before we'd left for New York, Clive suggested a single with direct appeal to the American market could be a good move and Ray came up with 'Wish I Could Fly Like Superman'. The first *Superman* film, with Christopher Reeve in the title role, had just been released and Ray's song, typically, flipped the idea of a 'superman' on its head. Humans are in reality weak, fallible creatures, who make stupid decisions, and busk their way through life, stumbling from one problem into the next: 'I'd like to fly, but I can't even swim.' With the song in the can at Konk, we flew to New York and we saw Clive only occasionally. He'd drop by the studio, perhaps to listen to the final mix or two of a track, but he understood his role very well. In some respects he operated like an old-school A&R guy. While largely keeping out of our way he provided all the resources we needed and relentless encouragement, which allowed us to get better and better.

My confidence in my own playing had increased because falling in love with Nancy was motivating. She stayed with me throughout the time we were working on *Low Budget*, and we lived a suitably low-budget existence. We stayed at an apartment in a shitty mid-town hotel called The Wellington, but I didn't care because Nancy and I could spend all the time we wanted together. We bought some tablecloths and cushions, lit the place with candles, and cooked for ourselves and made it home-from-home. The wallpaper peeled and flaked, and more than once I found a dishevelled drunk in the dark corridor that led to our room. The apartment had bad plumbing and bugs. One morning the pest-control guy knocked on our door at some ungodly hour. 'This is the exterminator, open up,' he said in a thick Brooklyn accent. And I thought, Bloody hell: Mafia. I refused to open the door and, much to my relief, he went away. Only later did I discover that visits from exterminators were daily occurrences in New York apartments. Quite honestly, we had a better class of vermin in Muswell Hill.

After our two weeks of recording, *Low Budget* was in the can and we flew back to London, and the post-production was finished off at Konk. Looking back all these years later I realise how far our music had travelled from a decade earlier when we were suffering the birth pangs of the *Village Green* album. With Ray's life now based in New York, his voice as a songwriter had changed and took on new perspectives. Where once he'd observed life in north London, now he was taking the mood of America. 'Gallon of Gas' was a cool blues number, but also about the recession and oil crisis that was crippling America in the late 1970s. 'Catch Me Now I'm Falling' was about America in decline too. *Low Budget*, as its title suggested, captured the moment and we were rewarded with the album going to number eleven in the American album charts. The single of Ray's *Superman* song did pretty well too.

In the autumn we returned to the US and toured the album to jam-packed arenas. We'd hired a terrific new keyboard player, Ian Gibbons, who could play anything we wanted and did so with unfailing good humour. Another great keyboard player, Mark Haley took over for a few years, but Ian came back and was always a real asset to the band, and we kept in touch until he died in 2019. Some of the concerts were recorded live and became the basis of our next album, *One For The Road*, released in 1980. It's a great document of the band during that era – things like 'You Really Got Me', 'David Watts' and 'Victoria' rubbing shoulders with 'Misfits', 'Superman', 'Low Budget' and 'Catch Me Now I'm Falling', every song a piece of the whole Kinks jigsaw.

Nancy and I spent all the time we could together during the *Low Budget* tour and then, in January 1980, she took the plunge and moved to London so that we could be together, staying at first in Highgate. I had wondered if we could all live together, which turned out to be a seriously silly idea. I raised the prospect with Nancy and Lisbet. Nancy was prepared to give it serious consideration, but Lisbet was implacably opposed. No. Way. Ever. Danish culture – and Lisbet came from an upper middle-class background – was very proper and pride was a big deal. But to my surprise they agreed to meet each other and I booked a table at a restaurant in Muswell Hill. Over dinner they behaved towards each other with complete civility and they were both curious, I think, to see what the 'other woman' was like. Lisbet and I went home together afterwards and she became distraught, like that was the moment the reality properly hit her. She burst into tears and told me that I might be leaving her – 'but you're not leaving your kids'. She was adamant that I kept an ongoing relationship with my sons.

For a while I was spending time with Nancy in Highgate and with Lisbet in Southgate, which was difficult emotionally and proved ultimately unsustainable. Soon enough Nancy became pregnant, and that December our son Daniel was born and we found a flat in St John's Wood. The day I finally left my family home in Southgate to move in with Nancy was horrendously painful. Daniel had appeared only six months after Russell, and I had to tell my older boys that I was moving out, and their bravery and understanding made it both easier and harder. A year or so after we finally split, my son Simon said he was pleased that we were seeing more of each other than before the break-up. Going to see Nancy in Highgate had been eating away at the time I could spend with my kids. Danish people are very proud by nature and perhaps Lisbet would rather have kept up some front of normality, but I felt relieved that everything was now in the open and that, over the years, I could develop meaningful relationships with my boys.

CHAPTER NINE

VISIONARY DREAMER

The deeper you dive, the more connections you see, and to make sense of The Kinks – and relations between Ray and me as the 1980s moved into the 1990s – you need to dive ever deeper into the turbulent waters. We played our final shows in June 1996 in Stockholm and Oslo, but The Kinks didn't suddenly crash and burn. That persistent and creative spirit, we tried to keep it alive. Throughout our existence we had managed, just about, to avoid falling off a precipice. Had 'You Really Got Me' flopped, it might have all ended in 1964; and again after the *Village Green* album in 1969; also at any point during *Preservation* and *Soap Opera*. The fear that the band could fall apart had always been a real and present danger.

The 1980s was a great period for us, creatively and commercially; we were doing bigger shows again and our albums were selling well. But Ray's move to New York necessarily changed the way we operated. Periods when the band recorded and toured were blocked out in advance and playing together was never anything other than intense and required my absolute commitment. But periods of free time opened up in London and, for the first time in years, I started thinking seriously about solo projects and about what *I* was going to do next. Having Ray out of my hair certainly made thinking easier. I'd been a steadfast supporter of Ray's music and helping him nurture his ideas had been just as important as doing my own stuff. But the energy required to deal with him on a day-to-day basis sucked my own creative juices dry, and too often my own work ended up on the backburner.

Through Elliot Abbott I met Ed DeJoy, then head of A&R at RCA in New York, and we hit it off right away; it turned out Ed was a good friend of Eddie Cochran's and I loved to hear his stories about him. Ed listened to my demos and immediately grasped what a solo Dave Davies record could be. But Ed understood that I had an identity of my own and, like Clive Davis, he got the balance right between enabling artists to make records and putting his nose where it wasn't welcomed. I was signed to RCA and my first solo album, *AFL1-3603*, was released in the summer of 1980. It couldn't have been a more personal record. I had written all the songs and, early on, I decided to play all the instruments myself, except on three tracks, where I used Nick Trevisick (drums) and Ron Lawrence (bass). I did the mixing, and I asked John Rollo to engineer because he understood exactly the sound I wanted. Everything you hear, other than on those three tracks with Nick and Ron – vocals, guitars, drums, bass, keyboards – that's all my playing. This was a big moment in my career and I was cheered by how seriously RCA took the promotion and marketing.

Playing most of the stuff myself wasn't about massaging my ego, it was about getting the album done with minimum fuss and how I wanted it. I'd tried to record my songs at various points during the 1970s, and always found it hard going. Recording solo material with various musicians connected with The Kinks – Mick, Baptist, Pyle – and also at Apple Studios on Savile Row with musicians not connected, like Phil Palmer and Ron Lawrence, and Neil McBain and Nick Trevisick – I had found it difficult to communicate my ideas. Beyond jottings that didn't mean much to other people, I couldn't write music down and within The Kinks I'd got used to working intuitively. When you're close to people, as I was with Ray and Pete in the early days, you don't need to explain too much. You find shortcuts and sometimes just a look is enough. Many of these recordings eventually saw the light of day in 2018 on an album called *Decade*, so called because I started making these recordings around the time Konk came into being, but before we signed to Arista and made it big in the US again – it provided a backstory of that ten-year period.

I didn't want to mess up the opportunity to release a solo project on RCA and the only way, I thought, I was going to achieve it was to play everything myself. I developed a way of working, a process of *feeling* each song deeply and from that working out how to play on it. I'd always played drums on my own demos and had a drum kit at home already. But I didn't spend hours working up a flawless drum technique, honing perfect snare drum rolls, which I then applied to the songs. Couldn't be arsed with that. Instead, I divined the technique I needed for a song from *out* of that song. Playing all the instruments helped me focus on how each song should sound, which gave me more confidence in my songs and in my writing. Songs don't care about whether the time is right. They appear when they appear and the challenge is to write them down before they disappear. I've always been one of those people for whom if it feels right, it is right.

AFL1-3603 was about how there is always more going on beneath the surface in life than anybody realises, and I was able to deal with feelings I had kept bottled inside for many years. It was a liberating experience. My song 'Nothin' More To Lose' suggested itself by thinking about Eddie Cochran. It was about where we were musically, politically and spiritually in a world where those who thought of themselves as 'leaders' had failed us. Perhaps the way forward, I thought, was reaching a point in our consciousness where all these things could fuse together. Building this song around Eddie Cochran was never about copying his style or sound, it was about allowing his spirit to speak again and being influenced in a surreal, creative way, like I was intoxicated by him. If this all sounds deadly serious, the song also gently takes the piss out of itself; it's funny too. Following on, 'The World Is Changing Hands' was a plea for younger people to grasp the future with bigger imagination and spiritual awareness than any president or prime minister had shown. 'Imagination's Real' was about the power of imagination to transform the world into whatever we want it to be, about making powerful imaginative ideas actually happen.

The album was very warmly received and sold pretty well in the US. I performed a couple of the songs during Kinks shows and the material transferred well to live performance, all of which made me feel good about what I'd achieved. When the time came to think about a follow-up, Ed DeJoy had left RCA to set up his own company and I worried that my first solo album might also have been my last; but *Glamour* was released almost exactly a year after *AFL1-3603*. This was the era of Margaret Thatcher and Ronald Reagan, and this new album was all about manipulation. Is that what we want at the end of the day? I thought it was so weird having a film actor as president. Perhaps they should have chosen Cary Grant instead. With my slicked-back hair and dapper suit I looked very debonair on the album cover, like a Golden Age of Hollywood star – Humphrey Bogart in *Casablanca* perhaps.

I approached making the album differently to *AFL1-3603*. I still played all the guitars, keyboards and percussion myself, but Bob Henrit came in to play drums. A few years later Bob would take over in The Kinks when Mick Avory left and he is a shithot drummer – almost too good, in fact. As we worked together on *Glamour* something didn't feel quite right at first. Bob was a highly skilled musician who over the years had played hundreds of sessions, and working under that sort of pressure, you learn certain tricks just to make it through the day. In a way, his chops, and knowing all those licks, impeded Bob's natural sense of listening to the songs and feeling his way into the music. I found myself counting the bars during one session, which I'd never done before. I thought: What the fuck am I counting this for? Then I realised Bob was counting and somehow it had transferred to me. Once we talked it all through, we had a lot of fun making the album. Bob's a charming guy and his drumming gave the album a real lift.

One track on the album drove people a bit crazy, especially at the record label. Was 'Reveal Yourself' too excessive? Perhaps so, but the world had reached a point when it was time to reveal what was going on inside of us; and also reveal the glamour of posing – the smart picture on the front – for what it was. That's what was going through my mind as I sang: 'Reveal yourself/For life is nothing but a movie show/Or free yourself/Your heart, your mind/Your soul, your sanity/Just got to see it, smell it/Know that it's reality.' Some people said it was too strident, too in-yer-face, and had problems with the other songs too. 'Telepathy' was about gaining knowledge from other people on an intuitive level, and the necessity to see beyond the words and the image. Telepathy between people who understand each other, and intuition, are beautiful things, completely at odds with fake corporate smiles that exist only to sell their brand. 'Too Serious' was a song about worrying about life too much, and was a play on the word 'Sirius', the star, and how maybe we're all on this intergalactic journey there together.

Glamour received some good press but landed at the wrong time to make a mark. Perhaps the album would do better now: Reagan was an actor who became president, and Trump was a game-show host. But back in the 1980s, pop reflected the spirit of greed and the attitude of me-me-me that might have blighted the decade. It asked questions relating to the general malaise. I suggested to the label an idea for a short promotional film which, tellingly, didn't go down well with their publicists. It was to have featured a 1940s film star – think Ronald Reagan meets Cary Grant – who somehow ends up as president. We see him poncing around the place as every PR person's dream: immaculate hair, designed suits, aware of how good he is at manipulating everyone around him. Playing in the background are visions of apocalyptic devastation, but he's oblivious to what's going on. So wrapped up in his own self-image – and the glamour of it all – that he's blind to the destruction around him. Then an alien from another time points to him from the sky, desperately trying to get him to see into the future and the consequences of his actions – or lack of them. But he gazes into the horizon as the film fades out, with a look of smug satisfaction on his face while the world is in chaos. Needless to say, the marketing guys baulked at the thought, thereby proving my point. This was a pop album, not an episode of *Panorama*. I had to back down.

I've never been interested in promoting one political point of view over another. In some ways, I'm an old hippy. If politicians can't act out of love, how are they ever going to help anybody? The Indian yogi Swami Vivekananda once said, 'Where love is absent, beware,' which stuck in my head. He also wrote, 'If a man believes God to be a stone, what's to say he is wrong?' That's pretty special, I think. It's playful and funny, and humour can lead us towards truth.

My next solo album, *Chosen People*, released in 1983, moved those ideas forward in quite an audacious way. RCA hadn't known what to do with *Glamour*, that much was obvious. Perhaps things might have been better had Ed DeJoy still been in charge, but Elliot Abbott managed to get me an 'in' at Warner Brothers and I swapped labels. I'd discovered a book by Black Elk, a famous Native American Indian and religious thinker whose writings had been collected under the title *Black Elk Speaks*, while The Kinks had been touring the US and that gave me a starting point for *Chosen People*. Black Elk had been present at the Battle of Little Bighorn and his philosophies resonated with me more than our politics. He advocated a more natural way of living and he told of how, in his culture, they were more harmonious with nature and with animals. They ate buffalo meat *because* the buffalo was a sacred animal and they would give thanks to The Great Spirit, what we refer to as God. They gave thanks for the things in life that helped you and the phrase 'Chosen People' is really about us. We're all chosen. We chose ourselves, to come into life, to do as good as we can. Using his philosophy, his people taught that the red-skin would one day meet his new white-brothers, and they would hold hands and work together in harmony. Not that it happened like that. Instead, the white-brothers did their best to help destroy an ancient race of people.

Towards the end of his life, Black Elk said, 'When I walk up to that hill and close my eyes, I join with the Great Spirit and my people. I am one with all that went before me. I am not alone.' Something white men failed to understand, as they blundered in, was the damage they did to the link between the people and the Great Spirit. In spiritualism they talk about psychometry, tapping into etheric matter and the subtle energy that surrounds everyone and everything; an object contains the energy of every person who touched it and there are ways of extracting the meaning it con- tains. Go into a room where great music has been played – a concert hall or jazz club – and it's not just an empty space. There are tan- gible vibrations, and that's why music is so powerful because it can affect us in ways we don't realise. *Chosen People* is about all those ideas and its more ethereal tone sounded nothing like *AFL1-3603* or *Glamour*.

After *Chosen People*, I didn't make a solo album again until *Bug*, which was released in 2002 on my dear friend Bob Frank's Red River label. Why the long gap? Life was busy with The Kinks, but more than that the record business can be treacherous terrain. My album was a sincerely felt piece of work with something to say about life and the world; but it turned out the record company didn't seem to be interested. I tried to get them to pay for a promo video of my song 'Mean Disposition' and they gave a little money, but I ended up putting my hand in my own pocket. The Kinks were on *Top of the Pops* the day we filmed and I had to sneak away for the afternoon, but I think we made a good video. The song was about how the idealism of youth can be eroded by the experience of life, but how it's important to live a 'Life full of dreams/And we really believe that they come true some day.' The video was pure slapstick, like Charlie Chaplin meets Eric Sykes. It's about a slobby bully who enjoys picking on people and generally being an oaf. He yanks the hat off an old lady's head in the street and, in a record shop, chucks a load of Kinks LPs on the floor; then he's roundly humiliated when the old dear returns and beats him up with her walking stick.

I'd hired Shelly Heber, a friend based in LA who was working on PR with lots of bands at the time, to help get my album some attention. One day she rang with the news that she'd heard the album had been released only as a way of offsetting tax; what's called an 'out of the box failure' in the business. Suddenly Warners' lack of interest and their reluctance to give it any push made sense. I was upset at how casually they were treating this project so close to my heart, and I began to suspect that Elliot had twisted arms at the label, calling in some favours, to get the record made. I did some press for the album in LA and when I talked about Black Elk, or anything spiritual, there'd be awkward silences and puzzled faces.

Shelly also told me about a conversation she'd overheard, someone in the office asking, 'Hey, he's not one of them, is he?' Because of my title *Chosen People*, he meant Jewish. What's wrong with people? There might not have been much American record industry, or Hollywood, without Jewish people. Things didn't much improve when I arrived in New York. One interview ended with me being taken to a basement where I was cross-examined by some very weird men who, in my paranoid state, I couldn't help wonder if they were from the FBI or NASA undercover agents. They certainly weren't interested in my music. Instead they fired a load of questions about alien abductions at me. 'Did they place implants inside your brain?' 'Did they examine your sex organs?' I spun them some yarn about little green men from Mars who, while I was sleeping as a kid, would come into my bedroom and feed tubes into my arms: 'I was *so* petrified, I didn't even tell my mum.' They looked at each other and nodded wisely. Yeah, he's off his rocker – although at least I wasn't gullible enough to fall for such obvious bullshit.

Another thing that pissed me off about the whole *Chosen People* experience: radio stations refused to play the single I'd chosen from the LP, 'Love Gets You', because the way I sang the line 'Do you want it, any way it can' sounded like I had something else in mind, which had never been my intention. From beginning to end, the whole thing had been a disaster. Thankfully, flying home to London allowed me to recover my strength and my spirit.

At least throughout this period I'd demonstrated to myself that I could enjoy being a solo artist and also a Kink at the same time. *AFL1-3603* was recorded around the time *One For The Road* was being edited and mixed. *Glamour* was released just a few weeks before the American release of The Kinks' next album, *Give The People What They Want* in 1981; *Chosen People* and The Kinks' *State of Confusion* were both released in the summer of 1983.

Ray was working on projects of his own too. As I was making *Glamour* he was writing his first musical, called *Chorus Girls*, which opened at the Theatre Royal in Stratford. Perhaps because we were also doing stuff independently, Ray and I were getting on really well. Typically, though, he didn't mention that his marriage to Yvonne had become shaky. Instead he began turning up at Kinks gigs with Chrissie Hynde, then she started accompanying him on tour, and clearly they were more than friends. I couldn't argue against the fact Ray seemed happier, and his moods were lighter, than they had been in a while. He was even seen to smile occasionally. But I worried that the last thing he needed in his life was another mammoth ego to compete against. Their relationship would surely burn itself out, I feared. It was only a matter of time. Their self-absorption and their thirst for constant affirmation and attention would surely lead to problems. They were two alpha cats both trying to occupy the same territory.

Like Ray, Chrissie had a knack of dominating any conversation to the point where she left me feeling depleted of energy. Only full attention when she was speaking would do – then her eyes would start to wander, looking for someone more important in the room. It was infuriating. During one gig she suddenly appeared next to Ray and expected to sing. I yelled at her to get off the fucking stage; last time I looked she wasn't in The Kinks. Eventually relations thawed. Chrissie and Nancy hit it off immediately and beyond her icy exterior I discovered a fun, humorous side of Chrissie. The four of us had some great nights out – and The Pretenders opened for The Kinks on a few US shows. One night, when we were playing in Toronto, Pete Quaife, who was by then living in Canada, turned up and sat in with us. Except I don't think he had any idea how to work with a modern sound system. It was always good to see Pete though and realise that, on some level, he was still interested in the band. When I recorded a live album at The Bottom Line in New York in 1997, again he turned up and sat in. Years earlier, around the peak of 'Lola', I'd seen him on a television chat show in Canada talking about the song – a bit of a cheek given he'd already left the band, but then again I thought, Good luck to you, mate.

Nancy and I spent November 1981 in North Devon, with Daniel, our young son. I loved rambling through the countryside and walking around Exmoor was restorative; after months on the road with The Kinks, I took refuge in the beauty and mystery of nature. But my emotions were starting to mess with me again. I was torn. The Kinks had been the backbone for most of my life, but the need to get away from Ray, for my own sanity and well-being, suddenly overwhelmed me. I'd had a taste of creative autonomy, and although I couldn't bring myself to break away from The Kinks altogether, every part of my being was crying out for creative independence. I became extremely depressed. Nancy nursed me through as best she could, but I wouldn't have been mentally strong enough to endure a ten-day tour of Germany scheduled for the beginning of December, and it was cancelled.

Reluctantly I agreed to pick up the pieces again in 1982 for a two-month tour of the US, Australia and Japan, beginning early January, but in hindsight I should have taken more time to myself. There was intense pressure to get back on the road; from Elliot, from Ray, from the record label, all of whom were concerned that upsetting promoters and fans was not the best idea when things were going so well for the band in the US and it wasn't like we had enough of a fanbase at home to risk alienating anybody. But things got weird very quickly. After a couple of days, when we were flying to play a show at the Coliseum in Hampton, Virginia, I began to feel oddly disembodied, like I was looking in from the outside. Must be jetlag, I thought, as I picked up my bags and the smiling aircrew led us off the plane. Then we had the afternoon to settle into our hotel before that evening's concert but, as I unpacked, I couldn't understand why I was feeling so peculiar.

I didn't feel physically ill. This was different. Suddenly I had a feeling like a boa constrictor had wrapped itself around my forehead and was pressing hard. What the fuck? I glanced over at Nancy half expecting her to run over in obvious concern. But no. She smiled back reassuringly and carried on doing her thing. Then I started hearing voices inside my head, like my brain had flicked on a new psychic switch. After the initial jolt, I didn't feel panicked or alarmed; these voices had a commanding presence, but were also non-threatening, calming even. My senses were overwhelmed. Where were these voices coming from? Were they floating close by? Or an alien force from many thousand miles away? I began to feel their presence. I could already hear them; then I felt them physically and my nostrils were filled with different smells, again nothing unpleasant or sinister. In fact, the smells – of fresh flowers like jasmine and magnolia – had a fragrance that was so full I felt like I could have scooped them up with a spoon.

What you're about to read might sound a bit crazy, but I can only describe it as honestly as I can. I called these voices 'the intelligences' and I realised they had taken over complete command of my senses. The feeling I'd had earlier in the day of being disembodied from my surroundings intensified. It was like viewing reality through the prism of a distorting mirror; I could feel the intelligences operating on my thoughts and emotions, opening up pathways so that they could communicate with me more directly. And they communicated via smell, the vibration around a particular scent becoming a conduit through which they fed me information. In life there is conscious thought, but also other layers of information – pure feelings – that are not facilitated by the conscious mind. And I felt they were gaining control over my consciousness to show me hitherto unseen sides of life.

I became twitchy and suddenly convulsed with terror. I reached over to Nancy and tried to explain to her what I was experiencing; that I'd entered into a telepathic exchange with mysterious beings.

The intelligences, though, would only let me tell her what they wanted her to know. But when she looked at me with full acceptance of my situation, I knew that her unswerving faith in me would prove vital over the next few days. I panicked about playing all the shows we had lined up, and held Nancy close to me; being alone would have been the worst. I'd panic, but then the convivial, soothing odours of those fragrances would calm my nerves and I'd feel temporarily elated. The intelligences revealed certain things about themselves. Two of them had always been my spirit guides; another two were not of this planet but had been sent to protect and mother our race; one intelligence was the projected consciousness of a sentient being living in a physical form on earth.

Their communications became more demanding, more challenging. They told me I must not have sex and, although I was able to walk normally, my groin and pelvis suddenly became numbed, like they'd blocked any sensation down there. The reason being, they told me, was they wanted to transmute my sexual energy to a higher vibrational level. At one point they took me deep into my various past lives and invited me to observe carefully as they revealed the things I'd done, deeds that were very painful indeed to be confronted with. Nor did they leave me alone during shows. The intelligences would collate information about the people around me and, suddenly, I'd be able to see behind the motives and look directly into the inner thoughts of the people I worked with. After one soundcheck I watched Ray as he walked back to his dressing room and he looked so vulnerable and desolate. His forced, lopsided smile looked ready to fall off his face. I had seen that same look so many times when he was a little boy, and it was like looking at a child.

I welled up inside. I felt protective of Ray, like all along I had been the big brother. Suddenly an intoxicating odour flooded my senses and touched my very being. In response, I closed my eyes and breathed it in. The intelligences showed me a picture of Ray, his body now the trunk of a bushy rose tree from which branches stretched in all directions where they blossomed into hundreds of different sorts of flowers. I was enchanted by the smell of the roses and reached out to touch. But then a horrible truth. These things of such beauty scratched and cut me, and I broke down in tears. I held Nancy close and told her that Ray had taken advantage of me all my life, and his behaviour had left me hurt and bruised. I'd spent a good portion of my life trying to help Ray nurture and tend to those flowers. But the intelligences helped me. The fragrances made my anger and bitterness melt away. I was overcome with forgiveness and compassion.

Back at the hotel, I felt empty, like I'd been hollowed out from the inside. The sadness was so acute I dropped to my knees and begged Nancy for help. The intelligences were flashing images at me of unimaginable suffering in the world. I was spellbound by what they showed me. They were manipulating senses within my own body to bring about these psycho-mystical visions, and I knew that man's mission on earth had to be to harness and channel these same forces. I was drawn inexorably towards Jesus, and immediately grasped that he had been a being of tremendous power, great learning and influence. The magnitude of his endeavours on earth hit me like a tornedo. My Jesus was a spiritual guru and, who knows, one day we might be ready to comprehend the depth of his teachings. I don't believe Jesus to be the only son of God. All of us have the potential within us to be sons and daughters of God. There is evil in the world, but also enormous goodness, and the tendency is to elevate the evil and overlook the good. We lean on God too much for answers and pin the blame on him when the bad stuff happens. I believe that the burden is on *us* to make our world a better and more thoughtful place.

So much more became clear to me once I'd met Dr George King, a mystic, a medium, a philosopher and a profoundly great writer on matters metaphysical; I lapped up his book *The Nine Freedoms* and I dedicated *Chosen People* to him. He lived in west London and I'd visit him for long talks, and his intellect was towering, his insights into the world profound and beautiful. We'd talk about the mystical elements within all of us, based on what Indian and Tibetan mystics call Kundalini – a force based on the coming together of the male and female forces in the body, and aligning in a way that creates a third force, an alignment of male and female energies. Talking with him was at first daunting. Although I'd encountered some of his ideas previously, he took me in deeper than I was used to, explaining in great detail about Eastern yogic traditions and aligning certain energies. And I was immediately able to make connections with what he'd told me and what I had learned from Regardie's *The Middle Pillar*.

I came to various conclusions about what happened to me in that hotel room in Virginia. It was psychological and it was spiritual, yet there are things I still can't explain. Very basically, the yoga system is centred around balancing the left and right sides of the body. The right side of the body is concerned with female energies and the left with male energy. When you do certain breathing and mental practices, you learn to align these forces. During my experience, the energies crossed over at the solar plexus and alignment took place in my physical body. So I could walk and everything but the sexual energy was numb, and the energies became focused in the higher body: the heart, throat and towards the forehead. This is what they call the 'third eye' in yogic practice – a place where all energies align and you can perceive far beyond normal seeing. There's an old occult adage, borrowed from the Bible: 'The light of the *body* is the *eye*: if therefore thine *eye* be *single*, thy whole *body* shall be *full of light*.' Christianity has a very strong belief in what they call the 'Christ force'. Tibetan yogis and Judaism have their own ways of perceiving Kundalini and chakras.

I realised all religions are, in their own way, founded on the same basic energy points in the human system.

When I nearly jumped out of the hotel window in New York, the voices had been demonic and teasing. But in Virginia they were benevolent and I believe that they had my interests at heart. They were benevolent spiritual guides or teachers, and that incredible experience changed me for ever and it took many years to fully understand the implications of what had happened to me; and that process may take many more years for all I know. These ideas were swirling around my head as The Kinks toured in 1982, through Japan, Australia and the US, where I discovered *Black Elk Speaks* and decided to call my next solo album *Chosen People*. Ray was working on a solo project of his own, a film with a tie-in album called *Return to Waterloo*. Sometimes it's been said that I angrily refused to take part. Ian Gibbons, Jim Rodford and Mick were all involved. But this felt like such a personal statement for Ray, he really didn't need me. I could have put down guitar parts, and filled out the harmony, but time now to cut each other some slack. Ever supportive, the best way now was to give him space to create.

After those miserable experiences in the US with *Chosen People*, I went to ground at home in London and ended up cancelling another Kinks tour, which enraged Ray and Elliot. Looking back, I realise I should have summoned up the strength to do the tour. At the time, though, my morale had been shot to pieces and I thought nobody, apart from Nancy, cared or understood me. Some American newspapers ran salacious articles about how I'd lost the plot and been admitted to a mental hospital: not true at all. Some fans sent goodwill messages via Konk, for which I was grateful, but the irony was not lost on me – when I was properly losing my mind during the 1970s nobody cared, but now I was on top of things, and was finding my path through life, the word on the street was that I had gone mad.

By the end of the year, The Kinks had reassembled and we played some East Coast shows in the US, with Cyndi Lauper opening for us, including at the Roseland Ballroom in New York on New Year's Eve. The album we were promoting at the time, *State of Confusion*, had just given us a hit record. A year earlier Ray had been playing with a promising idea for a song based around when our sisters used to go dancing to the big bands at the Palais in Muswell Hill on a Saturday night. It became 'Come Dancing'. The song was fun and feel-good, and also a very nice nod to the memory of Rene and Uncle Frank. Julien Temple directed the video and Ray dressed like a 1950s crooner – and looked the spitting image of Uncle Frank. The likeness was uncanny and brought the memories flooding back. One night Rene held a party at Denmark Terrace and Frank turned up with a radiogram in his van. He'd heard about a shop that lent them out on approval; try for a week and pay if you decide to keep it. But the next day, back in the van it went, and Frank returned it, full of fag burns and splashed drinks, to the shop and told them it was a load of crap. He was such a classic Cockney geezer.

For reasons best known to themselves, the BBC had refused to give 'Come Dancing' airplay and the record all but disappeared in the UK. In the US, Clive Davis had been worried initially that Americans wouldn't cotton on. The record was too quirkily English. But catch on it did in the US, and its popularity there led it to be re-released in the UK and audiences lapped it up. We went back on *Top of the Pops* for the first time in ten years. All good, although making *State of Confusion* helped to clarify that putting distance between Ray and me was becoming a necessity. The album was filled with good songs and Ray and I worked hard – *together* – to arrange songs like 'Don't Forget To Dance', designed as a follow-up to 'Come Dancing'. And also a cool track called 'Clichés Of The World', which I thought was brilliant. Knowing Ray like I did, I talked to him and to Elliot about making sure I got appropriate credit on the album, not just for playing but also for writing, arranging and collaborating. Elliot agreed. This was fair and he'd make sure the sleeve notes were truly reflective of the role I'd taken. 'I'll square everything with Arista,' he said.

When the liner notes finally appeared I was stunned to see everything credited, as per sodding usual, to Raymond Douglas Davies. I rang Elliot and, in my sheer frustration, yelled at him down the phone, only to find that he was as genuinely taken aback as me. We rang the office at Arista only to find it was too late – the printing presses were already rolling. Evidently Ray had phoned Arista late one night, after the liner notes were finished and everyone thought they'd been signed off, to demand changes. What an opportunistic and manipulative sod. The nectar smelt sweet, but yet again I'd spiked myself on Ray's meanness. In between tours, Ray was polishing and finessing his *Return to Waterloo* film and, although I hadn't wanted to get involved myself, I did him the courtesy of watching a rough cut and thought it was really good.

At the start of 1984 we went back to the US to play some of those shows cancelled during the previous year, and another problematic relationship finally hit the buffers. This was the beginning of the end of the road for Mick, whose playing I felt had become ever more slapdash. A sense of humour is essential to pull everyone through the trials and tribulations of touring, but I felt that Mick's clownish behaviour was creating a bad atmosphere. He was not taking it seriously and his presence no longer felt right. Either way, we could barely communicate without our words blowing up into a huge argument. One night, Mick had hurled his drumsticks at me during a concert and a scrap backstage would have escalated into something far more serious had people not pulled us apart.

It was the twentieth anniversary of The Kinks in 1984. Mick had invested his working life in the band, but I thought, OK, Mick, thanks for everything, but that's it. As far as he had moved away from The Kinks, The Kinks had moved away from him. In the beginning the group had been Ray, Pete and me, and Mick arrived as an add-on, Grenville's idea because his playing was just about good enough and he fitted image-wise. But now I had greater aspirations for what I wanted music to be and I couldn't be bothered with Mick arsing around. Ray sensed my feeling that we should move ahead and there was no question in my mind that Bob Henrit was the man to take over and Ray came round to my point of view. Mick didn't disappear though. Despite the tensions over so many years, Mick was like a third brother. He would invariably side with Ray, but he understood perfectly the dynamic between us. Ray kept him on as manager of Konk and after a while, with the pressures that came with working together gone, we patched up our differences and became friends again.

This was a period of change in other ways too. It was time to renegotiate our contract with Arista. We had one more album to deliver to them, which turned out to be *Word of Mouth*, and we were as keen to re-sign to the label as Clive was to have us. Then Elliot started dropping hints that he was cooking up a more lucrative deal with a bigger company, and we should hold our fire before signing with Arista again. That other deal turned out to be with MCA, whose Director of Marketing, Richard Palmese, had worked for Clive Davis back during our early days on Arista. Richard would essentially poach us by flexing financial muscle that outbid Clive. All is fair in love and business, I suppose, but with the benefit of hindsight it was a mistake – we would have been far better sticking with Clive, even if the dollars had been less favourable.

We didn't actually sign on the dotted line until January 1986, but only after sneaky manoeuvres – or smart, depending on how you look at it – from MCA. The November before we signed, their publicity department leaked the news that we were due to join the label. When the news was picked up by MTV, this gave a signal to Arista that the game was up and they backed off, when in fact the company still had a chance.

The handover period became very stressful. The worry that Arista had no reason to push our new album hung over us like a black cloud. Right from the get-go, my intuition told me that MCA would prove disastrous for The Kinks. When we went to their fancy offices I felt uneasy the second we walked through the door. Naff dance music was playing in the background and the atmosphere was sterile and stuffy. The head of promotions desperately tried to avoid eye contact and wriggled uncomfortably in his seat when I talked to him. He had nothing to say to us, and this was the guy whose job it was to represent out best interests with the press. Sure enough, when the time came, MCA proved itself incapable of selling Kinks records. I looked on in disbelief. Arista had managed perfectly well and with a fraction of the resources. MCA had offices scattered all over the US and the company maintained a massive publicity organisation, but somehow couldn't get their act together.

To shore up things in the UK, Ray called back someone from our dim and distant past, who we'd last encountered in a courtroom two decades earlier. Out of the blue, Ray phoned Larry Page and asked him to manage us at home. Larry, although surprised, agreed – and we let bygones be bygones and he stepped right back into the role without missing a beat. Around this time we were approached to see if we'd be interested in playing the Kray twins in a forthcoming film. Apparently, Reggie and Ronnie were big Kinks fans, but by that time the full horror of their crimes were known and I was against the idea. I didn't want to be seen in a film that glorified crime. When the film appeared, the director Peter Medak had Gary and Martin Kemp from Spandau Ballet playing the

Krays, and I thought they caught the atmosphere of time and place incredibly well. Chrissie Hynde flippantly said that we should definitely have done the film – we were a whole lot scarier than Reggie or Ronnie, she joked.

There was a whole two-year gap between *Word of Mouth* and our debut album for MCA, *Think Visual*. Mick's departure occurred during the *Word of Mouth* sessions and Bob played on the majority of the songs. We recorded two of my songs – 'Guilty' and 'Living on a Thin Line' – for the album, which both seemed to sum up life with The Kinks. I wrote 'Living on a Thin Line' for Ray to sing, but I ended up singing it myself. I thought about how for much of the history of the band, Ray and I had been delicately balanced on a tightrope. We'd wobbled on the line and fallen off continually and had to find countless ways to get back up on our feet. I began to think about all those other desperate people just about scraping by in life, their existence on the breadline and how they struggled to keep going – and how governments had consistently failed to make things better. It's a song that is, unfortunately, perpetually relevant and has had an unexpected afterlife, appearing in an episode of *The Sopranos*.

There were two singles released off the back of *Word of Mouth*, 'Do It Again' and 'Summer's Gone', both good songs, both by Ray. We had great fun making the video for 'Do It Again', filmed in Brighton and on the London Underground, and I got to tick one thing off my bucket list. I'd always wanted to drive a London tube train and now I did – for all of one minute. Ray was still feeling guilty about the manner of Mick's departure and invited him to take part in the video. He played the part of a busker on the platform who, having failed to make anything, walks off under Ray's steely gaze. The big question for me, though, was why 'Living on a Thin Line' was not being released as a single. It was receiving massive airplay on the radio, then it transpired Ray had had it written into his publishing contract that the first three singles from any Kinks album had to have been written by himself. By the time anyone realised what was going on, it was too late to put it out as a single.

Ray's relationship with Chrissie had unravelled and he was distressed at the news that she'd married Jim Kerr from Simple Minds, with surprising speed. Their split had been inevitable from the start. I once tried to act as peacemaker by going round to their house when they were having an intense argument, chucking chairs around; much good it did any of us. They were screaming at each other like hyenas and laughing manically, like it was a performance, but with real malice too. Ray suddenly turned on me, blaming *me* for *their* argument. But I just shook my head sadly: Shit like this happens all the time, I thought, before I went home.

Ray went to ground just at the time we ought to have been generating ideas for *Think Visual*; he just couldn't think straight and a load of insecurities came back to haunt him. Did we do the right thing getting rid of Mick and hiring Bob? Should we have stayed with Arista? How were we going to cope without Elliot, who felt our change of label was a good time to move on himself? He couldn't decide on anything, and probably kept himself awake all night worrying about what he was having for breakfast. I thought our change of label also provided a good opportunity to resolve basic issues that had been bugging me for a while – who owned the rights to the name 'The Kinks'? What was to stop Ray issuing music as 'The Kinks' that didn't include me? The negotiations, via lawyers, dragged on for longer than either of us wanted. But eventually we reached an agreement: the name was owned jointly and could only be used commercially with our mutual consent. We christened our new company Kinks 85.

We didn't get going properly on the new album until May, which ended up giving me much-needed breathing space. Nancy was pregnant with our second child and the baby was due at the end of February. Unfortunately she was having a very traumatic pregnancy with a condition called pre-eclampsia, which results in dangerously high blood pressure and can endanger both child and mother. We sat through some very stress-inducing hospital appointments and it was with considerable relief that our daughter, Lana, came into the world more or less on her due date. She was heartbreakingly beautiful and immediately I was overwhelmed with love for her. I couldn't help but think back all those years to the birth of a daughter I never knew and the painful void that had created in my life. I felt a sense of completion now – I had my fantastic boys and now a daughter.

I also began to think about a life outside London – and The Kinks. I had very fond memories of times I had spent in the West Country, and I decided to buy a small cottage in the heart of the Devon countryside, surrounded on one side by woods and the sea on the other. The pace was slower. We spent precious time there with my boys and family, and it was the perfect place to think about what I wanted from life. I meditated and painted, and saturated my ears in music by Mahler, Berlioz, Sibelius, Beethoven, Dvořák and Bach.

I had started writing screenplays for films, including one set during our early days in Muswell Hill, and this new obsession picked up on a love of film that had begun during my childhood. And Devon was a place that nourished my imagination. I always loved Exeter. It's built on a mound with far-reaching views, and you find chain coffee stores slammed next to ancient Roman ruins; the ancient and modern. I bought an old Citroën H-van which I overhauled, putting some beds inside to transform it into a camper van. I also installed a platform on the roof and bought a telescope so I could go UFO-spotting on Holdstone Down, which overlooks the Bristol Channel. Quickly I learned to distinguish possible

UFOs from other lights in the sky, like satellites, stars or weather balloons. The UFOs I saw moved at such a lick that my telescope turned out to be useless. They would hang completely still high in the sky – far higher than anything else I could see with the naked eye – then dart away abruptly towards the heavens, like starbursts of exploding light.

We'd recently returned from the US, where we'd been trying to make some sort of success out of *Think Visual*, when my sister Gwen phoned with very worrying news. Mum was in hospital. She'd been admitted with crippling stomach pains and the doctors had decided that surgery was the only option. I arrived at the Whittington Hospital to find Mum on a hospital bed on her way to theatre for her operation. I ought to have been the one doing the reassuring, but instead she was telling me not to worry – 'Everything's going to be fine, David.' But Gwen felt uneasy about the whole thing, and as it turned out with very good reason. The next day we heard from Mum's doctors that they had discovered cancer in her stomach and that in all likelihood she had only three or four weeks to live. The shock was like recoiling from a punch in the mouth but, once the initial pain and panic wore off, I realised what a privilege it was to help nurse Mum through her final weeks. The clan descended. Lisbet, who'd always adored Mum, dropped everything. Peg, Gwen and her husband Brian, and all my sisters, in fact, were brilliant; we all helped each other through this most difficult of times.

Witnessing Mum's decline was devastating, but alongside tears of deep sadness there were also tears of cathartic laughter as we remembered all her favourite family stories. Mum had good days and bad. One day she woke up feeling disorientated and confused. 'David, who are all these people?' she asked, gesturing into thin air. Not wanting to add to her distress by contradicting her, I asked her to describe these people to me and asked whether they were good people or not. Her eyes filled with tears and she told me they were beckoning her to come with them, but she wasn't ready – not yet. I told them, respectfully, to please leave us in peace. I could see how spooked Mum was, but she gradually began to accept them and, as the end approached, actually gained some comfort from their presence.

The one person who wasn't around was Ray, who was finalising some deal or other in New York. Ray will always be Ray, and people deal with grief in different ways, fair enough. But Mum desperately wanted to see him, and his continued absence was upsetting for everyone. I was going to say that occasionally he'd ring, but that is not strictly the case. Gwen or I would be the one to ring him in New York, and he'd mouth comforting words down the line – 'Hang in there, Mum, it'll all be fine.' One day a letter arrived from Ray in which he told Mum that she had been at the core of his inspiration and how deeply he loved her. She read it again and again, and held it close to her chest. Reading those words had meant everything to her, but why couldn't Ray fly back to London?

Late one night, Mum told me to go home and catch up on some sleep. I'd been with her all day and was exhausted by that time. I said goodnight and that was the last time I saw her. She died soon after I'd left. Clearly she knew the end was near and hadn't wanted me to see her die. This was her last caring act as a mother.

The day of her funeral, Ray made his grand entrance, fresh off a transatlantic flight. We were all aching with exhaustion and stress after tending Mum's bedside for the last few weeks, but I marvelled as Ray delivered an exceptionally eloquent eulogy – each word carefully thought through and filled with love. Mum would have lapped up every word and indeed I believe firmly that she was present in some form inside that room as Ray spoke; I imagined her standing in a corner, arms folded, listening intently, that face I had looked on with such love creased with laughter.

The day following the funeral, I drove to Devon to spend some time in quiet deliberation. I started writing, not music, but words about Mum which subsequently I shaped into a film script about her life. I felt Mum's presence as I wrote, like I was entering into an intimate dialogue with her. This wasn't just about exorcising grief. Mum had been my closest friend and my mentor; a part of me had died with her. Now I was finding new ways to communicate with her and, released from her physical form, the pathways were more open in some ways, from which I drew tremendous strength.

CHAPTER TEN

I WILL BE ME

Just my bloody luck I decide to write my autobiography and at that very moment the whole world drops off a cliff edge. This weird time of COVID-19, lockdowns, social distancing, wearing masks, speaking to people on Zoom and folks asking 'Are you double jabbed yet?' At least I've had time to think about my life, ample opportunity to sit in my favourite pub in Highgate and think about these words – more than I could ever have imagined when I started. I can't help wonder what Mum would have made of the pandemic. Her outlook on life was, of course, shaped by the war. After all that had happened in her life, she'd probably have said we just have to get on with it the best we can, while trying to remain cheerful and optimistic. 'We'll get there, don't worry, David,' she'd have said.

We'll get there with this book too! We're about to reach a point where The Kinks fade into the background somewhat. Not entirely obviously, but my desire for creative independence was growing all the time, and I could feel the same impulse gnawing at Ray. When *Think Visual* was released at the end of 1986, the prospects felt good and we tried to make the situation with MCA work. The album was, I felt, a great selection of songs, a typical Kinks pull-together of rock and roll with occasional hints of vaudeville and dark humour. My song 'Rock 'n' Roll Cities' ended up being the first single, and I was very proud of the other song I wrote for the album, 'When You Were A Child', about what happens when people lose touch with their memories of being a child and go through life either feeling resentful at the hand they have been dealt – or reflecting on the wonderful experiences they've had. I don't know how happy Ray was about 'Rock 'n' Roll Cities' becoming the single, but the decision was made because it was the song most likely to attract airplay. When I was making the demo, for some reason I couldn't lock into the rhythm. Mick Avory was upstairs in the office working on some admin, and he ended up playing drums on the track and did great.

Ray and I bust our balls promoting that album in the US, appearing on every radio and television programme that would have us. But slowly the realisation dawned that the record wasn't going to take off. Neither of our next pair of albums for MCA, *The Road* – recorded live – and *UK Jive* did that well either, and our frustration with MCA grew again. Ray vented his frustration about our label by screaming insults through the microphone at a gig, which wouldn't have endeared us to the MCA suits, but there it is. They never had a clue what to do with the band. Fuck knows we tried. We poured everything we had into those albums. We met a great guy called Kenny Laguna, who was a musician and was also working as a promoter. He loved The Kinks, and knew people at the record company, and reckoned he could help us and he did all he could. But it was too late. By the time Kenny got involved it was an uphill struggle. In the end we parted from the label by mutual consent. They were likely as pleased to see the back of us as we were to be released from our contract.

Quite honestly, there had been far too many hustlers and scam artists cheerfully waving large chequebooks and wodges of cash around during the 1980s. I'm not party political, but I'd hoped that Margaret Thatcher might shake things up a bit. But by the time she went in 1990, and John Major took over, I felt more disenchanted than ever. I'd written a song for *UK Jive* called 'Dear

Margaret' that summed it all up: 'Dear Margaret I beg of you/ Dear Margaret gonna tell on you/Don't want to be patronised/By those lying eyes . . . You're a model and example/Of a greed that will destroy.' The outlook for the country felt unremittingly bleak. Rich folks had lined their pockets nicely, leaving the rest of the country impoverished. Discontentment hung in the air. Things rarely change.

As 1989 was drawing to a close, The Kinks were invited to be inducted into the Rock & Roll Hall of Fame. The ceremony was to be held at the Waldorf-Astoria Hotel in New York the following January. Ray and I didn't know whether to accept at first. Flattering to be asked, for sure, but we didn't think our music belonged in a museum or fitted into any establishment. But the list of other inductees was quite something: Simon & Garfunkel, The Who, The Four Tops and, posthumously, Louis Armstrong and the great 1930s jazz guitarist Charlie Christian, whose playing I'd adored as a kid. Then we looked more kindly on the idea, realising it was a nod of respect towards thirty years of producing our work. We were introduced as a band that 'deliberately operated outside of fashion and trend to create a completely original music brand', and then we were inducted by Graham Nash, of Crosby, Stills and Nash fame, who we'd first met back in 1964 when he was playing with The Hollies, who had toured with us that year. He'd kept tabs on our work ever since and we were touched by his gracious speech. Pete and Mick joined Ray and me onstage to accept the award. Mick made the audience belly-laugh when he said the reason nobody recognised Pete was because shops always put the price label over his face on our album covers. Bono inducted The Who and Stevie Wonder spoke about The Four Tops. It was quite a night.

We might have been feted at rock and roll's top table, but we were still dealing with the fallout from the MCA situation and, thirty years after The Kinks had first cast around for a record label, we were doing so again. Some shit never ends. Ray and I thought the best thing to do would be to look for new management first, and after a few false starts, met Nigel Thomas who had once managed Joe Cocker and was currently working with Morrissey. We both liked the guy immediately and felt we could work with him. He was old-school, like Robert and Grenville, and spoke with a cut-glass English accent, like Robert and Grenville. He had an imperious quality – like Robert and Grenville – that appealed to us, and he also had an impish, dry sense of humour. In an earlier life he had been employed by the Kray twins to do stand-up. And if he could deal with Ronnie and Reggie, not to mention Morrissey, no sweat dealing with The Kinks.

We went into a meeting at Columbia Records, which had recently been taken over by Sony Music, and immediately had a good feeling and we signed to the label without too much fuss. When we started making our twenty-fourth album, *Phobia*, we had no idea that we were working on a possible last Kinks record – but, you know, never say never. The record took far too much time to finish, a whole eighteen months from beginning to end. There were numerous reasons for this. Ray was now living back in London, while Nancy and I decided to make the move to Los Angeles. So now I was the one on the red-eye flights back to London to make the recording sessions at Konk. Having the Atlantic Ocean between us, as before, proved beneficial for our relationship, and Ray and I got along better than we had in a long time during the *Phobia* sessions. Nigel, too, was a calming influence, and eventually all our hard work bore fruit. The album was released in March 1993, a whole twenty-nine years since our debut record *Kinks* appeared in 1964.

It was a big, complex album too, packed with emotional layers. I wrote a couple of songs – 'It's Alright (Don't Think About It)' and 'Close To The Wire' – but a song we made together, 'Hatred (A

Duet)', became the talking point of the album, and also the single. We were getting on really well so, Ray being Ray, decided to write a skittish song about our famously on–off, love–hate relationship. We'd been messing around with some guitar riffs in the studio and his lyrics fit them like a glove: 'You wanna be my friend, well it's too late/My love for you has turned to hate . . . I hate you and you hate me/now I guess we understand each other.' Some people took it all very seriously, but we could barely keep a straight face when we were recording the song. To promote the album we did interviews together for the first time in a while, and some interviewers seemed almost nervous of approaching the subject of 'Hatred'. We performed the song on *The Tonight Show With Jay Leno* in Los Angeles and Billy Crystal was also a guest on the show. He told this endless gag built around the pair of underpants he was holding and I thought he was never going to shut the fuck up. Eventually I snapped and grabbed the pants off him and pulled them over his head. A high-risk strategy on a talk show, but Billy saw the funny side.

How often in this book have I said something like 'and things seemed to be going well, but then . . .'? Not long after we'd finished *Phobia* and while the album was still in production, I took a phone call from Nigel's office. There was terrible news: the night before, Nigel had died suddenly in his sleep. He was a good man who had been taken far before his time and I spent the rest of the day walking around in disbelief. I flew back to the UK for the funeral and it said something about his spirit, and his lust for life, that the funeral turned into a celebration of a life well lived although of course I felt deeply sorry for his family. Ray was the last to leave the graveside because, he said, he wanted to make sure Nigel was actually dead. Perhaps someone had messed up. He wondered, perhaps, if Nigel might have pulled a Reggie Perrin-like disappearing act and was watching us from behind a tree. How else to explain what had happened?

While we'd been navigating our way around the end of the association with MCA, Ray and I met Gene Harvey, who had managed Whitney Houston and who was a really laidback, professional and intelligent guy. We hired him very quickly to pick up the pieces; it's what Nigel would have wanted. I can hear his caustic tones now: 'Don't mind me, bloody bad luck dying like that, charge my glass with an Armagnac and we'll say no more about it.' There were numerous other stresses around my life at that moment. Nancy was pregnant again, joyful news, but her previous pregnancy had been so difficult I couldn't help feeling nervous. I'd also had to sell my precious bolthole in Devon to cover some taxes, and the reality that at this stage in my career I was still scrambling around for cash, still living on a thin line, was very depressing. I was planning to fly back to LA a few days after Nigel's funeral and decided to pick up my mail at Konk. More shitty news, bound to be, I thought.

I sat down feeling grumpy and depressed, and plucked a letter out of the pile. The handwriting on the envelope . . . hmm . . . sort of familiar. I opened the envelope and, to my utter shock, realised it was from Sue. My palms went sweaty and I had butterflies flying round my stomach, like I was that teenage schoolboy again. She'd written to tell me that our daughter Tracey was about to turn thirty and that she was keen to meet me. Throughout her life, she had avoided contacting me in case I didn't want anything to do with her – little did she know how much agony and sadness being separated from Tracey had caused me. Sue signed off with her work number and proposed that I ring her first before arranging to meet Tracey. Not that I needed any invitation. I leapt towards the phone, my hands shaking in anticipation as I waited for Sue to pick up.

'Dave! Wow, it's been so long!' Sue's voice was quivering with excitement as we spoke for the first time in over thirty years. Tracey's need to meet her father had, she told me, become something of an obsession and she could wait no longer. Sue and I decided it would be better to meet first and there was no time like the present – we arranged to meet at Hatfield station that same evening. I was so excited I ended up catching a much earlier train than I needed to and arrived an hour and a half early. My nerves! I went to a local hostelry for a glass or two of Dutch courage, then went for a stroll to calm myself. When I walked back to the station, I heard a voice calling my name. I swung around and there was Sue with that same smile on her face I'd thought about for all those years. We were, of course, so much older and, although we'd led completely separate lives, oddly something still felt the same. There was everything to say, but neither of us knew where to begin, and we walked down the street with grins glued to our faces.

The smiles turned to deep sobbing suddenly as I blurted out how much Sue had broken my heart – I just couldn't help it. We held each other close in the street, and Sue explained how devastated she had been and how she'd never really got over it. All those feelings that I had been suppressing for years bubbled to the surface. I couldn't believe I was hugging my Sue again – and that Tracey was about to enter my life. We sat in a pub for a few hours and breathlessly caught up. Sue told me that her marriage had ended and that she lived on her own. Tracey had married. Sue showed me the wedding pictures and I was relieved to learn that her husband was a decent, honest man. Then, suddenly, I was a grandfather. Unbelievable. Tracey had two young boys. More photographs, more tears. I told Sue about Lisbet, about Nancy, and about my children. When I showed her a photograph of Nancy, she laughed and said they could have been sisters. I hadn't noticed any resemblance before but, yes, that was spot on.

After a couple of hours, Sue rang Tracey and told her to come find us. When she arrived I was at first completely tongue-tied. The two of us sat in Sue's car in a daze. What to say? Where to even begin? After a few mumbled, awkward questions about her job, I suddenly gave it to her straight: 'I know this is a curious thing to say, given we've never met, but my God I've missed you.' She burst into tears and told me how she'd missed me too. Nervy giggles kept interrupting the sobs. We talked a little more, then the three of us went back to the pub. If ever stiff drinks were needed, that time was now. When the pub closed we went back to Sue's place. She made some tea and put Enya's *Caribbean Blue* on the turntable, and it was nice to hear the music she liked. Even if Tracey moaned about her mother's tastes, the meditative pulses of Enya's record helped me tune into Sue's moods and feelings.

After Tracey went home to look after her kids – my *grandchildren* – Sue and I talked and talked and talked into the wee small hours. I told her about the scarf I'd bought for her birthday and had a giggle thinking about my mum swanking around the living room with it wrapped around her shoulders. And it turns out I *should* have given the scarf to Sue, who was terribly upset that I apparently hadn't got her a birthday present. Then she started to tell me about her parents and became very cross. Her parents had poisoned our relationship by telling Sue that I hated her and never wanted to see her again. Sue's parents had, she said, wrecked her life. It was time to leave and as I walked out and saw the early-morning sky, I realised that was how so many of our evenings had ended all those years ago.

A couple of days later I visited Tracey at her house and met my grandchildren for the first time, then I flew back to Los Angeles. I told Nancy the whole unexpected story and how important it was for me to fly back to London to spend time with Sue. To be clear: this was never about 'getting back together', but for so many years our emotional lives had been inexorably intertwined and yet we had been forced into living parallel lives. There was much to talk about. We could never, of course, regain the time that had been cruelly taken from us, but we needed space to come to terms with what had happened, to process our feelings. I bought a present for Sue: a dark purple silk scarf and this time I handed it over without any shyness. We vowed to stay friends always. This time, I told her, when I walk out that door, 'this is our choice, it hasn't been forced upon us by anyone else'. A little thing, but just to be able to say that after all those years made a huge world of difference.

When I came back to London, Sue met me at the airport, and handed me a poem she'd written about what had happened to us. She had written other poems too and I thought she was very talented.

For David
You brought me springtime daffodils,
But they would not let you in,
You were not allowed to see me or our beautiful new-born child,
They slammed that big door on you,
And you had to walk away.
The jailer's key turned in the lock and I knew we could not win.
Snow lay on the ground that day
But it must have felt so warm compared to some of the frozen
hearts, that surrounded the three of us.
Was what we did so very wrong that we could not share our joy?
When they sent you away that morning they sent away half my soul.
If I gave you a springtime daffodil, for every time I've missed you
You'd find that you'd be swimming in a vast yellow sea of Love.

My personal life was about to take another completely unforeseen turn. During that period of flying backwards and forwards between Los Angeles and London to record *Phobia*, Nancy and I lost the focus of our relationship. She had been fantastically accepting about my reunion with Sue, understanding how deeply I had been scarred by the situation, and how there were feelings I needed to resolve. But Nancy and I had already begun to drift apart anyway; we had been together since 1976, a long time. Around the time *Phobia* was released, The Kinks did a long promotional tour of the UK and one night in Manchester, playing at the Apollo Theatre, I met Kate. Gradually we became an item and were together for the next fifteen years.

Kate was a fan of the band; sometimes I thought she knew more about The Kinks than I did. She would come to gigs and I had noticed her in the audience, and we'd made eyes at each other. She was working at The Playboy Club in Manchester when I met her, and she had such good stories. That night at the Apollo, Kate managed to get backstage and we started talking, before we were ushered into our car and driven back to the hotel, Sachas, in the middle of the city. Kate must have been determined, because when we went for drinks in the lobby bar she was there, and we both immediately knew that this was something very special. She was about ten years younger than me, so old enough to appreciate the background of The Kinks and be inspired by it. She was obviously a Mancunian girl, which I really appreciated. I had always loved Manchester, especially the humour.

When I flew back to Los Angeles after the *Phobia* tour, I had to explain everything to Nancy and face once again the guilty pain of separating from a partner and very young children. At that point, I felt committed to being in Los Angeles, and later Kate came out to be with me. I wanted to divert all my attention into film. Living in LA, it wasn't hard to meet people involved in the industry. I became good friends with Danny Bilson, the producer and director who made films like *The Rocketeer* and *The Wrong Guys*, and we began working on scripts with various studios. The first thing I learned in Hollywood, everybody wants to take you out to lunch, but nobody wants to do a deal! I ate some tasty lunches, but getting them to sign off on anything? Far less easy.

One film Danny and I worked on together, with his little writing team, was based on an idea of mine I called *When the Moon Meets Two Rivers*. It was a UFO-cum-abduction story set in the Nevada desert, based around the mystical experiences of an American Indian and reflecting my love for Black Elk. I wanted to make it in black and white, and we ran the script through a load of rewrites. We worked with a development producer for Hollywood Pictures for about two months and we would talk about improving different aspects of the story and the characters. At the end of the final meeting, he said, 'Look, I really like the script, but we already have a film like this in development.' And that was the end of that – months of hard work went nowhere, and he must have known about this other film all along. Was this other film an easier-to-swallow version of the story we'd been developing for all those weeks? I got a little paranoid but Danny reassured me that stuff like this happens all the time.

A friend of my son Russell was a very talented artist and together we story-boarded a film called *Spiritual Planet*, about UFOs that came to earth and blended in as sailing ships. Russell helped me write a soundtrack for the film, and I spent days pitching the idea to the development team at Disney. I worked with someone from that team who outlined the original idea for *Toy Story*, then next thing I know I was told an offshoot of the same studio had a movie called *Treasure Planet* in development. When I saw that film, and that spaceships were flying in the solar wind to earth and into the sea, it felt like history repeating itself.

For the next couple of years, I spent time meeting various film industry people trying to make stuff happen, and I don't regret it. Before leaving for Los Angeles, I had already been in touch with the great director John Carpenter, who'd made epic films like

Halloween, *The Fog*, *Starman*, *Big Trouble in Little China*, *The Thing* and many others. I sent him some of my scripts and he wrote back to say he'd love to hang out once I arrived in LA. He'd always loved The Kinks and had harboured ambitions to be in a rock band, and was involved extensively in writing music for his own movies and other collaborations with other composers. Meanwhile I wanted to get into film! We used to play pool together in Hollywood bars and talk movies and music into the early hours. When John got married, I was his best man and, later, he became godfather to my son Daniel.

In 1994, John asked me to work with him on the music for a sci-fi film he was making called *Village of the Damned*, due for release the following year. It was a remake of a famous 1960s film, itself based on the novel *The Midwich Cuckoos* by John Wyndham. His production company put me up in a nice little hotel near Sunset Boulevard, and I had a fantastic time in the studio creating that soundtrack. Mark Hamill was in the film and he was already a great friend. We'd met in May 1980 at the British premiere of *The Empire Strikes Back*, the sequel to *Star Wars*, in which he played Luke Skywalker. I went with Nancy and we had great seats, and Mark came over to say hello. Turned out he was a big fan of The Kinks and we had drinks afterwards, and we've been close pals ever since. A year later we were playing in Minneapolis and Leonard Nimoy – Spock himself, from *Star Trek* – came backstage and he, too, loved The Kinks. He was playing Vincent van Gogh in a play he'd written himself. It was wonderful to talk to him and we asked Leonard to introduce the band. The cheer from the crowd when he went onstage was awesome. And he gave a clever, eloquent and humorous introduction and clearly knew all about the long history of the band.

Otherwise things were complicated as different threads of my life became entangled. Things had ended with Nancy by that point, and Kate was living with me in Los Angeles. Also Lana was staying with me in the hotel part of the time, but mainly with her mother, Nancy. On top of that, The Kinks were due to play at the opening of the Rock & Roll Hall of Fame Museum in Cleveland. After the gig, I lay awake all night in my hotel room wondering what the fuck to do. The next morning I felt very tired and overwhelmed with emotion. Part of me wanted to stay in Los Angeles, which had come to feel like home. But Kate wanted to go back to the UK and staying in LA would have put the future of our relationship in question. Thinking through all the possibilities was exhausting, but I decided to go back to London.

And that meant seeing where Ray and I were at with The Kinks. We were still digesting the news that the band had been dropped by Columbia. *Phobia* had charted only very briefly in the US and made no dent at all at home. Ray's song 'Scattered' from the album was due to be released as a single in the UK when Columbia abruptly deleted *Phobia*. A few copies of 'Scattered' managed to dribble out and promptly vanished into the hands of hardcore collectors, and our last single made little impression at all.

Around this time Ray would play solo shows without telling me, like I would have minded anyway. Usually when Ray wanted to do something different he wouldn't talk about it and I had to be a mind reader. Even within the context of Kinks shows he was pulling weird stunts and giving out strong signals that he wanted to go solo. During the last year or so of the group's existence, Ray would do a ten-minute solo introductory slot before The Kinks started. He'd perform some new songs and talk about his life. After a gig in Portsmouth, he asked me how I thought the show had gone and I said, 'Great – but I think you really want to get rid of the opening act.' We got into an argument. I'd been taking the piss, obviously, but suddenly it turned serious. Just go fucking solo if that's what you want!

I remembered the exhaustion of constantly flying between LA and London to make *Phobia*, recording for a few days and then flying back to see my family. Lana was a super-sensitive kid and she was having a difficult time at school, and her dad being away all the time didn't help. When on occasion Lana fell out with her mother, I felt I needed to be there for her. Some days my sadness on the way to LAX felt like torture and, actually, what had been the point if Ray wanted to pursue a solo career anyway? Why in that case had we put ourselves through the emotional strain, good and bad, of making a new album? Why were we still doing this? Were we afraid of letting go of the kudos and history of The Kinks? I knew I loved Ray, but that didn't mean I liked him that much, and at times I couldn't stand being around him.

When all my instincts were telling me to walk away, the support of our fans proved the biggest asset. The last Kinks album released before the group was paused, *To The Bone*, reflected the unusual affinity we'd always shared with our fans. With Columbia out of the picture, we released the album ourselves and I've always retained a fondness for it. We decided to mix up live recordings made on the road in the US during 1993, and a couple of things recorded in the UK in '94, with new material especially recorded for the album at Konk in front of an invited audience of Kinks fans. Some of those relationships with the fans stretch back decades. 'To the bone' because the new tracks were recorded in an intimate setting, like a return to the very earliest days of the band. We wanted to recreate a cosy family setting – and given half a chance we'd have recorded the album in the living room at Denmark Terrace. The intimate homeliness of the Konk material made for a telling contrast with the arena-rock vibe of the songs recorded in America. The set list served up a career retrospective of early Kinks hits like 'You Really Got Me', 'See My Friends' and 'Sunny Afternoon', through to songs of more recent vintage like 'Apeman', 'Come

Dancing' and 'State of Confusion'. But the album was never meant to be a conscious farewell. It is true, ever since playing at The Clissold Arms as a kid, I'd always felt at home onstage and I enjoyed playing for the fans at our home base. I remember once a psychologist – Ray's psychologist, in fact – telling me that if I didn't get away from Ray he would end up destroying me, which was a shocking thing to hear and maybe I had reached the point where I had nothing else left to give.

While I was living in LA, I'd done a few low-key gigs and also a little tour, my first solo tour, where I played places like New York and Boston. When I started playing with my own band, it was fun again, and there was no necessity to negotiate with Ray. I played some Kinks songs, stuff of my own and mixed in some old Eddie Cochran songs. Even though, technically, The Kinks still existed, Ray and I were doing solo things anyway and after those last Kinks shows in Stockholm and Oslo in 1996, the band waned. There was no big announcement, and Ray and I simply got on with our lives.

In 1997, when I turned fifty, and I happened to be in London, Ray rang out of the blue and said, 'Come and have a pint with the boys at The Clissold Arms.' I had a weird feeling. Why The Clissold Arms? We never normally went there. But I played the game and, when I arrived, saw a big curtain drawn across the middle of the pub. My sons tried to move me away and bought me a pint, then suddenly the curtain opened and a big cheer went up – Ray had organised a surprise birthday party for me. When the time came for my birthday cake, Ray gave a speech that was about himself mainly. Then when people started taking photos, he jumped up on the table and trampled all over the cake, kicking bits to the floor, like the whole evening had been a joke from beginning to end. I was shaken up and very nearly lost my temper. Then I thought, No, this is my birthday and that's probably the reaction

Ray was hoping for. Instead I got another beer and left the anger to one side.

I returned to LA pretty quickly after that, and the next few years were largely spent being a father, helping Lana through school, which in a grand Davies family tradition, she hated – and I couldn't blame her. I kept up my interest in film during this period and also formed a kickass band of which I was very proud. Kristian Hoffman (keyboards), Andrew Sandoval (guitar), Dave Jenkins (bass guitar) and Jim Laspesa (drums) were all young kids compared to me but they'd already played in a load of rock and punk bands; they were fantastic musicians and loved playing my songs and Kinks material. At The Bottom Line in New York, just before Christmas 1997, we recorded an album released as *Rock Bottom*, which, I think, captures the joy of that period and how at gigs the audience hung off every note.

On 13 June 2004, two weeks before my stroke, I played a show in Potsdam with a version of this band, which ended up being the last gig I played for years. *Bug* was already out and during the gigs I was singing that line about 'There's a bug in my brain and driving me sane/There's a bug in my mind of an alien kind . . .' which now feels like some weird premonition. We were due to leave for Germany when I had a call from Jim Laspesa: he had realised only that morning that his passport had expired and he couldn't make the flight. Jim was a lovely guy and utterly reliable and was mortified at how he'd fucked up. 'Dave, you fly as arranged to London and I'll sort my passport out and meet you there,' he said. So I arrived without my drummer and felt uneasy about the whole thing – then Jim called once again to tell me his new passport wouldn't be ready in time to make the gig, and suddenly I had to scramble to find a replacement. I rang Mick Avory and Bob Henrit but they both had gigs that same night. Bobby Graham had always said to give him a shout if ever we were stuck. I managed to find his number, rang him, only to find he was recovering from a hip replacement operation at home. He couldn't dep either. It was a curse!

Then I thought about asking my son Simon. He had been working with a band called Mash and played great drums, but he hadn't played for a couple of years at least. He was reluctant at first, but it was getting close to the wire, to the point where I'd have to cancel. So in the end I persuaded him to help me out. We dashed to Heathrow to fly to Potsdam and, bizarrely, as we arrived we saw Ray and Martin who were flying back from a gig. When we arrived for the soundcheck and set up in a big outdoor arena, I realised it was a much bigger gig than I'd imagined. I hadn't played with Simon in any sort of professional context before and this was his one and only chance to rehearse with the band. And then the heavens opened, and the electricity went down and we had to abandon the stage. Simon knew the songs as a listener, but the only opportunity he had to practise his parts was back at the hotel, banging on pillows, with my guitar player Jonathan Lea guiding him through. In the end, Simon did really well. We played a long set that included some Kinks songs, some of my songs – 'Death of a Clown', 'Living on a Thin Line', 'Creeping Jean' – and even a fun version of 'Twist and Shout'. We finished with 'You Really Got Me' and enjoyed a few beers afterwards, and then headed back to London the next morning, from where I flew back to LA. Little did I know then that I wouldn't be playing again in public until 2013.

Dealing with trying to find a drummer had been stressful, but I hadn't felt unwell. After the stroke happened, I had plenty of time to come to terms with what had happened and ask all the questions I could. One of my doctors thought my illness might have been related to the amphetamines I'd taken in my twenties, that the drug had created a weakness in my brain – a time bomb waiting to go off. Add to that all the drinking, the too much travelling, too much touring, too many time zones crossed, too much of trying to do too much in too short a space of time. Put your body under that amount of pressure over so many years and this is what happens.

After leaving hospital, and the period I spent with my sister Dolly and her husband Joe, I knew I still had a long way to go to regain my strength. I still couldn't walk and going back to Los Angeles would have been impossible. So Kate gave up the apartment in LA and came back to the UK, and we got a house in North Devon, then after a while we moved to East Devon, near Exeter. Every day I did my physio programme which I designed myself, based around what they'd taught me in hospital which I blended with my existing yoga regime of stretches and postures. Speech therapy became a daily part of life too and it's hilarious to think of all the weird things I had to do. I had a speech therapist who taught me to flex a muscle in the mouth that is very well developed in Americans, which is helpful in redeveloping speech. I also learned about sing-talk, which if you're recovering from a stroke can be much easier than talk-talk. You propel the words forward by singing rather than speaking, which helps develops the muscles. It also makes you sound very 'upper-class twit' and as part of my daily exercises I ended up imitating Grenville's posh accent.

I started thinking about playing music again, which meant re-learning how to play guitar. Part of me wanted to give up. The thought that I'd never get anywhere was terrifying, but eventually I figured out how to confront my demons. Inside my head I knew how to play the instruments, but the problem was to do it physically, and to rebuild my confidence. I learned that the more you think it's never going to improve, the more you *must* keep up with the exercises. My illness had wiped out certain pathways between my brain and the muscles in my arms and hands, and in therapy I found out that muscles retain memory but that they need encouragement. Building facility in my hands, and coordination between left and right, meant doing the exercises over and over and over again.

Playing any instrument you can never feel confident enough, but I found that those milliseconds of timing – the difference between a groove feeling right or wrong – was stubbornly difficult to get right. The weight of my fingers on the strings and controlling the shape of a note when I bent a string, also took a lot of hard work. A stroke is like a brick wall and there is only one way through it, and that's by headbutting. I learned a few shortcuts to get around especially tough technical challenges, and taking a practical view of overriding problems was how I'd always worked in The Kinks, so no change there. And after all those months of hard work, one day I turned a corner. True, things were not absolutely as they were, but I could play the guitar again and the relationship musicians have with their instruments changes all the time anyway.

In 2005, the news came through that The Kinks had been inducted into the UK Music Hall of Fame. The ceremony was to be at Alexandra Palace, which felt fitting because I had fond memories of the building from growing up in Muswell Hill, and The Kinks had played there in 1990. My son Martin, who was then working at Konk, arranged with the producers for a reunion of the original Kinks line-up and they agreed to fly Pete over, who by then was living in Denmark. That year Pink Floyd, Jimi Hendrix, Aretha Franklin, Bob Dylan, The Who, Eurythmics, Joy Division and Black Sabbath were also inducted, and it was fantastic to see so many old faces; Pete Townshend bounded over and wished me full health again after my stroke. The four of us did a fun interview with Mark Radcliffe for Radio 2, and we were inducted by none other than Geoff Hurst, a nice flashback to that summer of '66 when England won the World Cup and 'Sunny Afternoon' was racing up the charts. When we were at the podium, Pete gave a long acceptance speech – in Danish. The ceremony was broadcast on Channel 4, and Pete's words of no-doubt wisdom got cut from the television transmission. In a little filmed segment before we went up onstage,

Townshend said how influential The Kinks had been in the early days, and Alex Kapranos from Franz Ferdinand spoke about the importance of the band for musicians of his generation.

The inevitable question was asked – will the four of you play? – but it simply wasn't possible. I was still too debilitated following my stroke and Ray had problems of his own: he'd been shot in the leg while walking through New Orleans a few months earlier and was still recovering. Pete had health troubles too. He needed regular kidney dialysis, and couldn't travel willy-nilly around the place. It was obvious that opportunities to play together again were limited, and there was talk of the four of us getting together in the studio to record some new material, which never happened. Instead, at Ally Pally, Chrissie Hynde agreed to play a few Kinks songs with The Pretenders as a tribute and she did a very nice job. As the post-show festivities got underway we slipped away quietly and had a curry at the Fortis Green Tandoori in Muswell Hill, near to 6 Denmark Terrace – the last time the four of us original Kinks would be together.

In late 2006, Martin, who had been working for Ray at Konk, quit his job and suggested that together we made a film about my lifetime interest in spirituality and metaphysics. He came down to Devon – and we began filming at various locations, and later on in London. It was fulfilling to discuss on camera some major influences on me like Swami Vivekananda, Israel Regardie, Dion Fortune and Dr George King, also subjects like yoga, astrology, Tarot, the occult and psychology. We recorded conversations with my friend Dr Richard Lawrence, secretary of the Aetherius Society, and Geraldine Beskin of the legendary Atlantis Bookshop, near the British Museum. *Mystical Journey* was released on DVD in 2010, and featured some great artwork by the inspirational artist Charles Newington on the cover. I was pleased that people enjoyed the film and gained an insight into other aspects of my life. Also during this period, before I was fit enough to tour again, I held Satsang meetings in Devon, which were sacred gatherings where people interested in spirituality could come together to learn from each other. I'd invite specialists in yoga and other disciplines and those evenings became very important to me.

All the while, though, I desperately wanted to get back to playing and, after a number of years, I felt confident enough to begin putting material together again. In June 2013, a whole nine years after my stroke, *I Will Be Me* was released and making that album helped me get back into the swing of things. I was coming to the tail end of my rehab when I met John Lappin, who became a good friend. He reminded me of an old-fashioned A&R guy, with feelers out everywhere. We met up in Taunton and discussed putting a new solo record together based on all the song ideas I was coming up with and he arranged to have the album released on Cleopatra Records. Making *I Will Be Me* was like a training exercise. In the studio, I was nervous. My left hand wasn't up to full strength yet but that old wisdom about 'never giving up' proved to be true. Ideas spun around my head and, the more I played, and my muscles and brain caught up, the more I found I could play. And with a new album waiting to be released, I thought once more about touring – the old instincts were starting to stir again.

When we opened at the City Winery in New York, on 27 May 2013, I was shit-scared and buzzing with excitement in equal measure; but the second I stepped onstage and started playing again, I was immediately at home. We toured all over the place – through Connecticut, to Pennsylvania, Chicago, all over California, and I came back for a second leg of the tour in November. This meant a lot of driving across the US as we played in concert halls, auditoria, bars and old cinemas, and always it was heartening to see how often volunteers worked these community venues, in it only for the love of the music. The City Winery, managed by a great guy called

Shlomo Lipetz – with three different venues in New York, Chicago and Nashville – became like a home from home, and we always found Shlomo to be super-helpful and supportive. The New York shows had a terrific party atmosphere and we decided to record live there. *Rippin' Up New York City* was released in 2015 – my first live album since *Rock Bottom* in 1997. My son Simon produced and mixed the record and I couldn't have been happier with how it turned out.

Jonathan Lea had returned from the band I'd had before my illness, but otherwise I worked with a whole new line-up. On drums we had Teddy Freese for the earlier shows, then Dennis Diken took his place. Back in 1993 Ray and I had played a couple of songs with The Smithereens in Boston. Dennis was on drums and I loved his feel, and always wanted to work with him again. Tom Currier came in on bass, and we rehearsed at Tom's Manhattan condo. At one show, in October 2015, Jonathan suddenly became very ill and I decided we should play the show as a three-piece. It was punkier and heavier rock, one of my best ever shows, I thought, helped along by the energy of the crowd. I decided from then on to play as a three-piece permanently. David Nolte had played on some of my early solo tours and on the *Bug* album and I'd always had a special musical connection with him, so he came in on bass, although after a while our working relationship grew apart. I loved my well-honed power trio.

All those gigs felt like joyous occasions. In Los Angeles, Mark Hamill and Clem Burke came down. Bruce Springsteen's guitarist, Steven Van Zandt, came to a bunch of shows. Another night, I was amazed to meet the wrestler Mick Foley and we had a long conversation backstage about how much my mum had loved wrestling. Back in 2003, I'd played for the Chicago radio 'shock jock' Mancow Muller's Valentine's Day wedding party and I really enjoyed seeing him again. At his party, the stage had been balanced on top of big inflatable toys that looked like houses – then I looked out into the crowd and saw William Shatner, a big deal for a Trekkie like me.

There were always folks around from the old days, too. Goldie, from Goldie and the Gingerbreads, who had toured with The Kinks back in 1964, dropped by. The singer Billy J. Kramer turned up one night and told me how much he liked 'Lincoln County', so we played it for him, and we became good friends. Brian Ritchie from the Violent Femmes, the promoter Ron Delsener, who had put on so many Kinks shows back in the day, C. J. Ramone – how cool was it to swap stories about Joey Ramone – all came by, as did Doug Hinman who has become known as The Kinks' historian.

I played *The Tonight Show Starring Jimmy Fallon* in 2014, working with house band The Roots, promoting the album *Rippin' Up Time*, which I'd recorded with David Nolte in LA – not to be confused with *Rippin' Up New York City* – which I'd recorded in Los Angeles. We had only a very short time to rehearse, but the guys like the drummer Questlove and the guitarist 'Captain' Kirk Douglas were fast learners and it was cool playing songs like 'Rippin' Up Time' with them.

In Central Park, on 8 December 2015, I took part in an event organised by Yoko Ono, an attempt to make the world's largest peace sign in memory of John Lennon. Thousands of people showed up and were arranged into the shape of the peace sign, which was photographed by a helicopter above. I sang my song 'Strangers' and sat next to Yoko for some photos. Around this time I also met Dolores from the rock band The Cranberries in a favourite Indian restaurant in Edgewater, New Jersey. We became good friends and were going to work with each other but she died very tragically before we had a chance to reconnect. I'll always remember her fondly – she was hugely talented and special.

When we played Nashville a few years later, Bebe Buell – singer, muse to too many musicians to mention, and mother of Liv

Tyler – came to the show and, next day, Bebe and her husband Jim kindly showed us around the musical landmarks of the city. Life felt really good again.

And for another reason. In New York, I met up with a young writer, Rebecca G. Wilson, who a few months earlier had interviewed me online for *Punk Globe*, a magazine published by San Francisco-based Ginger Coyote, about *I Will Be Me*. As we fell into conversation online about the mystical world and artistic matters, there was a real spark and I found her inspiring to talk to – obviously very well educated and highly intelligent, a view that was reinforced during further conversations. When eventually we met in person in New York, around the time of the first City Winery shows, our relationship blossomed from there, which led to a very difficult period of reckoning with Kate. It seemed like Rebecca and I had always been friends – and then that friendship opened into other things. We fell in love and developed a profoundly supportive connection on so many levels. Because she loved singing, humour and poetry, we had lots to share together. Rebecca would sing backup with me on tour and we enjoyed performing together, and so connected on an artistic level too. Her family, I discovered, was very creative. Her sister, Diana Damon, was an independent filmmaker, and her mother, Marcia Sandmeyer Wilson, was a painter who lent me her studio so I could create art again. The evening Steven Van Zandt came down, the four of us – Rebecca and Little Steven's wife Maureen – all went for dinner. What a night that was! Little Steven and Maureen were, of course, both in *The Sopranos*. Ray loved that show and I quickly acquired a taste for it too. At gigs, Rebecca handled press and merchandise. Martin was tour manager, Simon supervised the sound and liaised between the band and the sound guys. After all those years of feeling sad and lonely while touring with The Kinks, now touring became a family affair. I was surrounded by the people I loved – a man blessed.

CODA

This book, really, has been all about that mysterious alchemy of music, and how to create music out of *feelings*; about how feelings can be transformed into sounds, and how the whole history of The Kinks has been about discovering how to make music through the experience of making music. During the fifties, America was growing up musically. Blues and rock and roll appeared in Britain, and it became clear that everything that happens socially is reflected through the arts. As young people who had grown up after the war, we were attempting to make art that reflected this new world, trying for the first time to work out what to do. It was all very spontaneous. We had to find ways to express ideas and feelings when often it wasn't clear to us what those feelings were. This is the value of art: you try things out, hopefully have a breakthrough, then you learn something about yourself and what it is you're feeling.

We didn't know what art was for! Fine art and all that bollocks – that belonged to another class. Art existed, and was contained within, very clear structures, and we were all looking for gaps in that social regime. There was a very definite sense within the music business around what you were allowed to do and what you were not. I was shocked when I heard an interview with the great jazz trumpeter Chet Baker, whose playing I adored. He was being interviewed by a musicologist and told him: 'I have to tell you, I don't know anything about music. I just get into a mode and play.' His playing was a way for him to get his feelings out there. Chet's music was about humanity and expression. His art was about itself, and what's wrong with that? We can't start learning unless we've identified who we are as individuals. When he sang, Chet's voice had a charm, charisma and individuality. And I could fully relate to everything about him, because I never studied music. I picked things up, I tried things out, I learned on the job, half the time not knowing what I was doing. I was very influenced by the jazz players of the era – Chet, Charles Mingus, Gerry Mulligan, Bill Evans and many other inspiring players – although it was their vibe more than copying their phrases. Listening to Chet, you wonder what could have been in his mind when he was playing that stuff. I like that it can never be fully explained.

In this book, I've tried to tell the truth about my relationship with Ray, and the time we shared together in The Kinks, as I see it. I'm aware of the endless fascination and speculation surrounding this subject, and I can't pretend that my life with Ray has been easy. Some of the stories I've told might make your hair stand up on end, but please remember that humour – and camaraderie – were always important elements in how The Kinks operated. I have said this many times, but it's worth repeating here, especially given all the bullshit I read on the internet about us – Ray is my brother and I love him. I've always felt protective towards him and have tried to support his work to the best of my ability – and sometimes that has meant telling him when I thought he was going wrong. I want this book partly to stand as a tribute to Ray and to The Kinks – and especially to Ray's writing. There is really nobody else like him.

When Ray picked up his knighthood in 2017, my initial thought was that it was a nice gesture, a tribute to The Kinks, rather than for Ray himself specifically. At first, I admit, I thought Where's mine? and then that rebellious side of me thought Fuck it – why would I want something like that anyway? The emotions were mixed. Our mum and dad would have burst with pride, no question about that, especially coming from a background like ours. And if they're giving out gongs to 1960s rock stars, Ray should be top of the list. Will The Kinks ever make music together again? Pete's death in 2010, although not unexpected, was a wrench, severing an essential link with the past. Ray, Mick and I have thought occasionally about doing something in the studio and, of course, I'd love to get back in the studio with Ray. These days, BMG looks after The Kinks' back catalogue and do a great job reissuing our albums. They're understanding and creative, and it's a real pleasure to be working with them. As is having a close and supportive work relationship with Bob Frank who has helped me with many of my solo projects over the years.

There was a period during the early 2000s when my daughter Lana moved to England under my care. She was a bright kid who loved music and she wrote some good songs. She ended up renting a flat near Leicester Square, and she'd hang out in Soho with Ray's daughter Natalie, and they became very close friends. Lana told me once how upset the constant Ray–Dave intrigue made her, which put me right in my place.

But it's never easy. In 2014 an idea came to fruition that had been around for a while. *Sunny Afternoon* was a musical based around the history of The Kinks, pegged around many of our greatest hits. The actor George Maguire played me, and it was fucking weird to sit in the audience and watch myself onstage.

The musical was initially staged at the Hampstead Theatre but, before it could transfer to the West End, I had to get lawyers involved. Ray had written the original script to gloss over my role in creating the guitar sound behind 'You Really Got Me' and I felt that the story be told properly – and we came to a compromise. Sometimes it is necessary to mess with the truth a little, to fictionalise, if you're trying to make a story work theatrically or on film. I get that. I could see what Ray was doing, but was he doing it for honourable reasons, to make the musical more streamlined? I hoped so and wanted to give him the benefit of the doubt. But where do you draw the line? How possessive can you be over an idea? A musical isn't a definitive report on history, but people think of it so. That's the problem. In the end I enjoyed the show, especially the nights I went with Grenville, who characteristically pointed out all the factual oversights in his very loud voice.

After all those shenanigans I tried to make the peace. This was the period after I'd released *I Will Be Me* and I was touring regularly again. In April 2014, I played at the Barbican, my first show in the UK since I was taken ill. And just before Christmas 2015 I had another show booked at Islington Assembly Hall and I thought it would be nice to invite Ray. I emailed him, and it was touch and go whether he'd turn up, but he arrived just as the show got underway. As the grand finale, he came onstage to gasps and screams from the audience. He gave a nice little speech, which led to a rousing version of 'You Really Got Me' – the first time we'd appeared onstage together since 1996. What a moment!

The story of The Kinks has always been a family story. Rene's death in 1957, a devastating tragedy, caused ripples that continued through the decades. Rosie and Joyce both died in 2014, within the space of a couple of weeks of each other. Dolly died in April 2020, just as the pandemic hit, and that was a horrible time. These days I speak to Gwen and Peggy most weeks. They are very loving and wise and they have become the matriarchs of the Davies family. Peggy's daughter Jackie, who came into our lives so unexpectedly when I was a kid, is still very dear to me and we always hang out whenever I'm in Los Angeles, where she has lived for many years. Ray and I are muddling along OK – and where would I be without my dear Rebecca? And all of my kids, who are my support network and I would feel completely lost without any one of them. Martin is now my manager, and Simon is a stalwart who inspires me creatively. Christian helps me in many ways, including with social media platforms, and Daniel, whom I love deeply, is a fine musician, composer and writer. I've made a few records with my son Russell over the years, including *Open Road* and *The Aschere Project*, and I've loved collaborating with him. My youngest son Eddie – my last child with Nancy – was very young when I was taken ill and I didn't see him for a number of years while I was recovering. Now we have a great relationship. He works as an actor in the US and I'm proud of all that he has achieved – and much more yet to come. I'm also the very proud grandfather of Russell's children, young boys Max and Leo, and Daniel has a gorgeous little girl, Jane. And Tracey's children, Andrew and Michael, are now in their late thirties.

Truth is, people live, people die. It'll happen to me one day, but perhaps I have been around the block before. On 3 February 1947, the day I was born, I moved down my mother's birth canal and saw a light in the distance. Oh fuck, I thought. Here we go again.

INDEX

ACKNOWLEDGEMENTS

Special love and thanks to my beloved children for their constant support, guidance, inspiration and kindness, always and throughout the writing of this book: Martin, Simon, Christian, Russell, Daniel, Lana, Eddie and Tracey. I love you all, deeply.

Thank you also to my dearly beloved Rebecca for her love, support, devotion and all those years of happiness, joy and continued inspiration and laughter.

I'd like to thank Philip Clark for all his hard work in helping me get the manuscript to this final form, and for his good humour – and patience.

And to my loving siblings and families – Rose, Rene, Dolly, Joyce, Peg, Gwen and Raymond.